CW01572592

COMMUNICATIONS AC

EXPLANATORY NOTES

INTRODUCTION

1.   These explanatory notes relate to the Communications Act, which received Royal Assent on 17th July 2003. They have been prepared by the Department of Trade and Industry and the Department for Culture, Media and Sport in order to assist the reader of the Act. They do not form part of the Act and have not been endorsed by Parliament.

2.   These notes need to be read in conjunction with the Act. They are not, and are not meant to be, a comprehensive description of the Act. So, where a section or part of a section does not seem to require any explanation or comment, none is given.

3.   The Act relates to matters within the responsibilities of both the Secretary of State for Trade and Industry and the Secretary of State for Culture, Media and Sport. References to the Secretary of State in the Act mean any Secretary of State. In practice, some of the functions conferred upon the Secretary of State will be exercised by the Secretary of State for Trade and Industry and the Secretary of State for Culture, Media and Sport jointly and others by only one of them. This will reflect their respective ministerial portfolios.

SUMMARY

4.   The Act gives effect to the Government's proposals for the reform of the regulatory framework for the communications sector, as set out in the Communications White Paper – *A New Future for Communications* (Cm 5010) – published on 12th December 2000.

5.   The main provisions of the Act provide for:

- the transfer of functions to the Office of Communications (OFCOM) from the bodies and office holders which currently regulate the communications sector (which broadly speaking encompasses telecommunications and broadcasting) and manage the radio spectrum;

- OFCOM's general duties in carrying out their functions;

- the replacement of the current system of licensing for telecommunications systems with a new framework for the regulation of electronic communications networks and services;

- the power to develop new mechanisms to enable spectrum to be traded in accordance with regulations made by OFCOM, and a scheme of recognised spectrum access;

*In these explanatory notes, "spectrum" refers to radio spectrum (or radio frequencies) that forms a small part of the electromagnetic spectrum. Radio spectrum is an important and versatile communications medium, used for terrestrial and satellite broadcasting, mobile telephony, fixed wireless access, and many other applications. Radio spectrum is a finite resource and key issues in the effective use of spectrum include the efficient allocation and sharing of frequency channels (both domestically and internationally) and the need to ensure that radio signals from different users and services do not significantly interfere with each other.

- procedures for appealing decisions relating to networks and services and rights of use for spectrum;

- the development of the current system for regulating broadcasting to reflect technological change, to accommodate the switchover from analogue to digital broadcasting and to rationalise the regulation of public service broadcasters;

- the establishment of a Consumer Panel to advise and assist OFCOM and to represent and protect consumer interests;

- the establishment of a Content Board to advise OFCOM, and undertake functions on their behalf, in relation to the content of anything broadcast or otherwise transmitted by means of an electronic communications network and in relation to media literacy;

- the concurrent exercise by OFCOM of powers under the Competition Act 1998 and the Enterprise Act 2002 across the whole of the communications sector (including broadcasting); and

- the application of the merger control regime under the Enterprise Act 2002 to mergers involving newspaper and other media enterprises.

6.   There are currently five bodies or office holders who exercise regulatory responsibilities in the communications sector and who will be replaced by OFCOM. These are:

- the Broadcasting Standards Commission, a non-departmental public body which has statutory responsibilities for standards and fairness in broadcasting. It has three main tasks, as established by the Broadcasting Act 1996 ("the 1996 Act"). These are to produce codes of conduct relating to standards and fairness; to consider and adjudicate on complaints; and to monitor, research and report on standards and fairness in broadcasting;

- the Director General of Telecommunications, who is responsible for running the Office of Telecommunications (Oftel) – the UK telecommunications regulator. Oftel is a non-ministerial government department. The Director General is responsible under the Telecommunications Act 1984 for administering and enforcing the licences that regulate telecommunications operators.   His duties include those of ensuring that adequate telecommunications services are provided throughout the UK; of promoting the interests of consumers; and of maintaining effective competition;

- the Independent Television Commission, the statutory body which licenses and regulates independent television services in the UK, including cable and satellite. Operating under powers derived from the Broadcasting Acts 1990 and 1996, their responsibilities include setting and maintaining the standards for programmes, economic regulation, public service obligations, research, TV advertising regulation and technical quality;

- the Radio Authority, which is the statutory body responsible for regulation and licensing of independent radio broadcasting in the UK, that is to say all non-BBC radio services. Operating under powers derived from the Broadcasting Acts 1990 and 1996, their responsibilities include frequency planning, the awarding of licences, the regulation of programming and radio advertising, and the supervision of the radio ownership system; and

- the Secretary of State, as far as she has a regulatory role in respect of the allocation, maintenance and supervision of non-military radio spectrum in the UK. This role is exercised through the Radiocommunications Agency, an executive agency of the Department of Trade and Industry.

The Office of Communications Act 2002 establishes OFCOM and gives them a single initial function - to prepare to assume regulatory functions at a later stage. It also gives the existing regulators additional functions and duties to assist OFCOM to prepare.

7. One of the central objectives of the Act is the transfer to OFCOM of the functions, property, rights and liabilities of the bodies and office holders that currently regulate the communications sector. OFCOM will then develop and maintain new regulatory rules for the communications sector within the context of a single set of regulatory objectives, and in the light of the changing market environment.

8. In February 2002 the European Parliament and the Council of Ministers adopted four Directives ("the EC Communications Directives"), which set out a package of measures for a common regulatory framework for electronic communications networks and services. Provisions in the Act implement a significant proportion of this new regulatory package in the UK (see Appendices 2 and 3).

OVERVIEW OF THE ACT

9. The Act is in six parts –

Part 1 – Functions of OFCOM

Part 2 – Networks, Services and the Radio Spectrum

Part 3 – Television and Radio Services

Part 4 – Licensing of TV Reception

Part 5 – Competition in Communications Markets

Part 6 – Miscellaneous and Supplemental

TERRITORIAL EXTENT AND TERRITORIAL APPLICATION

10.   The large majority of the provisions in the Communications Act are on reserved matters (the exceptions being training and equality of opportunity in broadcast employment). The Act applies to the whole of the United Kingdom (a few procedural matters being dealt with separately for England and Wales, Scotland and Northern Ireland to take account of the different legal systems), with power to extend it by Order in Council to the Channel Islands and the Isle of Man. The Act does not confer functions on the National Assembly for Wales, although the Secretary of State is required to consult the National Assembly for Wales when carrying out a review of the fulfilment by the Welsh Authority of its public service remits (section 339).

COMMENTARY ON SECTIONS

PART 1: FUNCTIONS OF OFCOM

Section 1: Functions and general powers of OFCOM

11.   This section sets out the functions of OFCOM. These consist of those functions that prior to commencement were carried out by the Secretary of State and the pre-commencement regulators and which are transferred to OFCOM, together with all other functions conferred on OFCOM by other legislation, including the present Act.

> *the meaning of *pre-commencement regulators* is given in *subsection (1)* of section 405. Those regulators are the Broadcasting Standards Commission, the Director General of Telecommunications, the Independent Television Commission and the Radio Authority. The expression does not include the Radiocommunications Agency, as the Agency is an executive agency of the Department of Trade and Industry and acts in the name of the Secretary of State and, although functions of the Secretary of State are transferred to OFCOM by the Act, the office of the Secretary of State will not cease to exist, unlike the other four regulators.

12.   *Subsections (3), (4) and (5)* provide that OFCOM have power to do anything incidental or conducive to carrying out their functions. This, in particular, includes the power to borrow money (provided that this is done with the consent of, or in accordance with a general authorisation given by, the Secretary of State), the power to undertake research and development work in relation to their functions as well as to promote and arrange for it to be carried out by others, the power to prosecute in England, Wales and Northern Ireland offences relating to matters in respect of which they have functions, and the power, at their discretion, to compensate (where no legal liability arises) persons adversely affected by OFCOM's activities.

13.   *Subsection (6)* requires OFCOM to establish and maintain offices in England, Wales, Scotland and Northern Ireland.

14.   *Subsection (7)* enables OFCOM to contract out their functions to a third party,

where an order providing for such has been made by the Secretary of State under the Deregulation and Contracting Out Act 1994.

Section 2: Transfer of functions of pre-commencement regulators

15.   *Subsection (1)* provides that, from such date as the Secretary of State may appoint for the coming into force of this section, certain functions of the Secretary of State and the functions of the pre-commencement regulators will be transferred to OFCOM. By virtue of section 411 the Secretary of State may appoint different dates for different purposes.

16.   Schedule 1 sets out those functions that will be transferred to OFCOM from the pre-commencement regulators. These functions relate to wireless telegraphy, the licensing of television and radio services, the Channel Four Corporation, the proscription of foreign satellite services, Gaelic Broadcasting, the national television archive, the reservation of digital capacity to the BBC, listed events, fairness and privacy in broadcasting, and standards for transmission services. The functions also relate to warrants to enter and search premises to enforce broadcasting licence provisions, variation of existing Channel 3 and Channel 5 licences, and reviewing digital broadcasting.

17.   *Subsection (2)* explains the effect of the transfer of functions to OFCOM on references in existing legislation to the pre-commencement regulators and the Secretary of State. Where necessary, references in existing legislation to any of the pre-commencement regulators or the Secretary of State should be read as if they referred to OFCOM.

18.   *Subsection (3)* provides that, from the appointed date, OFCOM will be able to exercise the functions transferred to them in respect of events or issues arising both before and after the appointed date.

19.   *Subsection (4)* provides that any function transferred is that function as modified by this Act.

20.   Paragraph 1 of Schedule 18 (transitional provisions) provides that any subordinate legislation made or any other thing done for the purpose of carrying out the transferred functions by the pre-commencement regulators or the Secretary of State shall from the date of the transfer made by virtue of section 2 have effect as if they had been done by OFCOM.

Section 3: General duties of OFCOM

21.   This section sets out the general duties of OFCOM when carrying out their functions. OFCOM's principal duty is: (i) to further the interests of citizens, and (ii) to further consumer interests in relevant markets, where appropriate by promoting competition. "Citizens" are defined in *subsection (14)* as all members of the public in the United Kingdom; "consumers" are defined in section 405(5).

22.   *Subsection (2)* provides that the particular things that OFCOM are required to secure in carrying out their functions include: (a) the optimal use of the radio spectrum; (b) the availability throughout the United Kingdom of a wide range of electronic communications services; (c) the availability in the UK of a wide range of TV and radio services, comprising high quality services of broad appeal; (d) the maintenance of a sufficient plurality of providers of different television and radio services; (e) the application, in television and radio services, of standards that provide adequate protection to members of the public from any offensive and harmful material; and (f) the application, in television and radio services, of standards that safeguard people from being unfairly treated and from unwarranted infringements of privacy.

23.   *Subsection (3)* requires OFCOM to have regard in all cases to the principles that regulatory activities should be transparent, accountable, proportionate, targeted and consistent, and to any other principles which appear to OFCOM to represent best regulatory practice.

24.   *Subsection (4)* sets out a list of factors to which OFCOM must have regard, wherever relevant, in the performance of their general duties. These are the desirability of promoting the fulfilment of the purposes of public service television broadcasting, the desirability of promoting competition in relevant markets, the desirability of promoting and facilitating the development and use of effective self-regulation, the desirability of encouraging investment and innovation, the desirability of encouraging the availability and use of high speed data transfer services, the different needs of all existing and potential users of the radio spectrum, the need to guarantee an appropriate level of freedom of expression when applying the standards falling within subsection (2)(e) and (f) to television and radio services, the opinions of consumers and of members of the public generally, the need to protect potentially vulnerable members of society such as children, the elderly, those with disabilities and those on low incomes, the desirability of preventing crime and disorder and the interests of those living in different parts of the country, including rural and urban areas, and of different ethnic communities. They may also have regard, in each case, to the extent to which it is reasonably practicable for them to further their duties under this section.

25.   OFCOM must also have particular regard to the interests of consumers in respect of choice, price, quality of service and value for money when performing their duty of furthering the interests of consumers.

26.   OFCOM are given a duty to resolve as they see fit any conflicts that arise between their various general duties. However, in cases where their general duties may conflict with their "European duties" (imposed by sections 4, 24 and 25), OFCOM's European duties must prevail.

27.   Where OFCOM are resolving conflicts in 'important' cases between their duties under subsection (1), they are required as soon as possible after the conflict has been resolved to publish a statement setting out the conflict, how they have

resolved it and why they have taken that particular approach, unless they are legally obliged not to publish something which would be in the statement.

28.   OFCOM's annual report must include a summary of the manner in which they have resolved conflicts arising from their general duties in 'important' cases.

29.   'Important' cases are those that include: a major change in OFCOM's activities; are likely to have a significant impact on communications businesses or the general public; or appear to OFCOM to have been of unusual importance.

30.   OFCOM's duties under this section do not apply in relation to anything done by OFCOM in the carrying out of their functions under the Competition Act 1998 or the Enterprise Act 2002, unless they are matters to which the Office of Fair Trading is entitled to have regard when operating under those Acts (section 370(11) and section 371(11) of this Act and section 119A(4) of the Enterprise Act 2002 (inserted by Chapter 2 of Part 5 of this Act)).

Section 4: Duties for the purpose of fulfilling Community obligations

31.   This section creates a duty, which applies only to certain functions of OFCOM. These are their functions under:

- Chapter 1 of Part 2;

- the enactments relating to the management of the radio spectrum;

     * Section 405(1) defines the *enactments relating to the management of the radio spectrum* as the Wireless Telegraphy Act 1949, the Marine, &c., Broadcasting (Offences) Act 1967, the Wireless Telegraphy Act 1967, Part 6 of the Telecommunications Act 1984, the Wireless Telegraphy Act 1998, Chapter 2 of Part 2 of the Act and the other provisions of the Act so far as relating to any of those enactments.

- Chapter 3 of Part 2 relating to network access disputes referred to them under section 185;

- sections 24 and 25, so far as they relate to information required for purposes connected with matters in relation to OFCOM functions specified in this section; and

- section 26, if carried out for the purpose of making information available to the customers of communications providers, the customers of persons who make associated facilities available and persons who use electronic communications networks, electronic communications services or associated facilities.

32.   The duty is a duty to act in accordance with six Community requirements. In the event that there is any conflict between this duty and the section 3 duties, the former, which is required by the EC Communications Directives, is to take precedence.

33.   The Community requirements are: (i) to promote competition; (ii) to ensure that OFCOM's activities contribute to the development of the European internal market; (iii) to promote the interests of all persons who are citizens of the European Union; (iv) to take account of the desirability of carrying our their functions in a manner which, so far as practicable, does not favour one form of network, service or associated facility, or one means of providing or making available such a network, service or facility over another; (v) to encourage the provision of network access and service interoperability; and (vi) to encourage compliance with international standards to the extent necessary to facilitate service interoperability, and to secure a freedom of choice for customers.

> * *network access* is defined in section 151 as meaning (1) interconnection of public electronic communications networks; or (2) any services, facilities or arrangements (other than interconnection) by means of which a communications provider or a person making associated facilities available is able, for the purposes of the provision of an electronic communications service (whether by him or by another), to make use of any network or apparatus comprised in a network, or any service or facility capable of being used to provide a service.

> **service interoperability* is defined in section 151 as interoperability between different electronic communications services.

34.   Requirements (i) to (iv) implement Articles 7(1) & (2) and 8 of Directive 2002/21/EC (the "Framework Directive"). Requirement (v) implements Article 5(1) of Directive 2002/19/EC ("the Access Directive") and Article 18 of the Framework Directive and requirement (vi) implements Article 17(2) and 18 of the Framework Directive. This section also implements Article 20 (3) of the Framework Directive and Article 7(3) of the Authorisation Directive.

Section 5: Directions in respect of networks or spectrum functions

35.   This section gives the Secretary of State a power to give directions to OFCOM in respect of: (i) their functions relating to networks, services and the radio spectrum under Part 2 of the Act; and (ii) their functions relating to the management of the radio spectrum not contained in Part 2. Such directions may only be made for one or more of the purposes listed in *subsection (3)*. Those purposes are: national security, relations with foreign countries, compliance with international obligations, public safety and public health.

36.   The Secretary of State may not use her powers under this section to direct OFCOM to suspend any person's entitlement to provide electronic communications networks or electronic communications services or to make available associated facilities. This can only be done by a direction given by the Secretary of State in accordance with the provisions of section 132. Section 132 gives the Secretary of State express power to direct OFCOM to suspend or restrict entitlement, where this appears to her to be necessary to protect the public from any threat to public safety or public health or in the interests of national security.

> **associated facilities* are defined in section 32.

8

37. The Secretary of State must publish a direction issued under this section unless publication is against the interests of national security or relations with foreign countries.

Section 6: Duties to review regulatory burdens

38. This section imposes on OFCOM a duty to review their functions so that regulation by OFCOM does not lead to the imposition or maintenance of burdens that are or have become unnecessary. OFCOM must from time to time publish a statement setting out how they propose to comply with this duty and must have regard to that statement when carrying out their functions. When reviewing their duties under this section, OFCOM must consider whether or not their general duties set out in section 3 may be furthered or secured, or are likely to be furthered or secured, by effective self-regulation and, in the light of that, whether it would be appropriate to remove or reduce regulatory burdens.

Section 7: Duty to carry out impact assessments

39. Unless the urgency of a matter makes it impracticable or inappropriate, before implementing an important proposal in connection with the performance of their functions, OFCOM must either carry out and publish their assessment of the likely impact of the proposals or publish a statement setting out their reasons for thinking that it is unnecessary for them to carry out such an assessment. A proposal is an important proposal if it would be likely to involve a major change of their activities or have a significant impact on communications businesses or the general public. OFCOM will decide the form and content of the assessment, having regard to relevant general guidance, but *subsection (4)* requires that the assessment must set out how the proposal would secure or further the performance of OFCOM's general duties, or how the performance of the duties would be secured or furthered in relation to the proposals. When OFCOM publish an assessment, they must provide persons who are likely to be affected by the proposal with an opportunity to comment on it. OFCOM's annual report must set out the assessments that have been carried out under this section and summarise the decisions taken by OFCOM in relation to proposals in respect of which impact assessments have been carried out.

Section 8: Duty to publish and meet promptness standards

40. This section requires OFCOM to publish a statement setting out promptness standards which they propose to meet in carrying out their functions or transacting business for purposes connected with the carrying out of their functions. Such time limits will not apply where the Act or any other enactment already sets time limits within which their functions are to be carried out. OFCOM's annual report must summarise the extent to which they have complied with the promptness standards set out under this section.

Section 9: Secretary of State's powers in relation to promptness standards

41.   Where the Secretary of State considers that the promptness standards set by OFCOM under section 8 are not satisfactory, she may notify OFCOM. If OFCOM fail to amend the promptness standards to her satisfaction, the Secretary of State may give a direction requiring OFCOM to issue or revise their promptness standards in accordance with its terms. Before issuing a direction, the Secretary of State must give OFCOM an opportunity to comment on her proposal. The Secretary of State cannot use her powers under this section until 12 months have elapsed after the commencement of section 8.

Section 10: Duty to encourage availability of easily usable apparatus

42.   This section places a duty on OFCOM to take such steps and enter into such arrangements as appear to them calculated to encourage others to secure that domestic electronic communications apparatus (defined in *subsections (4) and (5)*) is developed which is capable of being used without modification by the widest possible range of individuals, including those with disabilities; and to secure that such apparatus is as widely available as possible. OFCOM are also to review from time to time whether they need to take further steps to perform their duty under this section. For example, many users find TV remote controls and similar devices inconvenient to use because the buttons are so small. OFCOM might accordingly assist designers by dissemination of research results, ergonomic advice, etc., which might be helpful in identifying ways to minimise such inconvenience.

Section 11: Duty to promote media literacy

43.   This section provides that it shall be a duty of OFCOM to enter into arrangements calculated to bring about, or to encourage others to bring about, increased public awareness and understanding of material published by the electronic media, the processes by which such material is selected or made available for publication, the available systems by which access to such published material is or can be regulated, and the available systems by which persons to whom such material is available may control what is received. OFCOM are also required to encourage the development and use of technologies and systems for regulating access to such material, and for facilitating control over what material is received. These could include internet filtering systems, rating systems by which, for example, programmes and videos can be given a classification that indicates the nature of their content, and other technical devices such as PIN-based systems to control viewing. Promotion of the use of such systems could include OFCOM participating in the development of related educational materials.

Section 12: Duty to establish and maintain Content Board

44.   This section places OFCOM under a duty to set up and maintain a Content Board (a committee of OFCOM), the functions of which are set out in section 13.

45. *Subsections (2)* to *(11)* detail the composition of the Content Board, including OFCOM's duty to ensure that for each of England, Scotland, Wales and Northern Ireland, there is a different member of the Board, and to ensure that a majority of Board members is made up of individuals who are neither members nor employees of OFCOM. The chairman and at least one other member of the Content Board are to be appointed by OFCOM and must be non-executive members of OFCOM (other than their chairman). No governor or employee of the BBC, nor any member or employee of the Welsh Authority or the Channel Four Television Corporation can be a member of the Board, nor can any person whom OFCOM think has a conflict of interest (although such a conflict will not arise merely through being a member or employee of OFCOM).

46. *Subsection (13)* provides that, in addition to paying remuneration and expenses under paragraph 14(4) of the Schedule to the Office of Communications Act, OFCOM may pay such sums as they see fit by way of pensions, allowances or gratuities (or provide for the making of such payments) to members of the Content Board who are not members or employees of OFCOM.

Section 13: Functions of the Content Board

47. OFCOM are to determine which of their functions are to be delegated to the Content Board. To such an extent and subject to such restrictions as OFCOM may determine, these must include the functions set out in *subsection (2)*, namely, functions related to broadcast content and media literacy.

48. The Board must ensure that OFCOM are aware of the different interests and factors that need to be taken into account in the carrying out of OFCOM's broadcasting functions as respects different parts of the United Kingdom.

49. The Board may be authorised by OFCOM pursuant to *subsection (5)* to establish committees or panels to advise it in carrying out its functions. Members of those committees or panels may include persons who are not members of the Content Board.

Section 14: Consumer research

50. This section requires OFCOM to make arrangements to ascertain public opinion and the experiences of consumers on certain issues relating to the communications sector, including electronic communications networks and services, associated facilities and television and radio services and programmes distributed by other electronic media. In general, these arrangements may cover the carrying out of research by OFCOM, by the Content Board or by others. The arrangements must cover the carrying out of research into matters relating to the promotion of media literacy, the setting and observance of programme standards for radio and television, the prevention of unjust and unfair treatment of persons in those programmes and of unwarranted infringements of privacy resulting from those activities.

51.   OFCOM are not required to make arrangements under this section in respect of the incidence or investigation of any interference with wireless telegraphy.

Section 15: Duty to publish and take account of research

52.   This section requires OFCOM to publish, consider and, to such extent as they think fit, take account of research under section 14. This obligation does not extend to information that is confidential within the meaning of *subsections (3) or (4)*.

Section 16: Consumer consultation

53.   This section places OFCOM under a duty to establish and maintain effective arrangements for consulting with consumers, in the markets for services and facilities in relation to which OFCOM have functions, the markets for apparatus used in connection with those services and facilities and the markets for directories capable of being used in connection with an electronic communications network or service. This section implements Article 33(1) of the Universal Service Directive.

54.   Such arrangements must include the setting up of an advisory panel to be known as the Consumer Panel. The principal responsibilities of the Consumer Panel will be to advise OFCOM and others on the interests of domestic and small business consumers in relation to the matters listed in *subsection (3)*. Those matters include the provision of electronic communications networks and services and directory enquiry facilities; the making available of associated facilities; the supply of apparatus; service, quality and safety standards; financial and other terms of provision; complaints handling; dispute resolution and remedies; and the availability of information. The matters in subsection (3) about which the Panel are able to give advice do not, however, include matters that concern the contents of anything which is or may be broadcast or otherwise transmitted by means of electronic communications networks. OFCOM may also refer additional matters not included in subsection (3) to the Panel for advice. The Panel may publish such information as they think fit about their advice, the results of their research or the carrying out of their other functions.

*the meaning of *domestic and small business consumer* is given in *subsection (10)*, and covers customers of a communications provider who are not themselves a communications provider, nor an undertaking for which more than 10 people work.

55.   *Subsection (7)* places OFCOM under a duty, when carrying out their functions, to have regard to the advice and research of the Consumer Panel. OFCOM are also obliged to provide the Panel with such information as is necessary to enable the Panel to carry out their functions and such other information requested by the Panel as OFCOM can reasonably be expected to disclose (having regard particularly to confidentiality requirements). OFCOM must ensure that where they intend to disregard any of the Panel's published advice, they both publish this intention and inform the Panel of their reasons for disagreeing with this advice. Finally, the Consumer Panel must report on the carrying out of their functions on an annual basis and must publish their report as soon as practicable after it has been prepared.

Section 17: Membership etc. of the Consumer Panel

56.   This section provides for the appointment of the chairman and other members to the Consumer Panel. The power to make all these appointments is conferred on OFCOM, subject to the approval of the Secretary of State. In appointing persons to be members of the Consumer Panel OFCOM must ensure that for each of England, Scotland, Wales and Northern Ireland there is a different member of the Panel capable of representing the interests and opinions of persons living in those parts of the United Kingdom. Also, OFCOM must seek to ensure that the Panel they appoint will be able to represent the interests of the categories of persons listed in *subsection (4),* which includes persons living in rural areas, persons living in urban areas, small businesses, the disadvantaged, and the elderly. The Panel have a duty, when carrying out their functions, to have regard to the interests of those persons as well as the interests of persons from different parts of the United Kingdom.

57.   All appointments to the Panel will be for a fixed period with provision for re-appointment. Members may be removed from the Panel by notice given by OFCOM, but, again, only with the approval of the Secretary of State. Being a member or employee of OFCOM disqualifies a person from becoming a Panel member.

58.   *Subsection (9)* provides that OFCOM may pay to the chairman and to other members of the Consumer Panel such remuneration and allowances as OFCOM consider appropriate.

Section 18: Committees and other procedure of the Consumer Panel

59.   The Consumer Panel may make such arrangements as they think fit for committees established by the Panel to give advice to them about matters relating to the carrying out of their functions. The Panel may make arrangements, including those related to quorums and the making of decisions by majority, regulating their own procedure and the procedure for committees established by them. Persons who are not members of the Panel may be members of a committee established by the Panel; however, every committee must include at least one person who is a member of the Panel. OFCOM may pay non-Panel members of a committee such remuneration and expenses as OFCOM may determine.

Section 19: Power to amend remit of Consumer Panel

60.   The Secretary of State may by order add to (but not reduce) the list of matters in subsection (3) of section 16 in relation to domestic and small business consumers on which the Consumer Panel may advise OFCOM and other persons. Before making an order under this section, the Secretary of State must consult OFCOM and such other persons as she thinks fit.

Section 20: Advisory committees for different parts of the United Kingdom

61.   This section places OFCOM under a duty to exercise their powers under paragraph 14 of the Schedule to the Office of Communications Act 2002 to establish and maintain a committee for each of England, Wales, Scotland and Northern Ireland. *Subsection (4)* provides that each committee shall have the function of providing advice to OFCOM about the interests and opinions, in relation to communications matters, of persons living in the part of the United Kingdom for which the committee is established.

Communications matters has the same meaning as in section 3.

62.   *Subsections (2) and (3)* require each committee to be comprised of a chairman, appointed by OFCOM, and such number of other members as OFCOM think fit. In making the appointments, OFCOM must have regard to the desirability of ensuring that the person appointed is able to represent the interests and opinions in relation to communications matters of persons living in the part of the UK for which the committee has been established.

63.   Under *subsections (5) and (6)*, should the Consumer Panel so request, the committees for the different parts of the UK may also, with the consent of OFCOM, provide advice to the Consumer Panel on the interests and opinions of persons in the respective parts of the UK.

Section 21: Advisory committee on elderly and disabled persons

64.   This section places OFCOM under a duty to exercise their powers under paragraph 14 of the Schedule to the Office of Communications Act 2002 to establish and maintain a committee to provide advice on the interests in relation to communications matters of elderly persons and of persons with disabilities.

Communications matters has the same meaning as in section 3.

65.   *Subsections (2) and (3)* require each committee to be comprised of a chairman, appointed by OFCOM, and such number of other members as OFCOM think fit. In making the appointments, OFCOM must have regard to the desirability of ensuring that the members of the committee include persons who are familiar with the needs of the elderly and of persons who are familiar with the needs of persons with disabilities.

66.   Under *subsections (5) and (6)*, should the Consumer Panel so request, the committee may also, with the consent of OFCOM, provide advice to the Consumer Panel on the interests of the elderly and of persons with disabilities.

Section 22: Representation on international and other bodies

67.   The Secretary of State may, as respects the United Kingdom, require OFCOM to represent the Government on international and other bodies having

communications functions and at international meetings about communications. The Secretary of State may also require OFCOM to become a member of or subscribe to international and other bodies having communications functions.

68. OFCOM may also, as respects the Channel Islands, the Isle of Man or any British overseas territory, at the request of the Secretary of State, represent the Government on international and other bodies having communications functions and at international meetings about communications. However, the Secretary of State cannot require them to do this.

69. *Subsection (3)* provides that OFCOM must carry out these functions in accordance with directions by the Secretary of State; and *subsection (4)* provides that this does not allow the Secretary of State to direct that OFCOM must represent any of the Channel Islands, the Isle of Man and the British overseas territories but that if OFCOM do represent any of them, the Secretary of State may direct them how.

> **communications functions* are defined in *subsection (5)* as any function concerned with the use of the radio spectrum, television or radio broadcasting regulation, or any other matter in respect of which OFCOM have functions.
>
> **subsection (5)* also defines *international meetings about communications* as international meetings concerned with the use of the radio spectrum, broadcasting regulation or provision, or any other matter in respect of which OFCOM have functions.

Section 23: Directions for international purposes in respect of broadcasting functions

70. This section gives the Secretary of State the power, by order, to give directions in respect of OFCOM's functions under the enactments relating to broadcasting. Such directions may be given only for the purposes of securing compliance with an international obligation of the United Kingdom.

> **international obligation of the United Kingdom* is defined in *section 405(1)* to include any Community obligation (within the meaning of the European Communities Act 1972) and any obligation under an international agreement or arrangement to which the United Kingdom is a party.

Section 24: Provision of information to the Secretary of State

71. This section provides that when directed to do so, OFCOM must provide the Secretary of State with such information as is required by the Secretary of State in order to enable her to secure compliance with an international obligation of the United Kingdom. This provision enables the Secretary of State to provide the European Commission with information requested pursuant to Article 25 of the Framework Directive, Article 16 of Directive 2002/20/EC ("the Authorisation Directive"), Article 15(2) and 17 of the Access Directive and Article 36(3) of Directive 2002/22/EC ("the Universal Service Directive").

Section 25: Community requirement to provide information

72.   This section provides that OFCOM are under a duty to comply with a requirement to provide the European Commission with information for the purpose of enabling it to perform any of its functions in relation to electronic communications networks or services or associated facilities. This provision is necessary in order to implement Article 5(2) of the Framework Directive and Article 15 of the Access Directive.

Section 26: Publication of information and advice for consumers etc.

73.   This section allows OFCOM to publish information and advice for customers of communications providers; customers of persons who make available associated facilities; users of electronic communications networks, electronic communications services or associated facilities; and persons to whom radio and television services are, or may be, provided. OFCOM should, where practicable, not publish confidential or private information relating to a particular individual or body where this might seriously adversely affect the interests of that individual or body.

74.   This section implements Article 5(4) and (5) of the Framework Directive, Article 15(1) of the Authorisation Directive, Article 11(2)_and 15(1) of the Access Directive, and Article 21(2) of the Universal Service Directive.

Section 27: Training and equality of opportunity

75.   This section requires OFCOM to take all such steps as they consider appropriate to: (i) promote the development of opportunities for the training and re-training of persons for employment by broadcasters or for work in connection with the provision of the services that they provide, otherwise than as an employee; (ii) promote equality of opportunity in relation to employment by broadcasters and the training and retraining of persons for such employment; and (iii) promote the equalisation of opportunities for disabled persons in relation to such employment, training and retraining. It is envisaged that, under this section, OFCOM might, for example, carry out or commission research, publish such research or other information, hold conferences and promulgate codes of practice or other guidance.

Section 28: General power to charge for services

76.   This section gives OFCOM a general power to prescribe or agree fees to be charged for the services they provide, save in respect of any service that they are under a duty to provide, or for which fees are expressly provided (or prohibited) elsewhere.

Section 29: Secretary of State guarantees for OFCOM borrowing

77.   This section allows the Secretary of State to guarantee, in such manner and on such conditions as she thinks fit, the repayment of the principal of any

borrowing by OFCOM, the payment of any interest on such borrowing or the discharge of any other financial obligation incurred by OFCOM connected with such borrowing. *Subsection (3)* limits the total amount payable by the Secretary of State in fulfilling any guarantees she may give to a sum not exceeding £5 million. *Subsection (4)* enables the Secretary of State to substitute a different total amount, subject to a draft order to that effect being laid before Parliament and approved by the House of Commons (*subsection (5)*). Where OFCOM give a guarantee under this section, they must lay a statement of the guarantee before each House of Parliament. *Subsections (8) and (9)* provide that any sums paid by the Secretary of State in fulfilling any guarantee she has given must be repaid by OFCOM as the Secretary of State directs and that payments are to be made with such interest, at such times and in such manner as she may determine.

Section 30: Transfers of property etc. from pre-commencement regulators

78.   This section gives the Secretary of State a power to give directions requiring any pre-commencement regulator to make a scheme or schemes for the transfer to OFCOM of any of that regulator's property, rights and liabilities. The Office of Communications Act 2002 gives the Secretary of State a power to require that such schemes are prepared in draft form. Before making such a scheme the pre-commencement regulator must consult OFCOM.

79.   Such transfer schemes will become effective only if the Secretary of State approves them. *Subsection (6)* allows the Secretary of State to approve such schemes subject to modification.

> *the meaning of *modification* is given in *subsection (1)* of section 405 and includes omissions, alterations and additions. Cognate expressions shall be construed accordingly.

80.   *Subsections (10) and (11)* provide for the circumstances in which the Secretary of State may herself prepare a transfer scheme. These are: (i) in order to transfer property, rights and liabilities from herself to OFCOM; and (ii) in order to transfer property, rights and liabilities from a pre-commencement regulator to OFCOM where either (a) the regulator has not complied with a direction of the Secretary of State to prepare a scheme, or (b) the scheme prepared by the regulator is not approved by the Secretary of State.

81.   Schedule 2 covers the contents and effect of transfer schemes. It explains that a transfer scheme is to set out the property, rights and liabilities that are to be transferred. As soon as a scheme comes into force, property transferred by that scheme vests in OFCOM, and any agreement made by the transferor has effect as if made in the name of OFCOM. The Secretary of State may retrospectively modify the scheme as appropriate. The Schedule also describes the circumstances in which third parties whose interests are affected by the operation of a scheme – whether due to any diminution in value of their interests or rights, or any increase in the burden of their liabilities - are entitled to compensation. Any dispute as to compensation is to go to arbitration.

Section 31: Transitional functions and abolition of pre-commencement regulators

82.   This section imposes a duty on the pre-commencement regulators to take all such steps as are necessary or expedient for ensuring that OFCOM are able effectively to carry out their functions from the time that they are vested in OFCOM. The Secretary of State may direct the pre-commencement regulators as to how to carry out this duty. OFCOM and the pre-commencement regulators must give the Secretary of State all such information and assistance as she requires for the purposes of carrying our her functions under section 30.

83.   This section also gives the Secretary of State a power, by order, to appoint a day for the abolition of the offices of the pre-commencement regulators and of the advisory bodies established under section 54 of the Telecommunications Act 1984. The Secretary of State may appoint different days for the abolition of each of the different regulators and advisory bodies.

> *Section 54 of the Telecommunications Act 1984 provides for the establishment of various advisory bodies to advise the Director General of Telecommunications. The Secretary of State was required to set up an advisory body for matters affecting each of the following: England, Wales, Scotland, Northern Ireland, and the Director was required to establish advisory bodies for matters affecting small businesses, and matters affecting persons who are disabled or of pensionable age. In addition, the Director was empowered to establish such other advisory bodies as he thought fit. Section 54 is repealed by *subsection (5)* of section 31.

PART 2: NETWORKS, SERVICES AND THE RADIO SPECTRUM

Chapter 1: Electronic Communications Networks and Services

84.   Chapter 1 of Part 2 of the Act provides for a new regulatory framework that will apply to all electronic communications networks, electronic communications services and associated facilities. Networks and services make up the communications infrastructure by means of which voice, content and other data are delivered to the consumer (the regulation of television and radio content is dealt with separately under Part 3 of the Act). This new regulatory framework implements a significant proportion of the harmonised framework for the regulation of electronic communications networks and services established by EC Communications Directives (see Appendices 2 and 3). The remainder will be implemented by secondary legislation or, where appropriate, administrative action.

85.   The Act abolishes the criminal offence of running a telecommunications system without a licence currently contained in the Telecommunications Act 1984. In the new regulatory framework for electronic communications networks, electronic communications services and associated facilities, there will be no need to apply for a licence. Persons will automatically be entitled to provide an electronic communications network, electronic communications services or to make available associated facilities provided that, where required, they notify OFCOM of this

intention and comply with certain regulatory conditions (known as conditions of entitlement) set by OFCOM.

Section 32: Meaning of electronic communications networks and services

86.   This section sets out the meanings of the three key concepts – 'electronic communications network', 'electronic communications service', and 'associated facility' - that are referred to throughout this Part.

87.   This section implements Article 2(a), (c), (e) and (m) of the Framework Directive.

> *electronic communications network* is defined in *subsection (1)* as a transmission system for the conveyance, by the use of electrical, magnetic or electro-magnetic energy of signals of any description, and associated apparatus, software and stored data. Examples of such networks include satellite networks, fixed networks (whether circuit- or packet-switched, and including the Internet) and mobile terrestrial networks and networks used for radio and television broadcasting, including cable TV networks.

> *electronic communications service* is defined in *subsection (2)* as a service consisting, or having as its principal feature, the conveyance, by means of an electronic communications network, of signals except in so far as it is a content service. Examples of such services include telecommunications services and transmission services in networks used for broadcasting.

> *associated facility* is defined in *subsection (3)* as a facility which is available for use in association with an electronic communications network or service in order to make the provision of that network or service (or other services) possible, or to support the provision of other services. Examples of such facilities include conditional access systems and electronic programme guides.

> * content service* is defined in *subsection (7)* as so much of a service as consists in (i) the provision of material with a view to it being comprised in signals conveyed over an electronic communications network, or (ii) the exercise of editorial control over the contents of signals conveyed by means of such a network.

> *a *signal* is defined in *subsection (10)* as including anything consisting of speech, music, sounds, visual images and communications or data of any description, and signals serving for the impartation of anything or for actuating or controlling any apparatus.

Section 33: Advance notification to OFCOM

88.   This section allows OFCOM to designate certain classes of networks, services or associated facilities as requiring notification. Under *subsection (1)* no one may provide any network, service or associated facility that has been designated in this way, unless he has notified OFCOM in advance of his intention to do so. If a network, service or associated facility already being provided is subsequently designated by OFCOM as requiring notification, the person concerned must notify OFCOM within the time period specified in the designation. OFCOM must also be informed when a person intends to modify or to cease to provide a designated network, service or associated facility.

89.   *Subsection (5)* lists the information that OFCOM may require to be contained in a notification. This basically consists of the information necessary to enable OFCOM to identify the person giving the notification, such as his name and address, a

declaration of his proposal to provide, modify or cease to provide the network or service described in the notification or to make available, modify or cease to make available an associated facility, and details of when he intends to commence these activities. OFCOM may also require details of a person who can accept service on behalf of that person and a person who can be contacted if there is an emergency.

90.   This section implements Articles 3(2) and (3) and 6(1), of and condition 10 of Part A of the Annex to, the Authorisation Directive.

Section 34: Designations and requirements for the purposes of s. 33

91.   This section details the procedural requirements imposed on OFCOM regarding the making or withdrawal of a designation by them under section 33. *Subsection (1)* provides that OFCOM must consult with those likely to be affected by OFCOM's actions, and *subsection (2)* requires OFCOM to consult with the Secretary of State prior to making or withdrawing a designation.

92.   This section forms part of the implementation of Article 6(1) of the Authorisation Directive.

Section 35: Notification of contraventions of s. 33

93.   This section provides that where OFCOM have reasonable grounds to believe that a person has contravened his obligations under section 33, they may notify that person and allow him a specified period of time (usually one month) in which to make representations to OFCOM and to comply with his obligations.

94.   This section and sections 36 and 37 implement Article 10(2) and (3) of the Authorisation Directive in the context of the enforcement of the advance notification requirements.

Section 36: Enforcement notification for contravention of s. 33

95.   If, by the end of the period specified in the notification given under section 35, OFCOM are satisfied that a person has contravened section 33 and he has not provided them with all the information needed to remedy the contravention, *subsection (2)* allows OFCOM to serve an enforcement notification on the relevant provider. Such a notification requires the relevant provider to provide OFCOM with the information specified in the notification. Those persons to whom an enforcement notice has been given are under a duty, enforceable by OFCOM via civil proceedings, to comply with it.

Section 37: Penalties for contravention of s. 33

96.   If a person has contravened section 33 and, by the end of the period specified in the notification given under section 35, he has not provided OFCOM with all the information needed to remedy the contravention, OFCOM may impose a

penalty. OFCOM may also impose a penalty if a person contravenes a requirement of an enforcement notification given under section 36. In deciding on the amount of a financial penalty under section 37, OFCOM are required to consider whether the financial penalty is appropriate and proportionate, and to take account of any representations made by the person concerned, and any steps taken by him to comply with section 33. The financial penalty shall not, in any event, exceed £10,000.

Section 38: Fixing of charges

97.   This section gives OFCOM a power to require providers of particular designated networks, services or associated facilities, universal service providers designated by regulations under section 66 for the purposes of conditions relating to directories and directory enquiry facilities, suppliers of apparatus to whom SMP apparatus conditions apply (under section 93) and also persons to whom the electronic communications code has been applied who do not provide a designated electronic communications network (under section 106(4)), to pay a yearly administrative charge. Any such charges should be set by OFCOM in accordance with pre-determined "charging principles", designed to ensure that the aggregate charges collected in any one year will just cover OFCOM's costs - in that same year - of carrying out the administrative functions listed in *subsection (5)*. This section implements Articles 6(1), 12 and 13 of, and condition 2 of Part A of the Annex to, the Authorisation Directive. It should, however, be noted that although OFCOM are able to collect an administrative charge from a supplier of apparatus to whom an SMP apparatus condition (i.e. a condition set under set under section 45(9)) applies or from a provider of a system of conduits to whom the electronic communications code has been applied, the collection of the administrative charge for these purposes is not part of the implementation of those provisions.

98.   Charges must also be objectively justifiable, proportionate and transparent. This implements Article 12(1) of the Authorisation Directive.

99.   *Subsection (9)* obliges OFCOM to publish an annual statement of the aggregate charges collected (or to be collected) for that year, and the corresponding aggregate costs incurred in carrying out their administrative functions. Any deficit or surplus must be taken into account in setting charges for the following year. This implements Article 12(2) of the Authorisation Directive.

100.   Paragraph 12 of Schedule 18 (transitional provisions) provides that where any licence fees in respect of licences granted under section 7 of the Telecommunications Act 1984 remain outstanding on the abolition of such licences, that liability is to have effect after the abolition as a liability to pay OFCOM so much of the amount outstanding as does not relate to times after the abolition.

101.   For the purpose of ascertaining who is liable to pay an administrative charge, sections 135 and 137(6) enable OFCOM to publish a general demand for information.

Section 39: Supplemental provision about fixing charges

102.   This section lays down the procedures (including consultation and publication) OFCOM must follow when they are setting administrative charges and determining "charging principles".

103.   *Subsections (2)* to *(4)* provide that when setting an administrative charge, OFCOM may make provision for a deduction from the charge in cases where a network, service or associated facility has been provided, or the universal service condition, electronic communications code or SMP apparatus condition has applied, for part of a year only.   Conversely, a charge may apply to networks, services or associated facilities that were being provided, or to persons to whom the universal service condition, electronic communications code or SMP apparatus condition applied, in a particular year before the charge for that year was set, as long as this is consistent with the "charging principles" for that year.   This would, for example, mean that OFCOM would have the flexibility to set the amount of the charge for a particular year after that charging year has commenced.

Section 40: Notification of non-payment of charges

104.   This section allows OFCOM to notify persons who do not pay part or all of the administrative charges due to OFCOM, and sets out the procedures, such as giving notice and allowing for representations, to be followed by OFCOM in such cases. OFCOM may not bring proceedings for the recovery of administrative charges unless they have given a notification under this section.

105.   This section and sections 41 to 43 relate to the enforcement of the administrative charge requirements contained in the Act and implement Article 10 of the Authorisation Directive.

Section 41: Penalties for non-payment of charges

106.   If a person has failed to pay an administrative charge fixed under section 38 and has not paid the whole of the amount outstanding in the period allowed by the enforcement notification under section 40, OFCOM may fine the notified charge payer. In deciding on the amount of a fine, OFCOM are required to consider whether the fine is appropriate and proportionate, and to take account of any representations made by the person concerned and any steps taken by him to comply with section 38. The maximum fine that may be imposed under this section is twice the amount of the relevant administrative charge for the year in question.

Section 42: Suspending service provision for non-payment

107.   This section gives OFCOM a power to suspend a person's entitlement to provide networks, services and/or associated facilities where OFCOM are satisfied that that person is or has been in serious and repeated breach of his obligations to pay administrative charges to OFCOM, that the breaches are not breaches relating only

to charges in respect of the application of SMP apparatus conditions, that the bringing of proceedings and the imposition of penalties has failed to secure complete compliance and that such a response is appropriate and proportionate. However, under *subsection (6)* OFCOM may not issue a direction unless they have given the provider notice of the proposed direction and given him an opportunity to make representations about it and to propose steps to remedy the situation. *Subsection (7)* provides that this period must be at least one month.

108.   A direction by OFCOM under this section may suspend entitlement generally or in relation to particular networks, services or associated facilities, or may restrict the entitlement in the way specified. A direction may impose conditions on the provider in order to protect the provider's customers. *Subsection (8)* enables OFCOM to revoke or modify suspensions and restrictions where they consider it appropriate to do so.

Section 43: Enforcement of directions under s. 42

109.   It is an offence, punishable by a fine, for any person to provide an electronic communications network, electronic communications service or associated facility while he is subject to a direction suspending his entitlement to do so, or to provide such a network, service or associated facility in contravention of a restriction in such a direction.

110.   A contravention of a condition of a direction which results in any person sustaining loss or damage is actionable at the suit or instance of that person. It is a defence for the person providing the electronic communications network, electronic communications service or associated facility to show that he did all that was reasonable to avoid contravening the condition.

Section 44: Duty of OFCOM to keep publicly accessible register

111.   This section places OFCOM under a duty to keep an up-to-date public register of designations made under section 33 or section 38, withdrawals of such designations and notifications given to them, or treated as given to them, under section 33. OFCOM must publish (and comply with) a notification setting out the times during which the register is available for public inspection and the fees (if any) that must be paid to inspect the register.

112.   This section implements Article 3(3) of the Authorisation Directive.

Section 45: Power of OFCOM to set conditions

113.   Under the regulatory framework provided for in Part 2, any person to whom OFCOM applies a condition under section 46 must comply with that condition. Section 45 gives OFCOM the power to set two categories of conditions – general conditions and specific conditions, the latter comprising universal service conditions, access-related   conditions,   privileged supplier conditions or significant market

power (SMP) conditions. *Subsection (10)(e)* provides that the power to set conditions includes the power to revoke or modify conditions.

114.   General conditions are conditions of general application and must be set in accordance with sections 51, 52, 57, 58 or 64. The ability to set such conditions implements Article 6(1) of, and partially implements Part A of the Annex to, the Authorisation Directive. It also implements Article 4(1) and 4(3) of the Access Directive.

115.   Universal service conditions are conditions authorised or required under section 67 for the purpose of ensuring that certain minimum electronic communications networks and services and associated facilities are available at all times throughout the UK. The ability to set such conditions implements Article 6(2) of the Authorisation Directive and Articles 3 to 7 and 9 to 11 and Part A of Annex I to of the Universal Service Directive.

116.   Access-related conditions are conditions authorised under section 73 for the purpose of ensuring adequate network access within communications infrastructure. The ability to set such conditions implements Article 6(2) of the Authorisation Directive and Articles 5(1) and (2) and 6 of the Access Directive.

> * *network access* is defined in section 151 as meaning (1) interconnection of public electronic communications networks; or (2) any services, facilities or arrangements (other than interconnection) by means of which a communications provider or a person making associated facilities available is able, for the purposes of the provision of an electronic communications service (whether by him or by another), to make use of any network or apparatus comprised in a network, or any service or facility capable of being used to provide a service.

117.   Privileged supplier conditions can be applied where a communications provider enjoys special or exclusive rights in relation to the provision of any non-communications services.   They are intended to ensure the separation of the provider's activities as a communications provider from other aspects of his undertaking, and must comply with section 77. The ability to set such conditions implements Article 13 of the Framework Directive.

118.   SMP conditions may be either an SMP services condition authorised or required under sections 87 to 92 or an SMP apparatus condition authorised under section 93. The ability to set SMP services conditions implements Article 6(2) of the Authorisation Directive, Articles 8 to 13 of the Access Directive, Article 16(2) of the Framework Directive and Articles 17 to 19 of the Universal Service Directive. SMP apparatus conditions are out with the scope of the EC Communications Directives because the supply of apparatus is not part of the provision of an electronic communications network or service. The power to set such conditions is therefore additional to the requirements of the Directives.

Section 46: Persons to whom conditions may apply

119.   This section lists the persons to whom OFCOM may apply general conditions

and specific conditions set in accordance with section 45.

120.   Under *subsection (2)*, OFCOM may apply general conditions to all persons providing electronic communications networks or electronic communications services or to all persons providing networks and services of a particular description specified in the general condition. General conditions may not be applied to persons providing associated facilities.   Subsection (2) implements Articles 2(a) and 6(1) of the Authorisation Directive.

121.   Under *subsection (3)*, OFCOM may apply specific conditions to a particular person specified in the condition.   This implements Article ^(2) of the Authorisation Directive and Article 13 of the Framework Directive.

122.   *Subsection (4)* specifies that OFCOM may also apply a privileged supplier condition generally to public communications providers who enjoy special or exclusive rights in relation to the provision of services in other sectors (other than the provision of associated facilities) or to particular descriptions of public communications providers, as specified by OFCOM in the privileged supplier condition. Subsection (4) implements Article 13 of the Framework Directive.

123.   Under *subsection (5)*, universal service conditions may only be applied by OFCOM to particular communications providers, persons providing directories and persons providing directory enquiry facilities designated by OFCOM in accordance with regulations adopted under the provisions of section 66.   Subsection (5) implements Article 8 of the Universal Service Directive and Article 6(2) of the Authorisation Directive.

124.   Under *subsection (6),* where an access-related condition is imposed for the purpose of securing end-to-end connectivity as described in section 74(1), OFCOM may apply the condition to any person. In all other cases, access-related conditions may be applied by OFCOM to providers of electronic communications networks or associated facilities.   Subsection (6) implements Article 6(2) of the Authorisation Directive and Article 5(1)(a) of the Access Directive.

125.   *Subsection (7)* allows OFCOM to apply an SMP services condition to communications providers and persons providing associated facilities where (i) such persons have been designated as having significant market power in a specific market for electronic communications networks, electronic communications services or associated facilities; or (ii) for the purposes of compliance with an international obligation, it appears necessary to OFCOM to impose a condition that corresponds to an SMP services condition.   Subsection (7) implements Article 6(2) of the Authorisation Directive, Article 16(4) of the Framework Directive, Articles 8(2) of the Access Directive and Articles 17 to 19 of the Universal Service Directive.

126.   Finally, *subsection (9)* permits OFCOM to apply an SMP apparatus condition to persons who supply electronic communications apparatus and have been determined   by   OFCOM   to   have significant market power in a specific

market for electronic communications apparatus.

127.   "Significant market power" is defined in section 78.

Section 47: Tests for setting or modifying conditions

128.   OFCOM must not set or modify any general, access-related, privileged supplier, universal service or SMP conditions unless they satisfy the test in *subsection (2)*. This provides that the condition or modification must be objectively justifiable, non-discriminatory, proportionate, and transparent. This implements Articles 6(1) and 14(1) of the Authorisation Directive, Articles 5(3) and 8(4) of the Access Directive and Articles 3(2), 9(5) and 17(2) of the Universal Service Directive.

Section 48: Procedure for setting, modifying and revoking conditions

129.   This section sets out the procedural requirements for the setting, modification or revocation of conditions of entitlement. OFCOM are required by *subsections (2), (3)* and, where appropriate, *(4)* to consult on any proposal by them to set, modify or revoke a condition and to allow a period of at least one month for representations to be made to them on the matter. OFCOM are obliged by *subsection (5)* to set, modify or revoke a condition only after considering every representation received, and any international obligations of the UK drawn to their attention by the Secretary of State for this purpose. *Subsection (6)* requires OFCOM to publish each notification under this section in such manner as brings it to the attention of those to whom it is relevant. This implements Article 6 and 7 of the Framework Directive, Articles 5(3), 6(3), 8(4), and 15(1) of the Access Directive and Article 14(1) of the Authorisation Directive.

Section 49: Directions and approvals for the purposes of a s.45 condition

130.   This section sets out the procedure that OFCOM or other authorised persons must follow when giving, modifying or withdrawing a direction, approval or consent that may be given under a condition of entitlement.

131.   Where any authorised person other than OFCOM gives, modifies or withdraws a direction, approval or consent, that person must act in accordance with the six Community requirements set out in section 4.

132.   Before a direction, approval or consent may be given, modified or withdrawn, a notification must be published that states that there is a proposal to give, modify or withdraw it, that identifies the person making the proposal, that explains what he is proposing and that sets out the direction, approval or consent that he proposes to modify or withdraw, its effect, the reasons for his decision and the period during which persons may comment on the proposal. The representations period must be at least one month, though (provided the notification is not one which needs to be sent to the European Commission in accordance with section 50(4) or (5)) it may be shorter in exceptional circumstances. If the condition to which the direction, approval or consent relates requires the authorised person to publish the notification, he must

do so (*subsection (7)*). Otherwise OFCOM must publish the notification (*subsection (8)*).

133.   An authorised person may adopt the direction, approval or consent, provided they have considered each comment made about the proposal within the period specified by him for comments and he has had regard to the international obligations of the UK as notified to them by the Secretary of State for the purposes of section 49(9).

134.   Any direction, approval or consent given, modified or withdrawn must be objectively justifiable, non-discriminatory, proportionate and transparent. This section implements Articles 6 and 7 of the Framework Directive.

Section 50: Delivery of copies of notifications etc.

135.   This section requires the relevant person to send a copy of each of the following to the Secretary of State: (i) a notification under sections 48(1) or (2), (ii) a notification published under section 49(4), (iii) each direction, approval or consent giving effect to a proposal that must be published under section 49(4); and (iv) any instrument modifying or withdrawing a direction, approval or consent giving effect to such proposals.

> * *The relevant person* means, in relation to a notification, direction, approval or consent, the person by whom it is published or (as the case may be) by whom it has been or is to be given, modified or withdrawn. Where a direction, approval or consent is given, modified or withdrawn by a person other than OFCOM for the purposes of giving effect to a proposal published by OFCOM under section 49(4), OFCOM are the relevant person.

136.   The relevant person must also send to the European Commission a copy of each of the following: every notification that is published under section 48(1), which sets out his proposal with respect to an SMP services condition, every direction, approval or consent given under an SMP services condition and every instrument modifying or withdrawing them.

137.   OFCOM are required to send to the European Commission and to the regulatory authorities of every other member State, a copy of every notification that they publish under section 48(2), which sets out their proposals with respect to the setting, modification or revocation of an access-related condition falling within section 73(2) or (4) or an SMP services condition, where such proposals would, in OFCOM's opinion, affect trade between member States. This implements Article 7(3) of the Framework Directive.

138.   OFCOM must send to the European Commission and to the regulatory authorities of every other member State, a copy of every notification that they publish under section 49(4), which sets out their proposals relating to the giving, modification or withdrawal of a direction, approval or consent under an access-related condition falling within section 73(2) or (4) or an SMP services condition, and where such proposals would, in their opinion, affect trade between member States.   Where

another person publishes a notification mentioned in section 49(4), he is required by *subsection (5)* to refer the question of whether the proposal would affect trade between member States to OFCOM, who must decide the matter immediately, and the person publishing the notification must act accordingly.

139. In cases which OFCOM consider would not affect trade between member States, the relevant person must, where he considers it appropriate, send a copy of every notification published under sections 48(1), 48(2) or 49(4), every direction, approval or consent given pursuant to a condition set under section 45 and every instrument modifying or withdrawing them to the European Commission and to such of the regulatory authorities of other member States as the relevant person thinks fit. However, the relevant person is not required to comply with this obligation where the notification or the notified proposal relates to an SMP apparatus condition or to any direction, approval or consent modifying or withdrawing such a condition.

140. The requirements to send various matters to the European Commission and the national regulatory authorities of other member states set out in this section, implement Articles 8(5), 15(2) and 16(2) of the Access Directive and Article 36(2) of the Universal Service Directive.

Section 51: Matters to which general conditions may relate

141. Sections 51 to 64 set out the scope of OFCOM's power to set general conditions, and the procedural provisions applicable for that purpose.

142. Section 51 provides that, subject to sections 52 to 64, OFCOM may set general conditions only in relation to matters that are listed in *subsection (1)*. The matters listed in subsection (1) include protection of end-users of public electronic communications services; network access and interoperability of services; protection of the integrity of public electronic communications networks and services; prevention (in accordance with European Community obligations) of interference with networks and services; provision for financial contributions towards the cost of universal service; provision of networks and services in the event of disaster; protection of public health; and compliance with relevant international standards. Sections 52 to 64 relate to customer interests, the assignment and use of telephone numbers and must-carry obligations.

> *public electronic communications service* is defined in section 151 as an electronic communications service provided to the public.
>
> *public electronic communications network* is defined in section 151 as an electronic communications network provided principally for the purpose of making services available to the public.
>
> *network access* is defined in section 151 as meaning (1) interconnection of public electronic communications networks; or (2) any services, facilities or arrangements (other than interconnection) by means of which a communications provider or a person making associated facilities available is able, for the purposes of the provision of an electronic communications service (whether by him or by another), to make use of any network or apparatus comprised in a network, or any service or facility capable of being used to provide a service.

*relevant international standards are defined in section 151 as meaning (1) any standards or specifications from time to time drawn up and published in accordance with Article 17 of the Framework Directive; (2) the standards and specifications adopted by the European Standards Organisations; and (3) the international standards and recommendations adopted by the International Telecommunications Union, the International Organisations for Standardisation or the International Electrotechnical Committee.

143.   The subject matter set out in subsection (1) implements most of Part A of the Annex to the Authorisation Directive. For more detailed information see the Table in Appendix 2.

144.   *Subsection (3)* provides that general conditions must be of general application. This means that the same general conditions must apply equally to all providers of the particular class of network or service to whom they are expressed to apply.

Section 52: Conditions relating to customer interests

145.   Sections 52 to 55 place OFCOM under a duty to ensure that the communications industry has in place effective and accessible machinery for the protection of domestic and small business customers, including procedures for dealing with complaints and disputes. They allow OFCOM to take action if the industry does not voluntarily develop an effective regime for this purpose. Taken together these sections implement Article 34 of the Universal Service Directive and form part of the implementation of condition 8 of Part A of the Annex to the Authorisation Directive.

146.   Section 52 provides that OFCOM must set such general conditions (if any) as they consider appropriate for securing that public communications providers establish procedures for dealing with domestic and small business customer complaints, and for resolving domestic and small business customer disputes. OFCOM are to ensure that, so far as they consider appropriate, such procedures are simple, transparent and effective, and that they can be used free of charge. The procedures as respect complaints are to be met through securing compliance with a code of practice that has been approved by OFCOM. The requirement to establish procedures for resolving customer disputes is to be met by the public communications providers establishing dispute resolution arrangements approved by OFCOM. The voluntary Ombudsman scheme for communications disputes recently adopted by Oftel is likely to be submitted to OFCOM for approval under these provisions.

* *public communications provider* is defined in section 151 as the provider of a public electronic communications network or service or an associated facility.

* the meaning of *domestic and small business customer* is given in *subsection (6)* and covers customers of communications providers who are neither (a) communications providers, nor (b) undertakings for which more than 10 people work.

Section 53: Approval of codes of practice for the purposes of s. 52
147.   This section sets out the procedures and criteria for approval by OFCOM of codes of practice for dealing with customer complaints. OFCOM shall only approve such a code if it adequately protects the customers of public communications providers to whom the code applies.

148.   *Subsection (2)* places OFCOM under a duty to keep under review codes of practice previously approved by them and *subsection (3)* allows OFCOM to approve modifications made to an approved code, to withdraw their approval, or to make their continuing approval conditional on the responsible providers making appropriate modifications to the code within a defined period of time.

149.   In considering whether to approve (or to continue to approve) a code of practice, OFCOM are obliged to take into account whether the code is easily understandable by customers, the need for consistency between approved codes of practice and the need to keep the number of different approved codes to a minimum.

Section 54: Approval of dispute procedures for the purposes of s.52

150.   This section sets out the procedures and criteria for approval by OFCOM of dispute procedures.   Before OFCOM approve a dispute procedure, they must be satisfied that the procedure satisfies the criteria set out in *subsection (2),* including accountability, independence and transparency, and they must consult the Secretary of State.   The procedures and criteria for approval of dispute procedures are similar to those for approval of codes of practice (outlined in the notes to section 53).

Section 55: Orders by OFCOM in the absence of conditions under s. 52

151.   This section enables OFCOM, by order, with the consent of the Secretary of State, to take appropriate measures where public communications providers have failed to put in place suitable procedures, standards and policies for complaints handling and dispute resolution, and where OFCOM consider it necessary for the protection of customers or to comply with EU obligations.   Appropriate measures by OFCOM may include establishing an independent body corporate to administer and enforce the necessary arrangements, and obliging public communications providers to pay for the establishment and maintenance of such a body.

Section 56: The National Telephone Numbering Plan

152.   OFCOM are to publish a document (the National Telephone Numbering Plan) setting out the telephone numbers available for allocation and the restrictions on the adoption and use of telephone numbers allocated under the Plan.   One way in which OFCOM might choose to set the numbers out could be as blocks or series of numbers. This implements Article 10(3) of the Framework Directive and Article 27 of the Universal Service Directive.   OFCOM are under a duty to review and, if they think fit, to revise the Plan, but subject to the requirements of section 60.   OFCOM must also keep day-to-day records of the telephone numbers actually allocated by them under the National Telephone Numbering Plan.

> * references to a *telephone number* are, under *subsection (5),* references to any number used for identifying the origin, destination or route of an electronic communication.   A *telephone number* is also a number that may be used for selecting a service or for identifying by whose service or network a communication is to be sent; but under *subsection (7),* the Secretary of State may

exclude any description of number from the numbers to be treated as telephone numbers.

adoption of a telephone number occurs, under *subsection (6)*, where a communications provider allocates or transfers that number to a customer or piece of apparatus, or uses that number for identifying the origin, destination or route of an electronic communication, or designates that number for use in selecting a service, or authorises the use of that number by others for any of the purposes mentioned in subsection (5).

* *number* is defined in *subsection (10)* as including data of any description.

Section 57: Conditions to secure access to telephone numbers

153.   OFCOM may set general conditions to ensure that telephone users are able to communicate with every normal telephone number: this implements Article 6(1) of, and condition 4 of Part A of the Annex to the Authorisation Directive and Article 27 and 28 of the Universal Service Directive.

*a *normal telephone number* is defined in *subsection (2)* as a number allocated under the National Telephone Numbering Plan for the purpose of identifying the destination for, or the recipient of, communications which has been adopted by a communications provider as a number to be used for that purpose or which has been allocated in accordance with section 59 and is used for that purpose by a person other than a communications provider.

Section 58: Conditions about allocation and adoption of numbers

154.   *Subsections (1)* and *(2)* allow OFCOM to set general conditions which provide for the matters listed, which broadly cover the requirements to be complied with by communications providers in respect of the adoption and use of telephone numbers; procedures for applying to OFCOM for numbers to be allocated; procedures for the adoption of numbers by communications providers; the circumstances in which numbers are required to be transferred from one provider to another; and payments to be made for allocation and transfer of numbers.

155.   *Subsection (5)* provides that OFCOM may allocate particular telephone numbers by means of an auction.

156.   *Subsections (6)* to *(9)* apply to any conditions set by OFCOM that enable them to determine the payments (including periodic payments) to be made to them in respect of the allocation or transfer of telephone numbers. OFCOM must stipulate in such conditions the principles in accordance with which they will determine the amounts of any such payments. For example, the amount may be determined by reference to bids at an auction, or to the costs incurred by OFCOM, or to any other factors OFCOM may think fit. OFCOM may require payments to be made by means of a lump sum or periodic payments or both. Conditions set subsequently may modify the amounts of (or the method of determining) periodic payments, except where the amount of these payments has been set by auction. Paragraph 16 of Schedule 18 (transitional provisions) provides that any telephone numbers allocated to a holder of a licence granted under section 7 of the Telecommunications Act 1984 shall be treated as if they were allocated to that person under section 58. This section implements most of Part C of the Annex to the Authorisation Directive. For more detailed

information see the Table in Appendix 2.

Section 59: Telephone numbering conditions binding non-providers

157.   OFCOM may set conditions to be complied with by persons who are not communications providers in respect of the allocation, transfer and use of telephone numbers. The duty will be enforceable by OFCOM in civil proceedings. OFCOM must comply with sections 47 to 49 when setting, modifying or revoking any telephone numbering condition which applies to non-communications providers or giving, modifying or withdrawing any direction, approval or consent given by them for the purpose of any condition.

Section 60: Modification of documents referred to in numbering conditions

158.   This section sets out the procedure that OFCOM must follow when revising or otherwise modifying the National Telephone Numbering Plan or any other document referred to in a numbering condition authorised by section 57 or 58 or set by OFCOM under section 59.

159.   Before revising or otherwise modifying a provision of the National Telephone Numbering Plan or other document referred to in a numbering condition (a "relevant provision"), OFCOM must publish a notification that explains the effect of and the reasons for the revisions or modifications. OFCOM must also give no less than one month for persons to comment on the proposal. OFCOM may modify the National Telephone Numbering Plan or other document if they have considered each comment made about the proposal within the period specified by them for comments and they have had regard to international obligations of the UK notified to them by the Secretary of State for the purposes of this section.

160.   Any modification of a relevant provision of the National Telephone Numbering Plan or other document must be objectively justifiable, non-discriminatory, proportionate and transparent. This section implements, in part, Article 14.1 of the Authorisation Directive.

Section 61: Withdrawal of telephone number allocations

161.   This section sets out the circumstances in which OFCOM may withdraw an allocation of telephone numbers.

162.   *Subsection (2)(a) and (b)* provides that an allocation may be withdrawn by consent, or where this is necessary for a transfer of numbers. *Subsection (2)(c)* and section 62 provide that an allocation may be withdrawn to facilitate a "numbering reorganisation" in respect of a particular series of numbers. *Subsection (2)(d)* provides that an allocation may be withdrawn in circumstances specified in numbering conditions and for the purpose of securing the best and most efficient use of telephone numbers (*subsection (5)* provides that *subsection (2)(d)* does not apply to a numbering reorganisation and that any circumstances specified in a numbering

condition must not unduly discriminate between communications providers and users). *Subsection (2)(e) and (f)* provides that an allocation may be withdrawn where it consists of numbers, or part of a series of numbers, which have not been adopted by the communications providers concerned during the time period stipulated in the general conditions. Before withdrawing an allocation under subsection (2)(e) or (f), OFCOM must follow the procedures set out in *subsections (6)* and *(7)* with respect to notification and allowing for representations.

163.   An allocation may also be withdrawn where the person allocated the number has repeatedly and seriously contravened the numbering conditions and where no other remedy is likely to secure compliance. Any contraventions of numbering conditions may justify withdrawal of numbers from a non-provider (*subsection (4)*). This implements Article 10(2) and 10(5) of the Authorisation Directive so far as enforcement of numbering conditions is concerned.

Section 62: Numbering reorganisations

164.   An allocation can only be withdrawn for the purposes of a numbering reorganisation if it does not unduly discriminate against particular communications providers, users of the allocated numbers or a particular description of providers or users, and if OFCOM make a replacement allocation of similar numbers to the person affected. OFCOM may not require a new payment to be made for a replacement allocation. However, in cases where periodic payments are still outstanding in respect of the allocation which has been withdrawn, OFCOM may require the balance of those payments to be made in respect of the replacement allocation, with such adjustments as OFCOM may think fit. This implements condition 2 of Part C of the Annex to the Authorisation Directive.

Section 63: General duty as to telephone numbering functions

165.   This section places OFCOM under a duty, in carrying out their functions under sections 56 to 62, to ensure the best use of telephone numbers. OFCOM are also required to ensure that communication providers do not discriminate against other providers in relation to the adoption of telephone numbers: this implements Article 10.2 of the Framework Directive.

Section 64: Must-carry obligations

166.   General conditions may include provision to ensure that services on the must-carry list are carried by networks which are used by a significant number of end users as their principal means of receiving television.

167.   The must-carry list contains the following services: a service of television programmes provided by the BBC in digital form (where the service is one in relation to which OFCOM have functions), digital Channel 3, digital Channel 4, digital Channel 5, S4C Digital and the digital public teletext service.

168.   The requirement to carry a listed service will also apply to any ancillary services (such as subtitling or other assistance to disabled people) related to that service, and may be treated as consisting of such other services comprised in or provided with that service as may be determined by OFCOM.

169.   General conditions containing provisions authorised under section 64 must comply with any order made by the Secretary of State under *subsection (5)* to set the minimum and maximum capacity that a listed service must or may use on a network.

170.   The Secretary of State, when setting the maximum or minimum capacity to be used by a listed service, must have regard (a) to the objective of securing that the services on the must-carry list, together with any others to which provisions authorised under section 64 apply, are available for reception by as many members of the public in the United Kingdom as practicable, and (b) to the need to secure that the amount of capacity left available is reasonable and, accordingly, that the burden imposed on the cable operator under this section is proportionate to the public benefit obtained.

171.   The Secretary of State can also make an order which sets the terms on which a service on the must-carry list is to be broadcast (or provides for OFCOM to set such terms).   This can include a requirement that no payment is made by the service provider or the network provider.

172.   The Secretary of State must, from time to time, review the must-carry list and any requirements as to the terms on which services in that list must be broadcast. When carrying out a review the Secretary of State must consult OFCOM and other parties likely to be affected by a modification to the must-carry list. Following such a review, the Secretary of State may, by order, amend the must-carry list.   When determining whether or not it is appropriate to amend the list, she must consider the public benefit in doing so, the extent to which a service would otherwise be made available even if not added to the list, the amount of spare network capacity of providers of electronic communications networks to whom the must-carry obligations apply and whether the burden of compliance is proportionate to the objective of securing that must-carry services are made available to the public.

173.   She must consult OFCOM and such persons who, in her opinion, are likely to be affected by an order, or who represent any of those persons, as she thinks fit:

- before making an order under *subsection (5)* (to set minimum and maximum capacity); and

- before making an order under *subsection (11)* (as to the terms of carriage).

This does not apply when a review has been carried out under *subsection (7)*, as a full consultation is already required under *subsection (8)*.

174.   This section implements Article 6(1) of, and condition 6 of Part A to the

Annex to the Authorisation Directive and Article 31 of the Universal Service Directive.

Section 65: Obligations to be secured by universal service conditions

175.   Sections 65 to 72 describe OFCOM's and the Secretary of State's functions relating to universal service.

176.   Sections 65 and 67 to 69 implement Articles 3 to 7 and 9 to 11 of, and Part A of Annex I to, the Universal Service Directive. Section 66 implements Article 8 of the Universal Service Directive and Articles 4(2) and 6(2) of the Authorisation Directive and sections 70 to 72 implement Articles 12 to 14 of the Universal Service Directive.

177.   Under section 65 the Secretary of State is required by order (which may be varied at any time) ("the universal service order") to set out the electronic communications networks, electronic communications services, associated facilities, directories and directory enquiry facilities, and particular methods of billing for services or of accepting payment for them that must be provided throughout the UK by universal service providers. Before making or varying the universal service order, the Secretary of State must consult OFCOM and other appropriate persons.

178.   The objective behind "universal service" obligations is to ensure that the basic communications services which are used by the majority, and which are essential to full social and economic inclusion, are made available to everyone who reasonably requests them at an affordable price.

Section 66: Designation of universal service providers

179.   OFCOM have the power, by regulations, to provide for a procedure for designation of communications providers (or persons who are not communications providers, in the case of supplying directories or directory enquiry facilities) who will be subject to universal service conditions. Such regulations must establish an efficient, objective, transparent, and non-discriminatory procedure for designation. Regulations made under this section are also to provide for a designation to cease to have effect where all the universal service conditions applying to a provider are revoked.

180.   Where OFCOM designate a person as a universal service provider, or where a designation ceases to have effect, they must notify this fact to the European Commission. This implements Article 36(1) of the Universal Service Directive.

Section 67: Subject matter of universal service conditions

181.   This section enables OFCOM to set universal service conditions for securing the provision of the networks, services and facilities etc. set out in the universal service order published by the Secretary of State under section 65. In setting such

conditions OFCOM must have regard to any guidance about matters relating to pricing that is contained in the universal service order.

182.   Persons who are subject to universal service conditions will be required to publish up-to-date information demonstrating how successful they are in complying with their obligations. The information is to be framed in accordance with the quality of service parameters, definitions and measurement methods set out in Annex III to the Universal Service Directive. The person may also be required to finance the independent auditing – for accuracy and usefulness - of such information. OFCOM may also impose performance targets.

Section 68: Tariffs etc. for universal services

183.   This section requires OFCOM to keep under review universal service tariffs. Universal service conditions can require a common tariff (which includes any pricing structure) or, in specified cases, a special tariff for provision of the networks, services, apparatus, associated facilities, directories and directory enquiry facilities set out in the universal service order. At no time should the customer of a universal services provider be required to pay for any service which is not necessary for the provision of the universal service in question.

Section 69: Directories and directory enquiry facilities

184.   This section provides that where the universal service conditions require the provision of directories or directory enquiry services, the provider must not excessively discriminate against any provider who provides information for use in that directory, or against any information so provided.

Section 70: Review of compliance costs

185.   This section enables OFCOM periodically to analyse the financial cost to a designated provider of complying with universal service conditions applied to him. OFCOM must then have these costs audited by an independent auditor, or must themselves audit those figures. OFCOM are under a duty to publish their conclusions, alongside a summary of the audit report.

Section 71: Sharing of burden of universal service obligations

186.   If, following a study of costs pursuant to section 70, OFCOM conclude that a financial burden is imposed on the provider of universal services, OFCOM must assess whether it would be unfair for that provider to shoulder the entire burden. If OFCOM determine that it would be unfair, and if the provider applies to OFCOM, OFCOM may determine that contributions from other communications providers, who themselves are subject to general conditions, are to be made. *Subsection (4)* provides that all this should be carried out in accordance with regulations made by OFCOM.   These regulations should ensure that the calculation, collection and distribution of such contributions is to be done in an objective, transparent, and non-

discriminatory way, and in a manner that avoids or minimises any distortion to competition or demand.

187.   Section 51(1)(d) enables OFCOM to set general conditions giving effect to determinations or regulations made under this section. This implements condition 1 of Part A of the Annex to the Authorisation Directive.

Section 72: Report on sharing mechanism

188.   This section provides that where regulations that provide for the sharing of the financial burden of providing universal services are in place under section 71, OFCOM must prepare and publish an annual report. However, OFCOM are not obliged to publish any confidential material.

> *material is *confidential* if it falls within *subsections (7)* or *(8)*, i.e. if it relates specifically to the affairs of a particular body, or the private affairs of an individual, in each case where publication could seriously prejudice that body's or person's interests.

Section 73: Permitted subject matter of access-related conditions

189.   This section governs OFCOM's power to set access-related conditions. OFCOM may set access-related conditions only in relation to one or more of the matters listed in *subsections (2)* to *(5)*.

190.   *Subsection (2)* allows OFCOM to set access-related conditions for the purpose of ensuring a level of network access and interoperability which will secure efficiency, sustainable competition and the greatest possible benefit to end-users. These access-related conditions include, but are not limited to, the specific type of access-related conditions set out in section 74. This provision, together with section 74, implements Article 5(1) of and Part II of Annex I to the Access Directive and Article 2(p) of the Framework Directive.

191.   *Subsection (3)* allows OFCOM to set access-related conditions to secure the sharing of apparatus and the division of the costs incurred by those to whom the electronic communications code applies, in cases where there is no viable alternative. This implements Article 12(2) of the Framework Directive.

192.   *Subsection (4)* allows OFCOM to set access-related conditions of a technical or operational nature to ensure the proper operation of an electronic communications network in compliance with any SMP services conditions falling within section 87(3). Section 87(3) allows OFCOM to set SMP conditions requiring the dominant provider to give entitlements in relation to network access, use of relevant networks and availability of relevant facilities. This provision, together with section 75(1), implements Article 5(2) of the Access Directive.

193.   Finally, *subsection (5)* provides that OFCOM may set access-related conditions in respect of conditional access systems in accordance with section 75(2).

This provision, together with sections 75(2) and 76, implements Article 6 of, and Part I of Annex I to, the Access Directive and Article 2(f) of the Framework Directive.

conditional access system is defined in section 75 (see below).

Section 74: Specific types of access-related conditions

194.   Section 73(2) allows OFCOM to set access-related conditions for the purpose of ensuring a level of network access and interoperability which will promote efficiency and sustainable competition and the greatest possible benefit end-users. Section 74 provides that such conditions include those designed to ensure end-to-end connectivity. It also provides that conditions can be set for securing that the use of Application Programme Interfaces (APIs) and Electronic Programme Guides (EPGs) is provided on a fair, reasonable and non-discriminatory basis.

end-to-end connectivity is defined in *subsection (3)* as the ability for two parties to communicate with each other whether they are using the same or different public electronic communications services.

*the meaning of *application programme interface* is given in subsection (3) as a facility for allowing software to use facilities in other software in order to allow someone to access a programme service or become the ultimate user of any network or service by means of which any programme service is broadcast or otherwise transmitted.

electronic programme guide is defined in subsection (3) as any facility by means of which a person may ascertain what programmes are included in a service, and may access that service.

Section 75: Conditional access systems and access to digital services

195.   *Subsection (1)* provides that OFCOM must ensure, when setting an access-related condition of a technical or operational nature for providers with significant market power (SMP), that they take account of all relevant international standards (which are defined in section 151).

196.   *Subsection (2)* provides that OFCOM are under a duty to ensure that access-related conditions are applied to every person who provides a conditional access system in relation to a protected programme service, and that such conditions comply with Part I of Annex I of the Access Directive.

conditional access system is defined in *subsection (3)* as any arrangements by means of which access to a programme service requires either subscription or authorisation.

protected programme service is defined in subsection (3) as a service which is encrypted such that the programmes on it can only be viewed or listened to in an intelligible form by the use of a conditional access system.

Section 76: Modification and revocation of conditions imposed under s.75

197.   This section provides that OFCOM may not modify or revoke any access-related conditions that they have set falling within section 75(2) unless they have carried out a market analysis from which they have concluded that the provider of conditional access systems to whom the condition applies does not have SMP. They

must ensure that the proposed modification or revocation will not adversely affect the accessibility to persons of must-carry services or the prospects for effective competition.

Section 77: Imposition of privileged supplier conditions

198.   Where a public electronic communications provider enjoys special or exclusive rights in relation to the provision of services in other sectors (other than the provision of associated facilities), OFCOM must set such privileged supplier conditions as they think fit (unless that provider has an annual turnover in relation to all of his communications activities of less than €50 million, in which case OFCOM are not obliged to impose a condition, but may do so if they wish). Such conditions can require such providers to keep separate accounts (all of which should be audited and published), or to have structural separation between different activities. This implements Article 13 of the Framework Directive.

> *special or exclusive rights* has the same meaning as in Article 86 of the Treaty establishing the European Community. Although the Treaty does not itself define them, guidance is given in Article 2(1)(f) and (g) of the Commission Transparency Directive OJ [1980] L 195/35. These rights are often, but need not be, given to public undertakings. Exclusive rights are largely self-explanatory but should be analysed in a functional rather than formalistic manner. Case law indicates that special rights are rights granted by a Member State to a limited number of undertakings where this limits – otherwise than according to objective, proportionate and non-discriminatory criteria - the number of undertakings authorised to provide a service in a particular area.

Section 78: Circumstances required for the setting of SMP conditions

199.   Sections 78 to 93 concern OFCOM's powers and duties to identify markets, determine whether persons have significant market power (SMP) on those markets, and to impose SMP conditions on persons whom they have determined as having SMP.

200.   Section 78 sets out when a person shall be taken to have SMP in relation to a particular market. A person will only be taken to have significant market power where he is, alone or with others, in a position of dominance in a market. A position of dominance must be construed in accordance with any applicable provisions of Article 14 of the Framework Directive, which (at its paragraph 2) defines dominance as 'a position of economic strength affording the person the power to behave to an appreciable extent independently of competitors, customers and ultimately consumers'. A determination of joint dominance must take into account, in particular, the criteria for joint dominance set out in Annex II to the Framework Directive. This implements Article 14 of and Annex II to the Framework Directive.

Section 79: Market power determinations

201.   *Subsection (1)* provides that before making a determination that a person has SMP, OFCOM must first identify the markets in which they consider it will be appropriate to carry out a market analysis and then carry out that analysis. When

identifying appropriate services markets and when making SMP determinations in relation to a services market, OFCOM are obliged to take due account of all relevant European Commission guidelines and recommendations - the first such recommendation was published by the European Commission on 11 February 2003: the recommendation can be viewed on the European Commission website (http://europa.eu.int/information_society/topics/telecoms/regulatory/maindocs/docum ents/recomen.pdf). The way in which a market is to be identified or a market determination made is by the publication of a notification under *subsection (4)*. This section implements Articles 15 and 16 of the Framework Directive. The Electronic Communications (Market Analyses) Regulations 2003 (S.I. 2003/330) empower Oftel to carry out market analyses and to make proposals for market power determinations and the setting of conditions in advance of the passing of the Act. Paragraph 10 of Schedule 18 to the Act provides that proposals confirmed under those Regulations have effect under this section and other relevant sections after the provisions of the Act have been commenced.

Section 80: Proposals for identifying markets and for market determination proposals

202.   Before identifying a market for the purposes of making a market power determination or making a market power determination, OFCOM must publish a notification of what they are proposing to do. A notification under this section must state that OFCOM are proposing to identify that market or to make a market power determination, set out the effect of the proposal, give their reasons for making the proposal and specify the period (not less than one month from the date of the publication of the notification) within which representations about the proposal may be made to OFCOM.

203.   Subject to sections 82 and 83, *subsection (6)* provides that OFCOM may give effect, with or without notifications, to a proposal notified in accordance with this section, provided they have considered every representation about the proposal made within the period specified by them and they have regard to every international obligation of the United Kingdom (if any) notified to them by the Secretary of State.

204.   This section implements Articles 6, 7 and 16(1) of the Framework Directive.

Section 81: Delivery of copies of notifications under ss. 79 and 80

205.   OFCOM must send a copy of every notification published under section 79(4) or 80 to the Secretary of State. OFCOM must also send to the European Commission: (i) a copy of every notification published under section 79(4) with respect to a market power determination in relation to an SMP services market; and (ii) a copy of every notification published under section 80 which relates to a proposal to identify a services market or to make a market power determination in relation to such a market; and which in OFCOM's opinion would affect trade between member States. A copy of a notification falling within (ii) must also be sent to the regulatory authorities of every other member State.

206.   In all other cases when it appears to them appropriate to do so, OFCOM must send a copy of a notification published under section 80 which relates to a proposal to identify a services market or to make a market power determination in relation to such market to the European Commission and such of the regulatory authorities of the other member States as OFCOM think fit.

207.   The various requirements in this section to send matters to the European Commission implement Article 16(2) of the Access Directive, Article 36(2) of the Universal Service Directive and Article 7(3) and (5) of the Framework Directive.

Section 82: European Commission's powers in respect of proposals

208.   During the period given for representations under a notification under section 80 relating to an SMP services condition, the European Commission may inform OFCOM that they believe that the proposed market identified in the notice or OFCOM's proposed market determination may not be compatible with the single European market, or with any Community obligations. In such a case, OFCOM may not give effect to their proposal for a further two months. OFCOM must withdraw their proposal if in accordance with the procedure in Article 7(4) of the Framework Directive the Commission, within that two-month period, decides that the proposal must be withdrawn. This implements Article 7(4) of the Framework Directive.

Section 83: Special rules for transnational markets

209.   When the European Commission identifies a transnational services market that includes the United Kingdom, OFCOM are required to make arrangements with all other relevant regulatory authorities to deal with the following issues:

- the identification of the market;

- assessing whether a person has SMP in the relevant transnational services market(s);

- the setting of appropriate SMP services conditions as well as the modification or revocation of such conditions; and

- the procedures to be followed to secure that OFCOM and other regulatory authorities comply with their agreed arrangements.

210.   This implements Articles 2(b), 15(4) and 16(5) of the Framework Directive.

Section 84: Review of services market identifications and determinations

211.   Where OFCOM have identified and analysed a services market for the purposes of making a market power determination, OFCOM must, at such intervals as they consider appropriate, carry out further analyses of the identified market for the purposes of reviewing the determinations made on the basis of the earlier analysis and

deciding whether to modify any SMP condition set on the basis of that earlier analysis (*subsection (2)*). Where OFCOM determine that a person to whom any SMP conditions are applied no longer has SMP, they must revoke every SMP services condition applied to that person by reference to the market power determination made on the basis of the earlier analysis.

212.   *Subsection (3)* requires OFCOM to carry out further analysis of a services market as soon as reasonably practicable after the European Commission makes any recommendation that affects the matters that were (or could have been) taken into account in the earlier market analysis.

213.   Before carrying out further analysis for the purposes of subsection (2), OFCOM may review any of their decisions identifying the appropriate markets that they considered in their earlier analysis.   Where OFCOM conclude that the appropriate markets have changed, OFCOM must identify the markets they now consider to be appropriate and those markets must be the identified markets for the purposes of further analysis.

214.   Sections 79 to 83 apply in relation to the identification of a services market for the purposes of reviewing a market power determination and in relation to the review of such a determination.

215.   This section implements Article 16(1) and (3) of the Framework Directive, Article 7(3) of the Access Directive and Articles 16(3) and 18(2) of the Universal Service Directive

Section 85: Review of apparatus market identifications and determinations

216.   Where OFCOM have identified and analysed an apparatus market for the purposes of making a market power determination, OFCOM must, at such intervals as they consider appropriate, carry out further analyses of the identified market for the purposes of reviewing the determinations made on the basis of the earlier analysis and deciding whether to modify any SMP condition set on the basis of that earlier analysis (*subsection (2)*).   Where OFCOM determine that a person to whom any SMP conditions are applied no longer has SMP, they must revoke every SMP apparatus condition applied to that person by reference to the market power determination made on the basis of the earlier analysis.

217.   Before carrying out that further analysis OFCOM may review any of their decisions identifying the appropriate markets that they considered in their earlier analysis.   Where OFCOM conclude that the appropriate markets have changed, OFCOM must identify the markets they now consider to be appropriate and those markets must be the identified markets for the purposes of further analysis.

218.   Sections 79, 80 and 81(1) apply in relation to the identification of an apparatus market for the purposes of reviewing a market power determination and in relation to the review of such a determination.

Section 86: Cases where review required

219.   This section prohibits OFCOM from setting an SMP services condition by a notification (other than by a notification which also makes the market power determination by reference to which the condition is set) unless (i) the condition is set by reference to a market power determination which has been reviewed under section 84; or (ii) the condition is set by reference to a market power determination made in relation to a market in which OFCOM are satisfied there has been no material change since the determination was made.

> * A change is material for the purposes of this section if it is material to the setting of the condition in question or the modification or revocation in question.

220.   OFCOM must not modify or revoke SMP services conditions applying to a person except where: (i) for the purpose of determining whether to make the modification or revocation, they have carried out further analysis under section 84 of the market in question and reviewed the market power determination for the time being in force in that person's case; or (ii) they are satisfied that there has not been a material change in the market identified or otherwise used for the purposes of the market power determination by reference to which the condition was set or last modified.

221.   OFCOM must not modify SMP apparatus conditions applying to a person except where, for the purpose of determining whether to make the modification or revocation, they have carried out a further analysis under section 85 of the market in question; and reviewed the market power determination for the time being in force in that person's case.

Section 87: Conditions about network access etc.

222.   Sections 87 to 92 make provision about the subject matter of SMP services conditions.   Where OFCOM have identified a provider of a public electronic communications network or a person who makes available associated facilities in connection with such a network as having SMP in a services market, they may impose such SMP conditions authorised by this section, as they consider appropriate.   These may include conditions requiring the provider to confer entitlements on other providers regarding the provision of network access, the use of that network, and the availability of facilities.   Such conditions may include provision for securing fairness and reasonableness in the process and should be set having taken into account the matters set out in *subsection (4)*.   These include the feasibility of providing network access; the need to ensure effective long-term competition in the markets; the investment made by the person initially providing or making available the network or facility in respect of which an entitlement to network access is proposed; the technical and economic viability of installing and using facilities that would make the proposed network access unnecessary; intellectual property rights; and the availability of services throughout the European Union.

223.   *Subsection (6)* provides that SMP service conditions may require a person with SMP to publish such information as OFCOM may direct for the purpose of securing transparency in relation to network access. They may require such a person not to discriminate in relation to any matter connected with network access. They may require such a person to publish the terms and conditions on which the provider will enter an access contract and to modify those terms and conditions.

*an *access contract* is defined in *subsection (12)* as any contract for the provision, by a dominant provider, of network access, or of associated facilities made available in relation to a public electronic communications network.

224.   *Subsection (7)* provides that OFCOM may set SMP services conditions obliging a dominant provider to maintain separate accounts for such different matters relating to network access or the availability of associated facilities as OFCOM may direct.

225.   *Subsection (9)* provides that OFCOM may set SMP services conditions requiring a person with SMP to comply with price-controls, rules on cost-recovery and cost accounting systems in relation to matters connected with network access or the availability of associated facilities. OFCOM may also, by setting such conditions, direct the provider to adjust its prices.

226.   This section, together with sections 88 and 89, implement Articles 8 to 13 of the Access Directive, Article 6(2) of the Authorisation Directive and Article 16(4) of the Framework Directive.

Section 88: Conditions about network access pricing etc.

227.   OFCOM may not set conditions under section 87(9) unless it appears to them from a market analysis that the provider in question might charge excessive prices or engage in other anti-competitive pricing behaviour. The condition must also be perceived by OFCOM as being efficient and pro-competitive, and as resulting in the maximum benefit to end-users. In setting an SMP services condition falling within section 87(9), OFCOM must take into account the extent of the investment that the person to whom the condition is to apply would need to make if the condition were to be applied.

Section 89: Conditions about network access in exceptional cases

228.   In exceptional circumstances, OFCOM may decide that SMP services conditions additional to those set out in sections 87 and 88 (SMP services conditions about network access) need to be imposed on a provider. Such additional SMP services conditions must be submitted by OFCOM to the European Commission for approval and OFCOM can only apply them once they are approved.

Section 90: Conditions about carrier selection and pre-selection

229.   Where the relevant market is one relating to services for the provision of public fixed line telephone networks, OFCOM may set conditions obliging providers with SMP to make a relevant connection facility available to any person to whom they provide a public electronic communications service, or to make interconnection facilities available to a person providing an electronic communications service. OFCOM must also set pricing conditions to ensure that charges imposed by the provider with SMP do not constitute a barrier to use of the facility. Conditions set by OFCOM under this section may impose obligations relating to the manner in which a relevant connection facility is to be made available or in which the facilities for interconnection that are to be made available to a person providing an electronic communications service. This section implements Article 19 of the Universal Service Directive Article 6(2) of the Authorisation Directive and Article 16(4) of the Framework Directive.

> *relevant connection facility* is defined in *subsection (6)* as a facility which allows the end-user to select which carrier to use. This may be specified on every occasion of use (carrier selection), or by designating a carrier in advance (carrier pre-selection).

Section 91: Conditions about regulation of services etc. for end-users

230.   This section deals with the situation where the relevant services market is one for the end-users of public electronic communications services, and where access-related conditions, and SMP conditions set under sections 87 to 90, are not sufficient to allow OFCOM to perform their duty under section 4. In such a case, OFCOM may set conditions obliging the provider to comply with such regulatory controls as OFCOM consider appropriate.

231.   If such regulatory controls are imposed on tariffs, or on other matters to which costs are relevant, the provider may be obliged to use such cost accounting systems as OFCOM direct, to have those systems annually audited and to publish an annual statement as to its compliance with those obligations. OFCOM must provide the European Commission with whatever information they require about conditions authorised by this section. This section implements Article 17 of the Universal Service Directive, Article 6(2) of the Authorisation Directive and Article 16(4) of the Framework Directive.

Section 92: Conditions about leased lines

232.   Where the relevant services market relates to the provision of such leased lines as are identified by the European Commission in the List of Standards published in the Official Journal of the European Communities, OFCOM may set and apply SMP services conditions obliging the provider to apply, so far as required by Annex VII of the Universal Service Directive, the principles of non-discrimination, cost orientation and transparency to dealings regarding leased lines. This section implements Article 18 of, and Annex VII to, the Universal Service Directive, Article 6(2) of the Authorisation Directive and Article 16(4) of the Framework Directive.

*a *leased line* is defined in *subsection (4)* as an electronic communications service consisting in the reservation of a fixed amount of transmission capacity between fixed points on the same or different electronic communications networks.

Section 93: Conditions about apparatus supply

233.   Where OFCOM determine that a supplier of electronic communications apparatus has SMP in an apparatus market, OFCOM may set conditions requiring the supplier to maintain accounting separation between such activities and other matters and also may set price controls in relation to the hiring of telephones which are hardwired to an electronic communications network. The SMP apparatus conditions may only apply to apparatus in respect of which the supplier has been found to have significant market power.

* A telephone is hardwired to an electronic communications network if the telephone has to be physically attached to apparatus in the network by means of a tool before it can be used (*subsection (5)*)..

*Apparatus in relation to SMP apparatus conditions is defined in *section 151(1)*, as apparatus designed or adapted for a use which consists of or includes the sending or receiving of communications or other signals (within the meaning of section 32) that are transmitted by means of an electronic communications network.

Section 94: Notification of contravention of condition

234.   This section gives OFCOM powers of enforcement in respect of all types of conditions set pursuant to section 45. Where OFCOM have reasonable grounds to believe that a person is or has been in breach of any condition, they may notify that person accordingly, and allow him a specified period of time in which to make representations to OFCOM and to take steps to comply with the condition or remedy the breach. That period must be one month, other than in the circumstances provided for by *subsections (6) and (7)* or where the case is an urgent case (see section 98(3)).

235.   OFCOM must not give such a notification where they decide that a more appropriate approach lies under the Competition Act 1998, in which case they must publish a notification to that effect.

236.   This section, and sections 95 to 100 and 102 and 103, implement Article 10 of the Authorisation Directive and Article 11(6) of the Universal Service Directive in the context of the enforcement of the conditions of entitlement.

Section 95: Enforcement notification for contravention of conditions

237.   If, by the end of the period specified in section 94, OFCOM are satisfied that the condition about which the provider was notified has still not been fully complied with, *subsection (2)* allows OFCOM to serve an enforcement notification on the notified provider. Such a notification requires the notified provider to take such steps as are specified in the notification to comply with the notified condition and remedy

the consequences of any contravention, within the period specified in the notification. Those persons to whom an enforcement notification has been given are under a duty, enforceable by OFCOM via civil proceedings, to comply with it.

Section 96: Penalties for contravention of conditions

238.   This section allows OFCOM to impose a penalty on a notified provider where a notification of contravention under section 94, has been issued, and the notified provider is in contravention of any of the conditions specified there and has not, within the period allowed by OFCOM for the making of representations, taken steps to comply with the condition(s) concerned and to remedy the consequences. OFCOM may also impose a penalty where a person is in contravention of a requirement of an enforcement notice under section 95. OFCOM must notify the decision to impose a penalty, the reasons for it, and the period within which the penalty is to be paid to the person on whom it is being imposed within one week of that decision.

Section 97: Amount of penalty under s. 96

239.   In deciding on the amount of a financial penalty under section 96, OFCOM are required to consider whether the penalty is appropriate and proportionate, and to take account of any representations made by the person concerned, and any steps taken by him to comply with the notified condition. The penalty shall not, in any event, exceed 10 per cent of the turnover of that person's relevant business for the relevant period.

> * *relevant business* is defined in *subsection (5) to (7)* as, broadly, business consisting of the provision of an electronic communications network, electronic communications service or associated facilities, and the supply of directories, directory enquiry facilities or electronic communications apparatus. In the case of a penalty imposed for the contravention of an SMP apparatus condition, the relevant business is only the business consisting of the supply of electronic communications apparatus.

> * *relevant period* is defined in subsection (5) – subject to exceptions for providers who have not been carrying on business for a full year, or who have gone out of business - as the period of one year ending on the 31 March preceding the notification.

Section 98: Power to deal with urgent cases

240.   This section gives OFCOM additional powers where they determine that there are reasonable grounds for suspecting that a contravention of a condition of entitlement (other than an SMP apparatus condition) has caused, or creates a risk of, either a serious threat to public safety, public health or national security; or serious economic or operational problems or any communications provider or provider of associated facilities or any person who uses them.

241.   In such exceptional circumstances, OFCOM may in a notification of the contravention under section 94, reduce the one-month period allowed to the person who is alleged to be in breach of a condition to make representations and to take steps towards compliance. In addition, OFCOM may suspend the person's entitlement to provide networks, services and/or associated facilities, or may restrict that entitlement in some way (*subsection (4)*). OFCOM may postpone the entry into effect of the

suspension and may also impose such conditions on the person whose service is to be suspended as they consider necessary to protect customers. Those conditions may include requirements for payment of compensation to customers for loss or damage or for annoyance, inconvenience or anxiety caused in consequence of the suspension; however, such conditions have effect only where the direction is confirmed in accordance with section 99.

Section 99: Confirmation of directions under s.98

242.   As soon as reasonably practicable after suspending or restricting a person's entitlement under section 98(4), OFCOM must give that person an opportunity of making representations to them about the grounds on which it was given and its effect and of proposing steps to remedy the situation.

243.   As soon as practicable after the period allowed by OFCOM for making representations, OFCOM must determine whether the contravention providing the grounds for the suspension or restriction did occur and whether the circumstances made it an urgent case justifying the suspension or restriction. If OFCOM decide that the contravention did occur and that the suspension or restriction was justified, they may confirm the direction. If not, OFCOM must revoke the suspension or restriction. They must notify the person concerned of their decision.

Section 100: Suspending service provision for contraventions of conditions

244.   Subject to compliance with section 102, this section gives OFCOM a power to suspend or restrict a person's entitlement to provide electronic communications networks, electronic communications services and/or associated facilities where OFCOM are satisfied that that person is in serious and repeated breach of any conditions imposed on him (other than an SMP apparatus condition) and that an attempt, by the imposition of penalties or the giving of an enforcement notification under section 95 or both, to secure compliance has failed. The suspension or restriction must be appropriate and proportionate to the seriousness of the repeated contraventions.

245.   A direction by OFCOM under this section may suspend entitlement generally or in relation to particular networks, services or facilities and may take effect indefinitely or for a fixed period. A direction may also include, where appropriate, conditions, such as the payment of compensation, to protect the customers of a provider. Where appropriate, OFCOM may revoke the suspension or restriction.

Section 101: Suspending apparatus supply for contraventions of conditions

246.   Subject to compliance with section 102, OFCOM have the power under section 101 to give a direction suspending or restricting a person from supplying electronic communications apparatus where OFCOM are satisfied that the person is in serious and repeated breach of an SMP apparatus condition and that an attempt, by the imposition of penalties or the giving of an enforcement notification under section 95

or both, to secure compliance has failed. The suspension or restriction must be appropriate and proportionate to the seriousness of the repeated contraventions.

247. A direction by OFCOM under this section may take effect indefinitely or for a fixed period and may require the supplier to take measures to protect its customers. A direction may also include, where appropriate, conditions, such as the payment of compensation, to protect the customers of a supplier. Where appropriate, OFCOM may revoke the suspension or restriction.

Section 102: Procedure for directions under ss. 100 and 101

248. Unless a case is urgent, before exercising their powers under sections 100 and 101, OFCOM must notify a contravening provider or supplier of the proposed direction, allow him the least one month to make representations and consider each representation made by him.

> *The meaning of an urgent case is set out in *subsection (4) and (5)* and arises where there is a serious threat to public safety, public health or national security or a serious economic or operational problem that makes it inappropriate to give a contravening provider or supplier time to make representations.

249. If a case is urgent, OFCOM may give a direction without consulting the relevant contravening provider or supplier. However, as soon as practicable after giving a direction in an urgent case OFCOM must provide the relevant contravening provider or supplier with an opportunity to make representations and to propose steps to remedy the contravention (see *subsection (3)*).

Section 103: Enforcement of directions under ss. 98, 100and 101

250. It is an offence for any person to provide a network, service or associated facility or to supply electronic communications apparatus while he is subject to a direction given under sections 98, 100 and 101 suspending his entitlement to do so or where he does so in contravention of any restriction in such a direction. A person found guilty will be liable to a fine.

Section 104: Civil liability for breach of conditions or enforcement notification

251. This section provides that the obligation of a person to comply with any applicable conditions under section 45, or the conditions imposed by a direction under section 98 or 100, or any requirements imposed by an enforcement notification under section 95, is a duty owed to every person who may be affected by the contravention of the condition or requirement. Where a person sustains loss or damage as a result of a breach of that duty or of an act which induces a breach of the duty or interfering with its performance, that person may bring civil proceedings against the provider or supplier concerned. OFCOM's consent is required before proceedings can be brought in respect of a breach of condition under section 45. In any such proceedings, a person may defend himself by demonstrating that he did everything reasonable and exercised all due diligence to avoid breaching the condition or requirement in question.

Section 105: Consideration and determination of network access questions

252. This section applies where a network access question has arisen and needs to be determined and OFCOM consider that, for the purpose of determining that question, it would be appropriate for them to exercise their powers to set, modify or revoke access-related conditions authorised by section 73(2) or (4) or SMP services conditions authorised by section 87.

*A network access question is defined in *subsection (6)* as a question relating to network access or the terms or conditions on which network access is or may be provided.

253.   Before considering whether, for the purposes of determining the network access question, to set, modify or revoke access-related conditions authorised by section 73(2) or (4) or SMP services conditions authorised by section 84, OFCOM must publish a notification of their proposal. If, after considering the network access question, OFCOM decide not to set, modify or revoke such conditions, they must publish a notification of their decision. This section implements Article 5(4) of the Access Directive.

Section 106: Application of the electronic communications code

254.   Sections 106 to 119 and Schedule 3 amend the telecommunications code (set out in Schedule 2 to the Telecommunications Act 1984) in order to translate it into a code applicable to apparatus used in electronic communications networks and services. The telecommunications code is designed to facilitate the installation and maintenance of telecommunications systems. It confers rights on operators to install and maintain apparatus in, over or under land and results in considerably simplified planning procedures, similar to those given to other utilities. These provisions, along with Schedule 2 to the Telecommunications Act 1984, implement Articles 11 and 12(1) of the Framework Directive, and Article 4(1) and 6(1) of, and condition 5 of Part A of the Annex to, the Authorisation Directive.

255.   Sections 106 to 119 provide that "the electronic communications code" (as it will in the future be known) will no longer be applied to operators by way of licences (and licence conditions), but rather as a result of directions given by OFCOM in response to applications by individual providers of electronic communications networks or systems of conduits to be used for the provision of electronic communications networks. The principal changes to the code which will be effected under Schedule 3 include the replacement of references in it to telecommunications apparatus, services and systems with references to electronic communications apparatus, services and networks respectively; amendments to enable the application of the code to persons who provide a system of conduits by which an electronic communications network may be provided, but do not actually provide the network; and the addition of a provision to encourage the sharing of apparatus by operators to whom the code applies (which was previously contained in sections 10(3A), (3B) and (3C) of the Telecommunications Act 1984 and section 189 of the Broadcasting Act 1990; now see new paragraph 29 of the code).

256.   Section 106 provides that the electronic communications code will apply to any person in respect of whom OFCOM have given a direction for this purpose. *Subsection (5)* provides that such a direction may specify that the code is to apply to the person concerned only in relation to particular places, or particular networks or parts of networks or particular conduit systems or parts of conduit systems.

257.   *Subsection (3)(b)* provides that the electronic communications code will also apply to the Secretary of State or any Northern Ireland department if either of them is providing or intends to provide an electronic communications network.

258.   *Subsection (4)* provides that the code may only be applied to a person for the purposes of the provision of an electronic communications network or for the purposes of the provision of a system of conduits to be used in connection with the provision of an electronic communications network.

259.   Paragraph 17 of Schedule 18 provides that where, immediately before the coming into force of this section, the code applied to any person by virtue of the conditions of his telecommunications licence, that person shall be treated, after the coming into force of this section, as a person in whose case the code applies by virtue of a direction given by OFCOM.

Section 107: Procedure for directions applying code

260.   This section provides that OFCOM may only give a direction applying the code in response to an individual application for this purpose, and specifies the procedures that apply to such applications. *Subsection (2)* provides that applicants must comply with all requirements as to form, content and manner of application as have been set out by OFCOM in a notification.

261.   In deciding whether or not to give a direction applying the code OFCOM, in addition to their general duties and their duties for the purpose of fulfilling Community obligations under sections 3 and 4 respectively, must have regard to a number of factors, including the benefit to the public; the difficulty of providing the network or service without the code; the need to encourage shared use of apparatus; and whether the applicant has sufficient resources to meet any liabilities that may arise as a result of action taken by him under the code.

262.   *Subsections (6)* to *(10)* lay down the procedures that OFCOM must follow when they propose to give a direction applying the code. These include obligations to publish a reasoned statement of the terms of their proposal, and to allow at least one month for representations to be made by persons likely to be affected. This implements Article 6 of the Framework Directive.

Section 108: Register of persons in whose case code applies

263.   Section 108 places OFCOM under a duty to keep an up-to-date public register of persons to whom the code applies and to record in this register every direction given under section 106. OFCOM must publish (and comply with) a notification setting out the hours during which this register will be open to the public and the fees for inspection.

Section 109: Restrictions and conditions subject to which code applies

264.   The Secretary of State, following consultation with OFCOM and others may, by regulations, make the application of the code subject to restrictions and conditions. In making such regulations, the Secretary of State must consider OFCOM's general duties and their duties for the purpose of fulfilling Community obligations. She must also consider the environment, road-traffic management, the need to encourage the sharing of apparatus and the need to ensure that the provider will be able to meet any liabilities incurred due to the imposition of the code.

Section 110: Enforcement of restrictions and conditions

265.   This section gives OFCOM powers of enforcement in respect of the restrictions and conditions subject to which the electronic communications code applies. Where it appears to OFCOM that a person to whom the code applies is or has been in breach of any condition or restriction subject to which the code applies, they are obliged to notify that person accordingly and to allow him a specified period of time (usually one month) in which to make representations to OFCOM and to take steps to comply with the condition or restriction or to remedy the breach. This section and sections 111 to 113 implement Article 10 of the Authorisation Directive in the context of the enforcement of those restrictions and conditions.

Section 111: Enforcement notification for contravention of code restrictions

266.   If, by the end of the period specified in the notification under section 110, OFCOM are satisfied that the condition or restriction in question has not been complied with, they may serve an enforcement notice on the notified provider. Such a notice requires the provider to comply with the requirements set out in the notice. This duty is enforceable by OFCOM in civil proceedings.

Section 112: Penalties for contravention of code restrictions

267.   Where a notified provider has not complied with a requirement notified under section 110 or 111, or remedied the consequences of the notified contravention, OFCOM may impose a penalty. In deciding on the amount of a financial penalty, OFCOM are required to consider whether the fine is appropriate and proportionate, and to take account of any representations made by the person concerned, and any steps taken by him to comply with the condition or restriction in question. The maximum fine that may be imposed under this section is £10,000. The Secretary of State may by order amend this provision so as to substitute a different maximum penalty.

Section 113: Suspension of application of code

268.   *Subsection (1)* allows OFCOM, if satisfied that a person has been in repeated and serious contravention of the requirements under section 38 to pay an administrative charge, that proceedings to recover any outstanding amounts have

failed to secure complete compliance with section 38 and have no reasonable prospect of securing compliance and that the imposition of penalties under section 41 has failed to secure compliance, to give a direction suspending the application to that person of the electronic communications code. OFCOM must also be satisfied that the suspension of the application of the code is appropriate and proportionate to the seriousness of the repeated contraventions.

269.   *Subsection (2)* allows OFCOM, having given a direction suspending a provider's entitlement to provide an electronic communications network, or part of such a network under section 42, 100, 132 or 140, to give a further direction suspending the application to that provider of the electronic communications code.

270.   Similarly, under *subsection (4)*, if a provider has been in repeated and serious contravention of any restriction or conditions set out in the Secretary of State's regulations made under section 109, OFCOM can by giving a further direction suspend the code in relation to its application to parts of the provider's network which are not yet in existence, or where the disapplication of the code would not prevent the continued provision of the network.

271.   Suspension of the application of the code will continue for as long as the suspension of entitlement remains in force (in the case of suspensions under *subsection (2)*) or until revoked by OFCOM. Suspension means that the provider cannot exercise any right conferred on him by the code but, unless OFCOM otherwise provide in a scheme made under section 117, suspension does not have any other effect on agreements entered into or on actions taken under the code. In other words, the suspension should not affect the rights of the operator to maintain service on the parts of its network unaffected by the suspension. This section implements Article 14(2) of the Authorisation Directive.

Section 114: Procedure for directions under s. 113

272.   Except in an urgent case, OFCOM must not give a direction under section 113(4) suspending the application of the code to any person ("the operator") unless they have: (i) notified the operator of the proposed suspension and of the steps (if any) that they are proposing to take under section 113; (ii) provided him with an opportunity of (during a period of not less than one month after the date of notification) making representations about the proposals and of proposing steps for remedying the situation that has given rise to the proposed suspension; and (iii) considered every representation and proposal made to them during that period.

273.   As soon as practicable after giving a direction under section 113 in an urgent case, OFCOM must provide the operator with an opportunity to make representations about the effect of the direction and of any steps taken under section 113 in connection with the suspension and to propose steps for remedying the situation that has given rise to the situation.

Subsection (4) provides that a case is urgent for the purposes of this case if OFCOM consider that it would be inappropriate to allow time, before giving a direction under section 113, for the making and consideration of representations, because the circumstances appearing to OFCOM to require the suspension fall within *subsection (5)*.

* The circumstance listed in subsection (5) include a serious threat to public safety, public health or to national security, serious economic or operational problems for persons (apart from the contravening provider or supplier) who are communications providers or persons who make associated facilities available or serious economic or operational problems for persons who make use of electronic communications networks, electronic communications services or associated facilities.

Section 115: Modification and revocation of application of code

274.   OFCOM may, by a further direction, alter the code's application under section 106(5) to particular places or particular networks or parts of networks or particular conduit systems or parts of conduit systems. Under *subsections (2)* and *(3)*, OFCOM may, by a further direction, revoke a direction applying the electronic communications code either on the application of the person to whom the code applies or where such a person ceases to be a communications provider or a provider of a conduit system.

275.   Before giving such directions OFCOM must, in accordance with section 106, first publish a notification of their proposal to give the direction and consider any representations made about that proposal. This implements Article 14(1) of the Authorisation Directive.

Section 116: Notification of cessation by person to whom code applies

276.   Where the code has been applied to a person who provides an electronic communications network of a type not designated for the purpose of section 33 or who provides a system of conduits, and that person ceases to provide that network or system of conduits, he must notify OFCOM. Failure to do so may result in the provider being penalised an amount not exceeding £1,000. Secretary of State may by order amend this provision so as to substitute a different maximum penalty.

Section 117: Transitional schemes on cessation of application of code

277.   This section gives OFCOM a power to put in place a transitional scheme in cases where the code has ceased to apply to a provider by reason of the code being either suspended, revoked or modified in relation to that provider.

278.   *Subsection (3)* gives a non-exhaustive list of the type of provision that might be contained in a transitional scheme. The examples given relate to the removal or retention of apparatus installed under the code, and the restoration of land affected by the code. Such a scheme may also provide for the transfer of rights and liabilities arising out of agreements made or obligations incurred under the code; authorise apparatus on code land to be retained for use by other providers; and provide for any issues arising from the scheme to be referred to OFCOM.

Section 118: Compulsory acquisition of land etc.

279.   Schedule 4 confers on code operators the power to purchase compulsorily land in England and Wales and Scotland, where authorised by the Secretary of State and with the consent of OFCOM. In Northern Ireland, code operators may purchase compulsorily land by requesting (with the consent of OFCOM) the Secretary of State to order that land vests in them. This provision re-enacts sections 34 to 40 of the Telecommunications Act 1984 (which are repealed by the Act), with certain consequential amendments to take account of the abolition of the regulatory regime under the Telecommunications Act 1984.

> *A code operator is a provider of an electronic communications network to whom OFCOM have applied the electronic communications code.

280.   The power to purchase compulsorily extends to land that is required by the code operator for or in connection with the establishment or running of an operator's network. For the purposes of Schedule 4, an operator's network does not include a conduit system.

281.   In England and Wales, the Acquisition of Land Act 1981 and, in Scotland, the Acquisition of Land (Authorisation Procedure) (Scotland) Act 1947 applies to compulsory purchases by code operators as if they were local authorities within the meaning of those Acts. Under these Acts, code operators must make and publish an order so that land owners are given the right to object to the purchase and to have their objections heard. Only after objections have been heard can the Secretary of State be requested to confirm the order. In Northern Ireland, the Secretary of State must follow the procedures laid down in Schedule 6 to the Local Government Act (Northern Ireland) Act 1972 and Schedule 8 to the Health and Personal Social Services (Northern Ireland) Order 1972.

282.   Where land is acquired compulsorily in England and Wales and Scotland, the benefit of certain provisions in, respectively, the Town and Country Planning Act 1990 and Town and Country Planning (Scotland) Act 1997 applies to code operators.

283.   A code operator may not dispose of any land purchased compulsorily in England, Wales, Scotland or Northern Ireland except with the consent of OFCOM.

284.   Paragraph 19 of Schedule 18 (transitional provisions) provides that any compulsory purchase orders, vesting orders or authorisations made by the Secretary of State which are effective immediately before the commencement of Schedule 4 are to have effect after the commencement of that Schedule as if made or given under that Schedule.

285.   Paragraphs 6, 7 and 8 of Schedule 4 enable representatives of code operators authorised by the Secretary of State in writing to enter upon and survey (at any reasonable time) any land (except land covered by buildings or used as a garden or pleasure ground) in England, Wales, Scotland and Northern Ireland for the purpose of

ascertaining whether it would be suitable for use by them for, or in connection with, the establishment or running of their networks. The powers of entry conferred on code operators are subject to the following provisions:

- in England and Wales, sections 324(8) and 325(1) to (5), (8) and (9) of the Town and Country Planning Act 1990 (as modified);

- in Scotland, sections 269(9) and 270(1) to (5), (8) and (9) of the Town and Country Planning (Scotland) Act 1997 (as modified); and

- in Northern Ireland, section 40(2) to (5) and (8) of the Land Development Values (Compensation) Act (Northern Ireland) 1965 (as modified).

286.   Code operators must make good, or pay compensation for, any damage caused to land or chattels by the exercise of their power of entry. Compensation must also be paid for any disturbance in the enjoyment of land or chattels of any person by the exercise of their power of entry.

287.   Paragraph 9(1) of Schedule 4 applies certain provisions of Part 1 of the Compulsory Purchase Act 1965 for the purpose of the acquisition of land in England and Wales by agreement by code operators. Sub-paragraphs (2) and (3) apply the corresponding enactments in Scotland and Northern Ireland, respectively.

288.   In exercising her powers under Schedule 4, the Secretary of State must have regard to the duties imposed on OFCOM under sections 3 and 4 of the Act and the need to protect the environment, to ensure that highways are not damaged or obstructed, to minimise interference with traffic and to encourage the sharing of electronic communications apparatus (see paragraph 2).

Section 119: Power to give assistance in relation to certain proceedings

289.   This section provides that in actual or prospective proceedings on a question relating to the application of the code, any party to the proceedings (other than the operator) may apply to OFCOM for assistance. OFCOM may grant an application for assistance on any one of the following grounds: (i) that the case raises a question of principle; (ii) that assistance is necessary, for example, because of the complexity of the case; or (iii) by reason of some other special consideration. Examples of the kind of assistance OFCOM might provide are given in *subsection (4)*, and include giving advice or arranging for the giving of advice by a solicitor or counsel, facilitating settlement, or arranging for legal representation.

> *The meaning of *operator* is given in the electronic communications code, as amended by paragraph 3(1) of Schedule 3 and is, as the case may be, the person to whom the code is applied by a direction under section 106, or the Secretary of State or the relevant Northern Ireland department.

290.   *Subsections (6)* and *(7)* allow OFCOM to recover any expenses they incur in providing assistance under this section, by way of a charge on any costs or expenses awarded to the applicant in proceedings or under any compromise or settlement.

Section 120: Conditions regulating premium rate services

291.   This section gives OFCOM the power to set conditions for the purpose of regulating the provision, content, promotion and marketing of premium rate services. Such conditions are binding on premium rate service providers and may relate only to compliance with directions given in accordance with the premium rate services code approved by OFCOM under section 121 or, in the absence of a code, the provisions of an order made by OFCOM under section 122. A premium rate service for this purpose is defined in *subsections (7) and (8)*. Briefly, a service is a premium rate service if:

 it consists of the contents of communications transmitted by an electronic communications network (e.g. a product helpline or 'chatline') or if it allows the user of an electronic communications service to make use, by making a transmission by means of that service, of a facility made available to the users of the service (including in particular a facility to make payments for goods and services, to enter a competition or claim a prize or to register a vote or record a preference); and

 there is a charge for the service, and that charge is paid to the provider of the electronic communications service by means of which the service in question is provided (e.g. through the customer's telephone bill)

292.   Under s*ubsection (9)*, a person provides a premium rate service if he: -

- provides the contents of the service, or

- exercises editorial control over the contents of the service, or

- packages together the content of the service for the purpose of facilitating its provision, or

- makes available a facility comprised in that service.

293.   In addition, under *subsection (10)*, an electronic communications service provider who, by virtue of arrangements made with someone falling within any of the four categories set out at a) to d) who provides a service, is entitled to a share of the charges for the provision of that service or for the use of his electronic communications service for the purpose of that service is also taken to be a premium rate service provider. Likewise, (in accordance with *subsection (11)*) the provider of an electronic communications network used for the provision of a service who has an agreement relating to the use of that network for the provision of the service with a provider of the service falling within any of the four categories set out at a) to d) is taken to be a premium rate service provider, as is (under *subsection 12*) an electronic communications network provider whose network is used under an agreement made with a person falling within subsections (10 or (11) or with an intermediary service provider (as defined in *subsection (15)*). The obligations that may be placed on a person falling within subsection (12) are limited by section 121(3) and section 122(5) (see below).

294.   Conditions set under this section may apply generally to each provider of a premium rate service or individually to specified providers or providers of specified services. Sections 47 and 48 apply to the setting, modification and revocation of a condition under this section.

295.   In accordance with *paragraph 9 of Schedule 18*, OFCOM may issue continuation notices in respect of premium rate service conditions in licences issued under section 7 of the Telecommunications Act 1984 for a transitional period before the arrangements provided by sections 120 to 124 take full effect.

Section 121: Approval of code for premium rate services

296.   This section enables OFCOM, where appropriate, to approve codes regulating the provision, content, promotion and marketing of premium rate services made by any person. OFCOM may not approve a code unless they are satisfied that the criteria listed in s*ubsection (2)* are met.   These include the existence of a person whose function is to administer and enforce the code; adequate funding for the activities of that person; objective justification for the provisions in the code; provisions which do not unduly discriminate and are proportionate and transparent. *Subsection (3)* forbids OFCOM approving a code which places obligations on a communications provider falling within subsection 120(12), unless they are satisfied that the obligations only arise where the provider concerned is the only person against whom it is practicable to take regulatory action and only after notice has been given by the code enforcer identifying the premium rate service and the manner in which it is alleged to have breached the code, and the only obligation imposed is to secure that the network does not deliver the premium rate service to persons in the UK.   OFCOM may (in accordance with *subsection (6)*) approve modifications made to an approved code or withdraw their approval of a code at any time.

Section 122: Orders by OFCOM in the absence of a code under s.121

297.   This section permits OFCOM to make an order imposing requirements with respect to the provision, content, promotion and marketing of premium rate services (including pricing) and for the enforcement of such requirements, where OFCOM consider there is no third-party code which could be approved under section 121. OFCOM's power to make an order includes power to establish a corporate body to determine the jurisdiction of that body and any other person, to confer jurisdiction over any matter on OFCOM, to provide a person upon whom jurisdiction is conferred with the ability to compensate or reimburse expenses and to enforce any awards. *Subsection (5)* places restrictions comparable to those in section 121(3) on the obligations that an order may place on communications providers falling within subsection 120(12). OFCOM must obtain the consent of the Secretary of State before making an order under this section.

Section 123: Enforcement of s.120 conditions

298.   OFCOM may enforce conditions set under section 120 in accordance with

sections 94 to 96. In deciding on the amount of a financial penalty under section 96, OFCOM must consider whether the fine is appropriate and proportionate and take into account any representations made by the premium rate service provider concerned as well as any steps taken by him to comply with the notified condition and remedy any consequences of a contravention. The penalty may not exceed £100,000. The Secretary of State may by order amend the maximum penalty.

Section 124: Suspending service provision for contraventions of s.120 conditions

299.   Subject to compliance with sections 102 and 103, this section gives OFCOM a power to suspend or restrict the right of a communications provider to provide premium rate services where OFCOM are satisfied that that provider is in serious and repeated breach of any conditions imposed on him under section 120, and that the imposition of penalties and enforcement notifications under sections 95 and 96 have not resulted in compliance with those conditions. The suspension or restriction must be appropriate and proportionate to the seriousness of the breach and necessary for reasons of public policy. OFCOM may similarly direct the suspension or restriction of the right to provide a service where a communications provider has contravened the conditions set under section 120 and the circumstances of that contravention are such that it is appropriate for OFCOM to proceed without the conditions mentioned above being satisfied and there is an urgent need to give the direction for reasons of public policy.

300.   A direction by OFCOM under this section may suspend entitlement to provide any or all premium rate services and may take effect indefinitely or for a fixed period. A direction may also include, where appropriate, conditions to protect the interests of the premium rate service provider's customers, including requirements for the payment of compensation. Where appropriate, OFCOM may revoke or modify the suspension or restriction. Provisions for the procedures applying to the giving of directions under this section, equivalent to those applying to directions for breaches of other conditions of entitlement, are included via *subsection (8)*.

Section 125: Dishonestly obtaining electronic communications services

301.   Anyone who dishonestly obtains an electronic communications service and intends to avoid paying for that service is guilty of an offence under section 125. A person found guilty of the offence will be liable to a fine or imprisonment, or both. Under *subsection (2)*, it is not an offence under this section to obtain a service mentioned in section 297(1) of the Copyright, Designs and Patents Act 1988. This section replaces section 42 of the Telecommunications Act 1984 which is repealed by Schedule 19.

* Section 297(1) of the Copyright, Designs and Patents Act 1988 mentions programmes included in a broadcasting or cable programme service (as defined in that Act).

Section 126: Possession or supply of apparatus etc. for contravening s.125

302.   It is an offence under *subsection (1)* for a person to have in his possession or under his control anything, including data, which may be used for or in connection with obtaining an electronic communications service with the intent to use the thing or to allow it to be used to obtain, or for a purpose connected with the obtaining of, an electronic communications service dishonestly.

303.   It is an offence under *subsection (2)* for anyone to supply or offer to supply anything that may be used for or in connection with obtaining an electronic communications service when he knows or believes that the recipient of those things intends to use them or to allow them to be used to obtain, or for a purpose connected with the obtaining of, an electronic communications service dishonestly.

304.   A person found guilty of either offence will be liable to a fine or imprisonment, or both.

305.   This section replaces section 42A of the Telecommunications Act 1984 which is repealed by Schedule 19.

Section 127: Improper use of public electronic communications network

306.   Anyone who sends a message or other matter that is grossly offensive or is of an indecent, obscene or menacing character (other than in the course of providing a programme service) by means of a public electronic communications network, or who causes such a message or matter to be sent, is guilty of an offence. It is also an offence under *subsection (2)* for anyone to send or cause to be sent false messages by means of a public electronic communications network or persistently to make use of a public electronic communications network for the purpose of causing annoyance, inconvenience or needless anxiety.

*A *programme service* has the same meaning as in the Broadcasting Act 1990.

307.   This section replaces section 43 of the Telecommunications Act 1984, which is repealed by Schedule 19.

Section 128: Notification of misuse of networks and services

308.   This section gives OFCOM powers of enforcement in respect of persistent misuse of an electronic communications network or an electronic communications service. Where OFCOM determine that there are reasonable grounds to believe that a person has persistently misused an electronic communications network or an electronic communications service, OFCOM may notify that person accordingly, and allow him a specified period in which to make representations to OFCOM. The period to be allowed for the making of representations is one month, unless OFCOM consider that the misuse is continuing and the harm caused makes it necessary for it to be stopped as soon as possible, in which case, the period is 7 days. Under *subsection*

(8), the Secretary of State may by order specify uses of an electronic communications network or an electronic communications service that shall not be treated as a misuse of a network or service where she considers that appropriate alternative means of dealing with those uses exist.

> *A person misuses an electronic communications network or an electronic communications service, under *subsection (5)*, if the effect or likely effect of its use causes another person unnecessarily to suffer annoyance, inconvenience or anxiety or if he uses a network or service to engage in conduct the effect or likely effect of which causes another person unnecessarily to suffer annoyance, inconvenience or anxiety.

> *A person persistently misuses an electronic communications network or an electronic communications service under *subsection (6)* where his misuse is repeated on a sufficient number of occasions so that is clear that the misuse forms part of pattern of behaviour or constitutes recklessness as to whether persons suffer annoyance, inconvenience or anxiety.

Section 129: Enforcement notifications for stopping persistent misuse

309.   If, by the end of the period specified in section 128, OFCOM are satisfied that the person has persistently misused an electronic communications network or an electronic communications service and that he has not taken all appropriate steps to secure that the misuse ceases and is not repeated, and to remedy the consequences of the misuse, they may serve an enforcement notice. Such a notice requires the notified person to take all steps to secure that the misuse ceases and is not repeated, and to remedy the consequences of the misuse.

Section 130: Penalties for persistent misuse

310.   OFCOM may impose a penalty if a person notified under section 128 has persistently misused an electronic communications network or an electronic communications service. Where an enforcement notification issued in accordance with section 129 has not been complied with, OFCOM may also impose a penalty.

311.   When deciding on the amount of financial penalty, OFCOM are required to consider whether the fine is appropriate and proportionate, and to take account of any representation made by the person concerned and any steps taken to secure that the misuse ceases and is not repeated and to remedy the consequences of the misuse. The penalty may not exceed £5000. However, the Secretary of State may by order amend the maximum penalty.

312.   Under *subsection (8)*, people may be liable for an offence under sections 125 to 127 and have a penalty imposed on them by OFCOM under section 130 in respect of the same conduct.

Section 131: Statement of policy on persistent misuse

313.   This section places OFCOM under a duty to publish and keep up-to-date a statement of policy on how they will use their powers under sections 128 to 130.

Section 132: Powers to require suspension or restriction of a provider's entitlement

314.   This section gives the Secretary of State a power to direct OFCOM to issue a person with a direction to suspend or restrict that person's entitlement to provide an electronic communications network or service or an associated facility where she has reasonable grounds for believing that it is necessary to do so to protect the public from any threat to public safety or public health, or in the interests of national security. This is permitted by Article 3 of the Authorisation Directive.

315.   *Subsection (2)* places OFCOM under a duty to comply with any such direction by the Secretary of State. Once a suspension or restriction is in place, both the Secretary of State and OFCOM must allow the person in question an opportunity to make representations to them, and to propose steps for remedying the situation. OFCOM may modify the terms of a suspension or restriction imposed under this section. The Secretary of State may direct OFCOM to revoke a suspension or restriction imposed under this section.

316.   A direction by OFCOM under this section may suspend entitlement generally or in relation to particular networks, services or facilities, and may take effect indefinitely or for a fixed period. It may also postpone the suspension or restriction (and, if doing so, may also impose additional conditions - such as compensation of their customers for loss suffered - in order to protect the customers of the provider).

Section 133: Enforcement of directions under s. 132

317.   It is an offence for any person to provide a network, service or associated facility while he is subject to a direction under section 132 suspending his entitlement to do so, or to provide such a network, service or facility in contravention of a restriction contained in such a direction. A person found guilty will be liable to a fine. A third party who sustains loss or damage as a result of a breach of such a direction or of an act which induces a breach of the duty or interferes with its performance may bring proceedings against the person concerned. In such proceedings, a person may defend himself by demonstrating that he did everything reasonable and exercised all due diligence to avoid breaching the condition in question.

Section 134: Restrictions in leases and licences

318.   This section replaces section 96 of the Telecommunications Act 1984, which is repealed by Schedule 19. *Subsection (3)* amends any provision, in any lease, licence or other premises-related agreement granted or entered into after the commencement of this section, which prohibits or restricts an occupier's choice of electronic communications services providers to a person who has an interest in the relevant premises or a person selected by a person with an interest in the relevant premises. Where a lease, licence or other premise-related agreement contains a provision imposing such prohibitions or restrictions, that provision is to have effect as if it provided for the election of an alternative electronic communications

service provider by the occupier, subject to the prior consent of the lessor, licensor or other party to the agreement, such consent not to be unreasonably withheld.

* The meaning of lease is given in *subsection (8)* and includes a leasehold tenancy (whether in the nature of a head lease, sub-lease or under lease) and an agreement to grant such a tenancy.

319.   *Subsection (4)* amends any provision, in a lease of one year or more granted or entered into after the commencement of this section or more or in a premises-related agreement to which such a lease applies, that imposes any other prohibition or restriction on the lessee relating to an electronic communications matter where such prohibition or restriction relates to anything done inside a building occupied by the lessee or for purposes in connection with the provision of an electronic communications service by a communications provider to the lessee. Where a lease of one year or more or a premises-related agreement to which a lease of one year or more is applied contains a provision imposing such a prohibition or restriction, the provision is to have effect as if the prohibition or restriction applied only where the lessor had not given his consent, such consent not to be unreasonably withheld.

*For the purposes of this section, an electronic communications matter includes the provision of an electronic communications network, the provision of an electronic communications service, the connection of electronic communications apparatus to an electronic communications network specified in an order for the purposes of this section, the connection of an electronic communications network to another electronic communications network specified in an order for the purposes of this section, and the installation, maintenance, adjustment, repair, alteration or use of electronic communications apparatus for the purposes of providing an electronic communications network or an electronic communications service.

320.   Under *subsection (6)*, OFCOM have the power by order to exclude certain provisions in leases, licences or other premises-related agreements from the remit of this section. This section only applies to leases, licences or other premises-related agreements entered into before the commencement of this section to the extent that OFCOM makes an order under *subsection (9)* providing for it to do so. The provisions of this section apply without prejudice to the application of the electronic communications code.

Section 135: Information required for purposes of Chapter 1 functions

321.   This section gives OFCOM information-gathering powers. Subject to the restrictions in section 137, it allows OFCOM to require any person falling within *subsection (2)*, including a communications provider, to provide OFCOM with all such information as OFCOM consider necessary for the purpose of carrying our their functions under Chapter 1 of Part 2 of the Act.

322.   This includes information for the following purposes:

- investigating possible breaches of conditions of entitlement, or of the electronic communications code, or of a transitional scheme after the cessation of the application of the code;

- ascertaining or verifying the amount of any administrative charge payable under section 38, or of any financial contribution towards the cost of complying with universal service obligations;

- ascertaining whether a condition set under section 45 continues to be effective;

- designating a universal service provider under section 66;

- carrying out a review under sections 66 or 70;

- identifying markets and carrying out market analyses for the purposes of Chapter 1 Part 2 of the Act;

- assessing whether any network access question gives rise to a duty under section 105 and considering any matter while exercising that duty;

- statistical purposes connected with OFCOM's functions under Chapter 1 of Part 2 of the Act.

This section, section 136 and section 137, implement Article 5 of the Framework Directive, Articles 6(1), 10(1) and 11 of, and condition 10 of Part A to, the Annex to the Authorisation Directive, Article 11(2) of the Access Directive, and Articles 11, 21 and 22 (in so far as those Articles necessitate the provision of information) of the Universal Service Directive.

Section 136: Information required for related purposes

323.   Subject to the restrictions in section 137, section 136 allows OFCOM to require communications providers and persons making available associated facilities to provide OFCOM with information required by OFCOM:

- to carry out comparative overviews of the quality and price of services provided by communications providers or of associated facilities;

- for statistical purposes.

Section 137: Restriction on imposing information requirements

324.   OFCOM may not use their powers under sections 135 and 136 to request information relating to a potential breach of a general condition unless OFCOM's investigation is in response to a complaint; they have reason to believe that a breach has occurred; they have decided to investigate to see whether the condition is being complied with; or the condition concerns sharing the burden of providing a universal service.

325.   Any demands made by OFCOM must be proportionate to the use to which they intend to put the information, and must describe the information required and state the reasons why it is required. This implements Article 11(1) and (2) of the Authorisation Directive. Unless the demand is for the purpose of determining who is liable to a charge under section 38 (in which case other appropriate methods may be

used) any demand must be set out in a notice and be served on the person from whom the information is requested.

Section 138: Notification of contravention of information requirements

326.   Where OFCOM have reasonable grounds to believe that a person is or has been in breach of any requirement under section 135 or 136, they may notify that person accordingly, and allow him a specified period of time (usually one month) in which to make representations to OFCOM, and to take steps to comply with the notified requirement. This section, and sections 139 to 144 relate to enforcement of the information provisions applicable to communications providers or persons making associated facilities available and together implement Article 10 of the Authorisation Directive.

Section 139: Penalties for contravention of information requirement

327.   Where a notified provider has not complied with a requirement notified under section 138, has not remedied the consequences of the notified contravention and no proceedings for an offence under section 144 have been brought, OFCOM may impose a penalty. In deciding on the amount of a financial penalty, OFCOM are required to consider whether the penalty is appropriate and proportionate, and to take account of any representations made by the person concerned and any steps taken by him to comply with the condition or restriction in question. The maximum fine that may be imposed under this section is £50,000. Secretary of State may by order amend this provision so as to substitute a different maximum penalty.

Section 140: Suspending service provision for information contraventions

328.   This section gives OFCOM a power to suspend or restrict a person's entitlement to provide networks, services and/or associated facilities where OFCOM are satisfied that that person is in serious and repeated breach of any requirements imposed on him under section 135 or 136, that the requirements are not requirements imposed for purposes connected with the carrying out of OFCOM's functions in relation to SMP apparatus conditions and that an attempt by the imposition of penalties under section 139 or the bringing of proceedings for an offence under section 144, to secure compliance has failed. The suspension or restriction must be appropriate and proportionate to the seriousness of the repeated contraventions.

329.   A direction by OFCOM under this section may suspend entitlement generally or in relation to particular networks, services or facilities and may take effect indefinitely or for a fixed period. Where OFCOM exercise these powers, they must allow the person in question to make representations to them and, if appropriate, OFCOM may revoke the suspension or restriction. A direction may also include, where appropriate, conditions to protect the customers of a provider, including the payment of compensation.

Section 141: Suspending apparatus supply for information contraventions

330.   This section gives OFCOM a power to suspend or restrict a person from supplying electronic communications apparatus where OFCOM are satisfied that that the person is in serious and repeated breach of any requirement of OFCOM to provide information for the purpose of section 135, and that an attempt, by the imposition of penalties under section 139 or the bringing of proceedings for an offence under section 144, to secure compliance has failed. The suspension or restriction must be appropriate and proportionate to the seriousness of the repeated contraventions.

331.   A direction by OFCOM under this section may require a person to cease supplying electronic communications apparatus generally or in relation to particular electronic communications apparatus. The direction may take effect indefinitely or for a fixed period. A direction may also include, where appropriate, conditions to protect the customers of a supplier, including the payment of compensation. When OFCOM exercise these powers, they must allow the person in question to make representations to them and, if appropriate, OFCOM may revoke the suspension or restriction.

Section 142: Procedure for directions under sections 140 and 141

332.   Unless a case is urgent, before exercising their powers under sections 140 and 141, OFCOM must notify a contravening provider or supplier of the proposed direction, allow him at least one month to make representations and consider each representation made by him.

> *The meaning of an urgent case is set out in *subsections (4) and (5)*. Such a case arises where there is a serious threat to public safety, public health or national security or a serious economic or operational problem that makes it inappropriate to give a contravening provider or supplier time to make representations.

333.   If a case is urgent, OFCOM may give a direction without consulting the contravening provider or supplier. However, as soon as practicable after giving a direction in an urgent case, OFCOM must provide the relevant contravening provider or supplier with an opportunity to make representations and to propose steps to remedy the contravention.

Section 143: Enforcement of directions under ss. 140 and 141

334.   It is an offence for any person to provide an electronic communications network, an electronic communications service or an associated facility while he is subject to a direction issued under section 140 suspending his entitlement to do so or where he does so in contravention of any restriction specified in the direction. It is also an offence for any person to supply electronic communications apparatus while he is subject to a direction issued under section 141 suspending his entitlement to do so or where he does so in contravention of any restriction specified in the direction. A person found guilty of either offence will be liable to a fine.

Section 144: Offences in connection with information requirements

335.   It is an offence for any person to fail to provide information in response to a demand from OFCOM under section 135 or 136 and any such person shall be liable to a fine. However, *subsection (2)* makes provision for a defence where it is not possible for the recipient of a notice to provide the information within the period specified by OFCOM but the recipient has taken all reasonable steps to provide the information after that period. However, no proceedings for this offence may be brought in respect of failures for which OFCOM have imposed a financial penalty under section 139.

336.   It is also an offence intentionally or recklessly to provide OFCOM with any false information in response to a request under section 135 or 136 and a person guilty of this offence is liable to a fine and/or imprisonment.

Section 145: Statement of policy on information gathering

337.   This section places OFCOM under a duty to publish and keep up-to-date a statement of policy on how they will use their information-gathering powers under sections 135 and 136 and how they will use any information obtained in exercise of those powers. When exercising their information-gathering powers under sections 135 to 144, OFCOM must have regard to their published policy statement.

Section 146: Provision of information by OFCOM

338.   This section places OFCOM under a duty to respond fully, within one week, (unless they have already conveyed the requested information) to any request made to them for information about any of the following:

- whether or not the person making the request is required under section 33 to notify OFCOM in advance of his intention to provide a network, service or associated facility;

- whether a notification submitted by that person under section 33 is satisfactory;

- that person's rights, in order to allow him to negotiate his right to network access; or

- what is required of that person under section 106 in order to make an application in respect of the electronic communications code.

This section implements Article 9 of the Authorisation Directive.

Section 147: Repeal of provisions of Telecommunications Act 1984

339.   This section repeals certain sections of the Telecommunications Act 1984. One of the principal effects of these repeals will be to abolish the current requirement for persons running telecommunications systems to hold individual or class licences.

*Sections 5 to 8 of the Telecommunications Act 1984 make it a criminal offence to run a telecommunications system without a licence and set out the powers of the Secretary of State and the Director General of Telecommunications to grant licences. Section 9 allows the Secretary of State to designate certain telecommunications systems as "public telecommunications systems". This designation confers additional rights and imposes additional duties on the licensee. Sections 10 and 11 relate to the telecommunications code (see the notes on section 106). Sections 12 to 15 set out the circumstances in which the Director General of Telecommunications may modify the conditions of telecommunications licences. Sections 16 to 19 deal with the powers of the Director General to enforce compliance with licence conditions. Finally, sections 27A to 27L make provision for standards of performance and service to customers in the telecommunications industry and for procedures for dealing with complaints and billing disputes. These sections also govern the terms upon which deposits may be required from customers, and the circumstances in which operators may disconnect customers.

340.   As a result of the abolition of telecommunications licensing it is necessary to make certain savings and transitional provision. These are set out in paragraphs 3, 4, 9, 11-14 and 16-18 of Schedule 18 (transitional provisions).

341.   Paragraphs 3 and 4 provide savings for the effects of certain agreements expressed by reference to licences. Paragraphs 9 and 11 deal with the saving of certain licence conditions relating to the regulation of premium rate services, to significant market power or access, and to accounting, respectively. Paragraph 12 makes provision in respect of the payment of licence fees. Paragraph 13 enables OFCOM to enforce the licence conditions saved in paragraphs 9 and 11 and any liabilities saved under paragraph 12 which were previously enforceable by the Director General of Telecommunications under the Telecommunications Act 1984.

342.   Paragraph 14 provides that where an agreement entered into for the purposes of a condition of a licence granted under section 7 of the Telecommunications Act 1984 entitles a party to it to terminate the agreement if he or another party ceases to be a Schedule 2 public operator, that right is not to be exercisable by reason of the coming into force of provisions of the Act, providing that corresponding general conditions, access-related conditions or a provision made by an SMP condition are imposed on one or both of the parties to the agreement.

343.   Schedule 2 public operator has the same meaning as in Schedule 1 to the Telecommunications (Licence Modifications) (Standard Schedules) Regulations 1999 (S.I. 1999/2450).

344.   Paragraphs 16-18 provide savings for allocated telephone numbers, the grant of powers under the telecommunications code, and guarantees of liabilities of code operators.

Section 148: Powers of local authorities in connection with networks

345.   This section replaces section 2 of the Telegraph Act 1899 and permits local authorities in England, Wales and Scotland to borrow money to provide public electronic communications networks or services, including where those networks or services extend outside their local authority areas.

Section 149: Grants by Department of Enterprise, Trade and Investment

346.   This section confers power on the Northern Ireland Department of Enterprise, Trade and Investment ("DETI") to fund expenditure on electronic communications infrastructure and to fund expenditure for any other purposes prescribed by regulations made with the approval of the Department of Finance and Personnel. DETI will have discretionary powers to support financially the development of a regional electronic communications infrastructure in Northern Ireland, specifically the provision of electronic networks and services, and the improvement of the extent, quality and reliability of such networks or services.

Section 150: Grants by district councils

347.   This section provides that district councils in Northern Ireland may award grants to persons providing a public electronic communications network, a public electronic communications service, or a facility connected with such a network or service where they believe such network or service benefits their area. Such grants must be for the purposes of compensating such persons for losses sustained in the provision of such networks, services or facilities. Any grant would also need to comply with the European Community rules on state aid. This provision repeals and re-enacts section 97 of the Telecommunications Act, with certain consequential amendments, but only in so far as that provision relates to Northern Ireland.

Section 151: Interpretation of Chapter 1

348.   This section provides for the interpretation of defined terms used in Chapter 1 of Part 2 of the Act.

Chapter 2: Spectrum Use

349.   The existing law governing access to and use of radio spectrum is contained in the Wireless Telegraphy Acts 1949, 1967 and 1998, the Marine, etc., Broadcasting (Offences) Act 1967 and Part VI of the Telecommunications Act 1984. Under section 1(1) of the 1949 Act, it is an offence for any person to establish or use any station for wireless telegraphy or to install or use any apparatus for wireless telegraphy, otherwise than under and in accordance with a licence granted by the Secretary of State. Since radio spectrum is a finite resource, users of spectrum will continue to be licensed as at present, although the licensing and enforcement functions under the above legislation will be transferred to OFCOM (in accordance with section 2 of and Schedule 1 to the Act – see the notes for those provisions above).

*The expressions *wireless telegraphy, apparatus for wireless telegraphy* and *station for wireless telegraphy* are defined in section 19 of the Wireless Telegraphy Act 1949. *Wireless telegraphy* means the emitting or receiving of electromagnetic energy of a frequency not exceeding three million megacycles a second, which is equivalent to 3000 Giga-Hertz in modern terminology, (essentially radio signals) for the purposes of conveying messages, sounds or visual images or for the determination of position or distance. *Stations and apparatus for wireless telegraphy* are stations and apparatus for the emitting or receiving of radio signals.

350.   Chapter 2 of Part 2 of the Act sets out new functions of OFCOM in relation to radio spectrum (which are in addition to the existing wireless telegraphy functions transferred to OFCOM under section 2 and Schedule 1). It introduces a new scheme of recognised spectrum access and continues the market-based approach to spectrum management introduced by the Wireless Telegraphy Act 1998 by allowing trading as a means of gaining access to spectrum. Additionally, Chapter 2 of Part 2 and Schedule 17 contain a large number of amendments to the existing law on wireless telegraphy, mainly for the purpose of implementing the new Directives.

Section 152: General functions of OFCOM in relation to radio spectrum

351.   This section sets out general functions of OFCOM in relation to radio spectrum. These functions are:

- to give advice in relation to the use of radio spectrum and to provide other services and maintain records with respect to radio spectrum use within and outside of the United Kingdom, as OFCOM consider appropriate for the purposes of spectrum management.

- OFCOM may also be required by the Secretary of State to give other advice and to provide other services or to maintain other records for the purpose of securing United Kingdom compliance with any of its international obligations. The services, records and advice may be in respect of spectrum use outside the United Kingdom.

352.   For the purpose of the carrying out of these functions, OFCOM may carry out or commission research and development work on use of radio spectrum, including future developments and any connected matters. OFCOM may, with the consent of the Treasury, also make a grant to any person in order to encourage efficient spectrum-management or use.

353.   Where OFCOM are required to give advice or provide another service, they may charge for doing so (if they are not required to do so, any charge would be under section 25).

Section 153: United Kingdom Plan for Frequency Authorisation

354.   This section places OFCOM under a duty to publish a plan (to be known as "the United Kingdom Plan for Frequency Authorisation") setting out the frequencies allocated for particular radio purposes in the UK that are available for assignment, and the purposes for which they have been allocated. This implements the requirement in Article 5(3) of the Authorisation Directive that there should be a national frequency plan.

Section 154: Duties of OFCOM when carrying out spectrum functions

355.   This section sets out the duties of OFCOM when carrying out their functions under the enactments relating to radio spectrum management. OFCOM must have regard in particular to (i) the amount of spectrum available for use; (ii) the present and future demand for spectrum; and (iii) the desirability of promoting efficient management and use of the radio spectrum, the economic and other benefits of radio spectrum use, the development of innovative services and competition in the provision of electronic communications services. In regard to functions other than setting fees for licences or grants of recognised spectrum access under section 2 of the Wireless Telegraphy Act 1998, OFCOM may disregard such of these matters as do not appear relevant to the case in question. OFCOM must resolve any conflict between their duties under this section in the manner they think best in the circumstances. However, OFCOM must give priority to their duties under sections 3 to 6 in the event of any conflict between those duties and their duties under this section. This implements Article 9(1) of the Framework Directive.

Section 155: Advisory service in relation to interference

356.   OFCOM may advise and help people complaining of interference with wireless telegraphy - in other words where the fulfilment of the purposes of the wireless telegraphy is prejudiced by any emission or reflection of electro-magnetic energy.

Section 156: Directions with respect to the radio spectrum

357.   This section gives the Secretary of State a power, by order, to give general or specific directions to OFCOM about the carrying out of their spectrum functions. They may include a direction (i) to reserve certain frequencies for different classes of use, for example broadcasting, mobile telecommunications, private business systems, air traffic control or radio astronomy, or within a class, for example for the provision of additional digital television services or radio broadcasting multiplexes; or (ii) to exercise their powers under the proviso to section 1(1) of the Wireless Telegraphy Act 1949 and under sections 1, 3 and 3A of the Wireless Telegraphy Act 1998 in accordance with the provisions of the direction. This power is in addition to the power conferred on the Secretary of State by section 5 to give directions for limited purposes in accordance with which OFCOM must exercise their functions.

*The proviso to section 1(1) of the Wireless Telegraphy Act 1949 allows classes or descriptions of wireless telegraphy stations or apparatus to be exempted from licensing requirements by regulations made by the Secretary of State (such regulations will be made by OFCOM when the relevant provisions of the Act come into force). Section 1 of the Wireless Telegraphy Act 1998 (as amended by section 161) allows the Secretary of State to make regulations setting the fees to be paid on the issue and renewal of wireless telegraphy licences and grants of recognised spectrum access, and is subject to section 2 of that Act (which, as substituted by paragraph 147 of Schedule 17 to the Act, allows the Secretary of State to charge licence fees above the cost of exercising wireless telegraphy functions ("administrative incentive pricing")). Section 3 of the 1998 Act allows the Secretary of State to make regulations providing for wireless telegraphy licences to be awarded by means of spectrum auctions. Finally, section 3A of the 1998 Act is introduced by section 161. The regulations provided for in sections 1 to 3A of the 1998 Act will be made by OFCOM when the relevant provisions of the Act come into force.

Section 157: Procedure for directions under s.156

358.   An order containing a direction under section 156 must state its purpose, unless the direction requires OFCOM to reserve certain frequencies for specified uses or requires OFCOM to exercise their powers under the proviso to section 1(1) of the Wireless Telegraphy Act 1949 or under section 1, 3 or 3A of the Wireless Telegraphy Act 1998 in a certain way.   Before making an order containing a direction under section 156, unless urgency makes it inexpedient to do so, the Secretary of State must consult OFCOM and such other persons as she thinks fit. A draft of the order must be laid before Parliament and approved by each House, except where the Secretary of State considers the urgency of the case requires the order to be made straight away. An order containing a direction given by the Secretary of State in an urgent case ceases to have effect at the end of 40 days (excluding Parliamentary recesses) unless it is approved by a resolution of each House of Parliament.

Section 158: Special duty in relation to television multiplexes

359.   If OFCOM reserve frequencies for the broadcasting of television programmes, they are under a duty, so far as practicable, to secure that sufficient multiplex capacity is available for qualifying services on television multiplexes licensed under the Broadcasting Act 1996. This is in accordance with condition 1 of Part B of the Annex to the Authorisation Directive.

qualifying service has the same meaning as is given in section 2 of the Broadcasting Act 1996.

Section 159: Grant of recognised spectrum access

360.   Sections 159 to 162 introduce a new scheme of grants of "recognised spectrum access".   Grants of recognised spectrum access ("RSA") will be available, in circumstances to be specified by OFCOM in regulations, to persons who transmit radio signals for reception in the United Kingdom, but who are not, for whatever reason, required to hold a licence under the Wireless Telegraphy Acts. Possible examples include certain satellite services, radio astronomy and Crown users of spectrum.

361.   Section 159 sets out the procedures that apply to the making by OFCOM of grants of recognised spectrum access. *Subsection (3)* allows OFCOM to specify, amongst other things, the frequencies used, reception coverage and strength and type of signal that are the subject of the grant. *Subsection (5)* allows OFCOM to make a grant of RSA subject to such restrictions and conditions as they think fit, for example as to strength and type of signal, times of use or sharing of frequencies.

362.   Schedule 5 makes additional detailed provision about the procedure for the grant, modification and revocation of grants of RSA. OFCOM are to prescribe

procedures for applications for a grant of RSA including requirements that must be fulfilled before, and restrictions and conditions subject to which, a grant will be made. Where an applicant fails to provide all the information reasonably required by OFCOM, their application may be refused. Any proposed refusal of an application must be notified to the applicant, stating the reasons and specifying the period (at least a month) within which the applicant may make representations about the proposed refusal. Similarly, if OFCOM propose to revoke or modify a grant or the restrictions or conditions to which it is subject, they must notify the person to whom the grant was made and give him the opportunity to make representations or, if applicable, to remedy a contravention of the restrictions or conditions of the grant.

Section 160: Effect of grant of recognised spectrum access

363.   This section places OFCOM under a duty to take into account any grants of RSA to the same extent as if a licence under section 1 of the Wireless Telegraphy Act 1949 had been granted when (i) granting wireless telegraphy licences; (ii) making grants of RSA; and (iii) carrying out any of their other functions under the enactments relating to radio spectrum management where it is appropriate to have regard to whether wireless telegraphy licences are in force or to their terms.

Section 161: Charges in respect of grants of recognised spectrum access

364.   This section amends section 1 of the Wireless Telegraphy Act 1998 to allow OFCOM to set the fees to be paid on the making of a grant of RSA. This section also inserts a new section 3A into the 1998 Act that makes provision for OFCOM to determine applications for the grant of RSA by means of an auction and for the procedures to be followed in such cases.

Section 162: Conversion into and from wireless telegraphy licences

365.   Upon application, OFCOM may (in accordance with regulations made by them) convert a wireless telegraphy licence into a grant of RSA and vice versa.

Section 163: Payments for use of radio spectrum by the Crown
366.   This section allows the Secretary of State to make payments (out of money provided by Parliament) for the operation by the Crown of stations and apparatus for wireless telegraphy or in respect of any grant of RSA made to the Crown. The Wireless Telegraphy Act 1949 does not bind the Crown, which is therefore exempt from the obligation to obtain a licence for its use of spectrum. However, in order that public sector users should have incentives to use spectrum efficiently, a commitment was given during the passage of the Wireless Telegraphy Act 1998 that the Crown would pay for access to spectrum on a comparable basis to the private sector.

Section 164: Limitations on authorised spectrum use

367.   Where OFCOM consider it appropriate to limit the number of wireless telegraphy licences or grants of RSA on certain frequencies, or for certain uses, for

the purpose of securing efficient spectrum use, they must make an order imposing the limitations. The purpose of this duty is to ensure fairness between potential users. The order must set out the criteria OFCOM will apply in limiting the number of licences and grants and deciding to whom to issue licences or grants of RSA. The criteria must be objective, non-discriminatory, proportionate and transparent. OFCOM must keep the order under review. This section implements Article 7 of the Authorisation Directive.

Section 165: Terms etc. of wireless telegraphy licences

368. This section adds three new subsections to section 1 of the Wireless Telegraphy Act 1949. Subsection (2A) provides that any terms, provisions and limitations of a licence granted under that Act may include (i) provisions relating to the strength or type of signal, times of use, and frequency sharing, and (ii) prohibitions on or obligations requiring the transmission or broadcasting of particular content by the licence holder. Subsection (2B) enables licences to be granted in relation to stations or apparatus described by reference to specified factors or in relation to a particular station or apparatus. Subsection (2C) provides that a licence must not duplicate conditions already imposed by general conditions under this Act: this new subsection implements Article 6(4) of the Authorisation Directive.

Section 166: Exemption from need for wireless telegraphy licence

369. This section amends the Wireless Telegraphy Act 1949 to require OFCOM to exempt certain stations or apparatus from the requirement to be licensed under that Act where their use would not cause undue interference (as redefined in section 183). This implements Article 5(1) of the Authorisation Directive.

Section 167: Bidding for wireless telegraphy licences

370. This section makes some procedural amendments to section 3 of the Wireless Telegraphy Act 1998, which governs the conduct of spectrum auctions for wireless telegraphy licences. The principal changes are to combine the separate regulations and notices which at present govern spectrum auctions, to introduce greater flexibility on how bids may be expressed and to add a new provision allowing OFCOM to require payments to be made by a person who successfully bids for a wireless telegraphy licence but subsequently refuses to take the licence applied for.

371. Paragraph 21 of Schedule 18 (transitional provisions) provides that any procedures set out in a notice issued by the Secretary of State under regulations made under section 3 of the Wireless Telegraphy Act 1998 before the commencement of this section shall have effect as if prescribed by OFCOM by regulations under that provision.

Section 168: Spectrum trading

372. This section gives OFCOM a power to make regulations authorising the

holder of a wireless telegraphy licence or the holder of a grant of RSA to transfer the rights and obligations under their licence or grant of RSA to another person. This will enable the development of a secondary market in licences and grants of RSA where this is permitted by OFCOM.

373.   *Subsections (1)* and *(2)* provide that regulations authorising spectrum trading may allow some or all of the rights and obligations attached to a wireless telegraphy licence or grants of RSA to be transferred to another person, or for such rights and obligations to be exercised concurrently by the transferee and the transferor. Sharing of rights could occur, for example, if it were intended that the licence or grants of RSA would revert after a period of time to the original holder, who meanwhile would remain responsible for ensuring compliance with the terms and conditions. *Subsection (2)* will thus allow secondary spectrum trading to take place in different ways and is designed to allow maximum flexibility.

374.   *Subsection (3)* sets out the range of provisions that may be included in regulations authorising spectrum trading. For example, under *subsection 3(c)* and *(e)* regulations may require the approval of OFCOM before a trade can be made, and may make trades subject to compliance with conditions imposed by OFCOM. Under *subsection (3)(i)*, the regulations may require that trades be notified to OFCOM both before and after the trade takes place (and notification before the trade will be made a requirement because Article 9(4) of the Framework Directive requires it).

375.   *Subsections (4)* and *(5)* provide that a transfer of rights and obligations under a wireless telegraphy licence or grant of RSA will be void unless it is made in accordance with either: (i) regulations authorising spectrum trading made under this section; or (ii) the provisions of an existing wireless telegraphy licence which allows the holder to confer the benefit of the licence on another.

376.   This section implements Article 9(3) and (4) of the Framework Directive and condition 5 of Part B of the Annex to the Authorisation Directive.

Section 169: Variation and revocation of wireless telegraphy licences

377.   This section substitutes a new section 1E of the Wireless Telegraphy Act 1949. The principal changes are an increase from 28 days to one month as the standard period of notice that OFCOM must give, new provisions about shorter notice in cases of serious and repeated breaches and urgency, and removal of the need for notice when the variation or revocation is at the request of, or with the consent of, the licence-holder. The first two of those changes implement paragraphs 2, 5, 6 and 10 of Article 10 and Article 14(1) of the Authorisation Directive (see also the notes on section 172 below).

378.   In addition, paragraph 8 of Schedule 17 amends section 1D of the Wireless Telegraphy Act 1949 to provide that any application for a grant of a wireless telegraphy licence shall be determined in accordance with procedures prescribed in regulations made by OFCOM. Any decision on such an application must, in

most cases, be published by OFCOM within six weeks. Paragraph 20 of Schedule 18 (transitional provisions) provides that any procedures set out in a notice under section 1D of the Wireless Telegraphy Act 1949 prior to the commencement of paragraph 8 of Schedule 17 shall be treated as if they are regulations made under the amended section 1D.

Section 170: Wireless telegraphy register

379.   OFCOM may, by regulations, set up a public register of information about the holders of wireless telegraphy licences and persons to whom grants of RSA have been made. This may also include details about the licences and frequencies assigned.

Section 171: Information requirements in relation to wireless telegraphy licences

380.   This section amends the Wireless Telegraphy Act 1949 by inserting new sections 13A and 13B. Section 13A allows OFCOM to require, by issuing a notice, any user of a wireless telegraphy station or apparatus to provide information relating to their use of the station or apparatus and any related matters to OFCOM for statistical purposes: the limitation on the purpose for which information may be required implements Article 11(1)(e) of the Authorisation Directive. Such a request must be proportionate (which implements the requirement in Article 11(1), and OFCOM must explain why they are demanding that information and the statistical purposes for which the information will be used (which implements Article 11(2). A person who fails to provide such information is guilty of an offence, although it is a defence to show that it was not reasonably practicable for him to comply within the period allowed, but that he took all reasonable steps to comply after that period had expired. It is also an offence for a person to provide information to OFCOM under this section that is materially false if he knows, or is reckless as to whether, it is materially false.

381.   Section 13B imposes a requirement on OFCOM to publish a statement of their policy on the use of their powers under section 13A and the statistical purposes for which they will use any information gathered and to have regard to such statement for the time being in force when exercising the powers under section 13A.

Section 172: Contraventions of conditions for use of wireless telegraphy

382.   Where OFCOM have reasonable grounds to believe that a wireless telegraphy licensee is or has been in breach of any term, provision, or limitation of that licence or any person is or has been in breach of any term, provision or limitation of an exemption under the proviso to section 1(1) of the Wireless Telegraphy Act 1949, they may notify that person accordingly, and allow him a specified period of time in which to make representations to OFCOM and to take steps to comply with the notified term, provision or limitation. The specified period of time must usually be one month, except, for example, in cases of repeated contraventions. This section implements Article 10(2) of the Authorisation Directive (see also the notes on sections 169 and 174).

Section 173: Meaning of "repeated contravention" in s. 172

383. This section defines a "repeated contravention" for the purposes of section 172. This section implements Article 10(2) and (5) of the Authorisation Directive.

Section 174: Procedure for prosecutions of wireless telegraphy offences

384. Proceedings for an offence under section 1 of the Wireless Telegraphy Act 1949 cannot be brought unless OFCOM have first notified the potential defendant under section 172 and considered any representations made by him (this implements Article 10(2) and (3) of the Authorisation Directive - see also the notes on section 172 above). However, OFCOM do not have to follow section 172 procedures in urgent cases, i.e. where there is a threat to public safety or health, or to national security, or where a person other than the defendant would suffer serious economic or operational problems (this implements Article 10(6) of the Authorisation Directive).

Section 175: Special procedure for contraventions by multiplex licence holders

385. This section gives OFCOM a power to impose fines for breach of terms, provisions or limitations falling within new section 1(2A)(b) or (c) of the Wireless Telegraphy Act 1949 (terms, provisions and limitations about service content) inserted by section 165. OFCOM may impose a fine under this section where they have notified the general multiplex licensee of their belief that he is in breach of the licence condition in question, provided that criminal proceedings have not already been commenced under the Wireless Telegraphy Act 1949 against that licensee in respect of that alleged breach. Once a fine has been imposed by OFCOM, *subsection (4)* provides that no criminal proceedings may be brought under the 1949 Act for that breach.

> *a general multiplex licence* is defined in *subsection (5)* as a wireless telegraphy licence issued for the purposes of a multiplex service, when no licence under the Broadcasting Act 1996 is held in respect of that multiplex service.

> *multiplex service* is defined in *subsection (6)* as a service broadcast for general reception which provides, or is capable of providing, two or more digital services.

386. OFCOM must notify a general multiplex licensee on whom they decide to impose a fine, giving the reasons for their decision and allowing a reasonable period within which the fine must be paid.

Section 176: Amount of penalty under s. 175

387. This section provides that the maximum penalty that OFCOM may impose for a contravention of section 175 will be the greater of £250,000 and 5% of the relevant amount of gross revenue (which term is defined in section 177). *Subsection (3)* provides for the Secretary of State to amend by order the amount of £250,000. When determining the amount of a penalty to be imposed, OFCOM must have regard to their guidelines for fixing penalties published in accordance with section 392.

Section 177: "Relevant amount of gross revenue" for the purposes of s. 176

388.   The relevant amount of gross revenue for the purpose of section 176 is to be calculated in accordance with a statement of principles made by OFCOM. Before making or revising a statement under this section, OFCOM must consult the Treasury and the Secretary of State. OFCOM must publish the statement or revision and send a copy to the Secretary of State, who must lay it before each House of Parliament.

Section 178: Proceedings for an offence relating to apparatus use

389.   This section amends sections 11 and 12 of the Wireless Telegraphy Act 1949 in order to bring the mechanism for appeals against decisions of OFCOM about apparatus which causes or may cause undue interference (which are currently taken by the Secretary of State) into line with the new provisions for appeals in Chapter 3 of Part 2 of this Act.

390.   The current arrangements for appeal to a tribunal established under section 9 of the 1949 Act, which is repealed by Schedule 19, have very rarely, if ever, been used.

Section 179: Modification of penalties for certain wireless telegraphy offences

391.   *Subsections (1) and (2)* amend section 14 of the Wireless Telegraphy Act 1949. They alter the penalties and mode of trial for offences under sections 1 and 1A of the 1949 Act committed after the commencement of this section consisting of unlicensed transmission other than for broadcasting, or possession of apparatus for such transmission: these offences become triable summarily only, and the maximum penalties are now six months imprisonment and/or a fine not exceeding level 5 on the standard scale (currently £5,000). *Subsection (3)* amends section 79(1) of the Telecommunications Act 1984 so that, where authorised by warrant, apparatus and other property suspected of being used in connection with an offence under section 1A of the 1949 Act consisting of possessing apparatus for unauthorised transmission (whether broadcasting or not) may be seized and detained.

> *As mentioned above, section 1(1) of the 1949 Act makes it an offence for any person to establish or use any station for wireless telegraphy or to install or use any apparatus for wireless telegraphy, otherwise than under and in accordance with a licence granted by the Secretary of State. Section 1A makes it an offence to possess or have control over any equipment with intent to use it in contravention of section 1 or knowing, or having reasonable cause to believe, that another person will so use it. The mode of trial and penalties for broadcasting offences are not affected by the 1949 Act.

Section 180: Fixed penalties for certain wireless telegraphy offences

392.   This section gives effect to Schedule 6 to the Act, which introduces a fixed penalty regime for summary offences under the Wireless Telegraphy Act 1949.

393.   Schedule 6 allows OFCOM to send a "fixed penalty notice" to any person they believe has committed any summary offence under the 1949 Act. This notice must

give particulars about the alleged offence, and will offer the alleged offender the opportunity to discharge any liability to conviction for the offence by payment of a fixed penalty within the specified period, which must be at least one month. The amount of the penalty may be prescribed in relation to that offence by regulations made by the Secretary of State, but must not be more than 25 per cent of the maximum fine on summary conviction). No proceedings may be brought for the alleged offence during the specified period, unless the alleged offender asks to be tried in accordance with the provisions of the notice. If the penalty is paid within the period specified in the notice, no further proceedings for that offence can be brought against the notified person.

Section 181: Power of arrest

394.   This section applies the summary arrest powers contained in Schedule 1A to the Police and Criminal Evidence Act 1984 (which is being inserted by the Police Reform Act 2002) to offences under section 14(1) of the Wireless Telegraphy Act 1949. Section 14(1) provides that certain offences under the 1949 Act are triable either summarily or on indictment ("triable either way"). This section also amends the equivalent provision in the Police and Criminal Evidence (Northern Ireland) Order 1989.

Section 182: Forfeiture etc. of restricted apparatus

395.   This section gives effect to Schedule 7, which replaces sections 80 and 81 of the Telecommunications Act 1984.

396.   Schedule 7 sets out the procedures which apply to the seizure and forfeiture of apparatus the custody or control of which is restricted under an order made under section 7 of the Wireless Telegraphy Act 1967. OFCOM are to notify each owner of such apparatus about its seizure and the grounds for that seizure. The principal change from the previous regime will be that restricted apparatus that has been seized will be deemed to be forfeited unless any person claiming that the apparatus is not liable to forfeiture gives notice of his claim in writing to OFCOM within one month of the date of the notice of seizure. In such cases OFCOM may take the matter to court. They must decide as soon as reasonably practicable after receipt of the claim either to do so or to return the apparatus to its owners.

> *Section 7 of the Wireless Telegraphy Act 1967 provides for the Secretary of State to make orders restricting certain actions in relation to specified apparatus for the purpose of preventing or reducing the risk of interference. Restricted apparatus may be seized either under warrant under section 15 of the Wireless Telegraphy Act 1949 or in accordance with a power in section 79(3) of the Telecommunications Act 1984 to seize any apparatus or thing used in connection with offences specified in section 79(1) of that Act.

Section 183: Modification of definition of "undue interference"

397.   This section modifies the definition of "undue interference" in section 19(5) of the Wireless Telegraphy Act 1949 (i) in implementation of condition 3 of Part B of

the Annex to the Authorisation Directive, which refers to "harmful interference" as defined in Article 2(2)(b) of that Directive, and also (ii) in implementation of Article 7(2) of Directive 1999/5/EC on radio equipment and telecommunications terminal equipment, which refers to "harmful interference" as defined (in the same terms) in Article 2(i) of that Directive. The new definition provides that interference with wireless telegraphy will not be regarded as "undue interference" unless it is also harmful. "Harmful" interference means that the interference creates dangers or risks of dangers in relation to any radio service used for navigation or for any other purpose connected with safety, or that it degrades, obstructs or repeatedly interrupts lawful radio transmissions.

Section 184: Modification of definition of "wireless telegraphy"

398. This section gives the Secretary of State the power (exercisable by order, subject to the affirmative resolution procedure in both Houses of Parliament) to modify the definition of "wireless telegraphy" in section 19(1) of the Wireless Telegraphy Act 1949 so as to vary the upper frequency limit (currently 3,000 Giga-Hertz) of the electromagnetic spectrum to which the Wireless Telegraphy Acts apply. Although current technology does not permit the use for radiocommunications of frequencies anywhere near that limit, as technology progresses it may be necessary to raise the ceiling.

Chapter 3: Disputes and Appeals

399. The dispute provisions in the Act reflect the requirements of Articles 20 and 21 of the Framework Directive. Article 20 enables disputes under the Framework Directive and the other Communications Directives between persons providing electronic communications networks and electronic communications services in the same jurisdiction to be referred to OFCOM by either party. Article 21 of the Framework Directive stipulates the procedures to be followed when cross-border disputes arise. Sections 185 to 190 implement these provisions of the Directives accordingly.

400. The appeals mechanisms in the Act have been devised to meet the specific requirements of Article 4 of the Framework Directive. Article 4 of the Framework Directive, in effect, requires that any person who is affected by a decision of OFCOM or the Secretary of State which relates to networks or services or rights of use of spectrum must have the right of appeal on the merits against that decision to an appeal body that is independent of the parties involved. The Act therefore sets out a mechanism for appeal on the merits to the Competition Appeal Tribunal (CAT) against any decision (with specified exceptions) taken by OFCOM under Part 2 of the Act or the Wireless Telegraphy Acts 1949 or 1998, against certain specified decisions of the Secretary of State and against directions, approvals and consents pursuant to conditions under section 45. Once the CAT has reached its decision it must remit the decision under appeal to OFCOM, the Secretary of State or the person responsible for the direction, approval or consent as appropriate, with such directions, if any, as it considers necessary.

Section 185: Reference of disputes to OFCOM

401.   This section enables parties to certain disputes relating to network access or dealing with obligations under Part 2 of the Act and other legislation relating to radio spectrum management to be referred by a party to OFCOM. The types of disputes that may be referred are: (i) network access disputes between different communications providers, between communications providers and persons making associated facilities available or between different persons making associated facilities available; (ii) disputes concerning the access-related conditions set under section 74(1) between communications providers or persons making associated facilities available and persons to whom that section applies or between different persons to whom that section applies; (iii) disputes between different communications providers dealing with obligations under Part 2 of the Act (other than disputes about obligations imposed by SMP apparatus conditions, the persistent misuse of networks or services, restrictions in leases and licences or offences relating to networks and services) or under other legislation relating to radio spectrum management.

402.   Under *subsection (4)*, OFCOM may stipulate the manner in which a reference may be made by a party to the dispute. Any requirements imposed by OFCOM must be published in a notice. This section implements Article 20(1) of the Framework Directive.

403.   Paragraph 22 of Schedule 18 (transitional provisions) makes provision for OFCOM to deal with disputes arising under 'old' rules (notably, the Telecommunications (Interconnection) Regulations 1997). Such disputes will in effect continue to be resolved under the 'old' rules as regards their substance. This means that, for example, only the latter's (more restricted) range of remedies can be applied; in particular, OFCOM cannot award costs or compensation. However, these disputes will be handled under the new *procedural* arrangements – so that, for example, the decisions will be appealable to the CAT, and must be taken within 4 months (rather than 6 as in the present rules) –(see subparagraph (1)). After the end of the transitional period (specified in section 408), OFCOM will only be able to deal with these disputes if they are satisfied that the circumstances are 'exceptional' – e.g. if it was not reasonable or possible for the issue in dispute to have been discovered before (subparagraph (2)(d)). Where they take a decision under these provisions, OFCOM must also take steps as soon as possible to decide whether or not to replace the direction giving effect to such a decision with a condition of entitlement under the new regime, and then to either introduce such a condition or else abandon the old direction.

404.   Any direction given under regulation 6 before the Telecommunications (Interconnection) Regulations 1997 are revoked will be enforceable under paragraph 13 of Schedule 18. Paragraph 22 also provides (subparagraphs (5) to (7)) for directions made by Oftel to resolve disputes under the Interconnection Regulations to have continued effect even after the revocation of the Regulations by the Act. However OFCOM's powers to continue such directions are restricted to obligations which could be replaced by new-style obligations and are subject to the duty to

review and either replace or abandon them as described above.

Section 186: Action by OFCOM on dispute reference

405.   If a dispute is referred to OFCOM by a party under section 185, OFCOM must handle the dispute unless they believe that there are alternative means, which would promptly and satisfactorily resolve the dispute consistently with the European Community requirements in section 4. Where OFCOM conclude that it is appropriate for the referred dispute to be resolved by alternative means, they must inform the parties to the dispute of their decision as soon as practicable. However, if the dispute is not resolved by the alternative means within 4 months, under *subsection (6)* either party to the dispute may refer it back to OFCOM. Section 186 implements Article 20(2) of the Framework Directive.

Section 187: Legal proceedings about referred disputes

406.   Subject to *subsection (8)* of section 190 (determinations bind the parties) and the terms of any agreement between the parties to a dispute, a reference of a dispute under section 185 or a reference of a dispute back to OFCOM under *subsection (6)* of section 186 is without prejudice to the rights of the person referring the dispute, the other parties to the dispute, OFCOM or any other person to bring or continue any legal proceedings dealing with the dispute. Any reference or reference back also does not prevent OFCOM from taking enforcement action in relation to the subject matter of the dispute. OFCOM, however, must comply with any court order requiring OFCOM to stay their handling of a dispute for the period of time specified by the court (which may be indefinite). The period of time specified by the court shall not be counted towards the 4 months that OFCOM have to resolve a dispute under section 185. Section 187 implements Article 20(5) of the Framework Directive.

Section 188: Procedure for resolving disputes

407.   This section requires OFCOM to consider and determine any dispute referred under section 185 that they decide to handle or any dispute referred back to them under *subsection (6)* of section 186. Unless there are exceptional circumstances or it is reasonably practicable for OFCOM to make a determination in a shorter period of time, OFCOM must determine a dispute within 4 months of the date on which OFCOM determines that it is appropriate for them to handle the dispute or on which the dispute is referred back to them. OFCOM must send a copy of their determination and the reasons for their decision to each party to the dispute. Subject to commercial confidentiality, OFCOM must also publish its determination. Section 188 implements Article 20(1) and (4) of the Framework Directive.

Section 189: Disputes involving other member States

408.   This section requires OFCOM to consult with the regulatory authorities of other member States prior to handling, considering or making a determination of a dispute referred to them under section 185 or referred back to them under *subsection*

(6) of section 186 if the dispute relates partly to anything done by means of an electronic communications network falling with the jurisdiction of those authorities.

Under subsection (2), a dispute falls within the jurisdiction of other regulatory authorities when it relates to the activities that are carried out by a party to the dispute in more than one member State or by different parties in different member States and the other regulatory authorities are the authorities for those activities in the other member State or one of the other member States.

409.   Where a dispute involves other regulatory authorities, *subsection (5)* imposes a duty on OFCOM to agree with them, so far as practicable, the steps to be taken in relation to the dispute. *Subsection (6)* requires OFCOM to resolve the dispute within such period of time as may be agreed with the other regulatory authorities.

410.   This section implements Article 21(2) of the Framework Directive.

Section 190: Resolution of referred disputes

411.   When determining a dispute under Chapter 3 of Part 2 of the Act, OFCOM may:

- issue a declaration setting out the rights and obligations of each party to the dispute;

- fix terms or conditions of transactions between the parties to a dispute (except where the dispute relates to radio spectrum management legislation);

- impose enforceable obligations requiring the parties to enter into a transactions on terms or conditions set by OFCOM (except where the dispute relates to radio spectrum management legislation);

- direct a party to the dispute to make payments to adjust under- or overpayment (except where the dispute relates to radio spectrum management legislation);

- require a party to make payments in respect of costs and expenses incurred by another party;

- require a party to make payments in respect of costs and expenses incurred by OFCOM, where the dispute relates to radio spectrum management legislation or where it appears to OFCOM that the reference was frivolous or vexatious or that a party otherwise abused his right of reference under Chapter 3;

- take account of any decisions made by others and ratify any such decisions, where a dispute has been referred back under subsection (6) of section 186.

412.   These powers to resolve a dispute do not prevent OFCOM from separately exercising their powers to (i) set, modify or revoke general conditions, specific

conditions dealing with universal service, access, privileged suppliers or SMP, (ii) to modify or revoke wireless telegraphy licences or grants of recognised spectrum access; or (iii) to make, vary or revoke any regulations under section 1 or 3 of the Wireless Telegraphy Act 1949.

413.   Any determination made by OFCOM is binding on the parties to the dispute; however, they may appeal against the determination in accordance with section 192.

Section 191: OFCOM's power to require information in connection with dispute

414.   This section gives OFCOM powers to require parties to disputes and other persons to provide them with information that enables OFCOM to:

- decide whether they should handle a dispute;

- determine whether they need to consult the regulatory authorities of other member States; and

- consider and determine a dispute.

415.   Information requested by OFCOM must be provided within the period specified by OFCOM. Requests for information under this section may be enforced by OFCOM using the procedure set out in sections 138 to 144. This section implements Article 5 and 21 of the Framework Directive.

Section 192: Appeals against decisions by OFCOM, the Secretary of State etc.

416.   This section provides for appeal to the Competition Appeal Tribunal (CAT) against decisions (with specified exceptions) made by OFCOM under Part 2 of the Act and the Wireless Telegraphy Acts 1949 and 1998 and against decisions made further to a condition of entitlement set under section 45. The specified exceptions are set out in Schedule 8 and are either (i) decisions that do not have immediate effect on a person, but are of a legislative or quasi-legislative nature that require a further act or decision to be given effect, or (ii) decisions on matters which fall outside the scope of the Communications Directives.   For example, a decision taken by OFCOM relating to the making or revision of a statement of policy on information-gathering under section 145 would not have immediate effect on any person. It would only be where OFCOM exercised their powers under section 135 to require the provision of information, in accordance with that statement, that there would be a decision that would actually have effect on any person. Another example is decisions under section 175 (special procedure for contraventions by multiplex licence holders), which fall outside the scope of the Directives.

> * For the purposes of this section and the rest of this Chapter, a decision includes OFCOM's exercise of any power and any failure by them to grant an application or to exercise any power following a request (*subsection (7)* and *(8)*).

417.   Section 192 also applies to specific decisions of the Secretary of State given

under section 5 (directions in respect of Part 2 functions) or section 156 (directions with respect to radio spectrum) (in both cases, excluding decisions specified by Schedule 8), under section 109 (restrictions and conditions subject to which the electronic communications code applies) or under section 132 (suspension or restriction of a communication provider's entitlement).

418.   The right of appeal extends to any person affected by a decision to which this section applies. *Subsections (3)* to *(6)* provide that an appeal can be made only by sending a notice of appeal to the CAT, and prescribe the contents of the notice. This section and sections 193 to 195 implement Article 4 and 11(3) of the Framework Directive and Article 10(7) of the Authorisation Directive.

Section 193: Reference of price control matters to the Competition Commission

419.   If an appeal under section 192(2) raises a price control matter specified in the rules of the CAT, the matter must be referred to the Competition Commission for determination in accordance with the rules and directions of the CAT and (subject to that) using such procedure as Competition Commission consider appropriate.

> *A price control matter as defined in *subsection (10)* relates to the imposition of any form of price control by an SMP condition set under section 87(9), 92, or 93(3).

420.   The Competition Commission must notify the CAT of a determination concerning a price control matter and the CAT must follow the determination of the Competition Commission unless it would be set aside under the principles of judicial review.

Section 194: Composition of Competition Commission for price control references

421.   This section requires the Secretary of State to appoint not less than three members of the Competition Commission for the purposes of references of price control matters to them under section 193. In selecting a group to determine a matter referred to the Competition Commission under section 192, the chairman of the Competition Commission must select at least one, but no more than three, of the members appointed by the Secretary of State to be members of the group.

Section 195: Decisions of the Tribunal

422.   The CAT is to decide an appeal on the merits, and then decide the appropriate action to be taken by the maker of the decision that is being appealed. Where an appeal is made against a decision under section 109 (restrictions and conditions subject to which the electronic communications code applies), the CAT must decide the appeal in accordance with the principles of good administration. The CAT's decision should be communicated to the original decision-maker along with directions regarding the implementation of the CAT's decision. However, the CAT cannot require the original decision-maker to take any action that he would not otherwise

have the power to take.

Section 196: Appeals from the Tribunal

423.   A decision of the CAT may be appealed on a point of law, with the permission of the CAT or the appellate court, to the Court of Appeal or, in Scotland, to the Court of Session.   Such an appeal maybe brought by a party to the original CAT proceedings, or by any third party who has sufficient interest in the decision.

Section 197: Interpretation of Chapter 3

424.   This section provides for the interpretation of defined terms used in Chapter 3.

PART 3: TELEVISION AND RADIO SERVICES

Chapter 1: The BBC, C4C, the Welsh Authority and the Gaelic Media Service

Section 198: Functions of OFCOM in relation to the BBC

425.   This section provides for OFCOM to have the function of regulating the BBC's services to the extent that there is provision for them to do so in the BBC Charter and Agreement (as defined by section 362(1)), in this Act and in Part 5 of the Broadcasting Act 1996 (that is, in relation to unfairness and unwarranted infringement of privacy).   For the purposes of that regulatory function, OFCOM may, where authorised by the Charter and Agreement, act on behalf of the Secretary of State.

426.   The existing Agreement between the Secretary of State and the BBC supplements the Royal Charter in setting out in more detail the provision and content of the BBC's services. It is intended that the Agreement will be amended to give effect to the new regulatory obligations placed on the BBC and to provide for OFCOM to impose financial penalties in the event of the BBC failing to comply with them. Under *subsection (3)* of this section, the BBC are required to pay to OFCOM any penalties which OFCOM impose for contraventions of provision made by or under Part 3 of the Act or the Charter and Agreement. The maximum penalty that OFCOM may impose under such a power is £250,000, but the Secretary of State will be able to change this figure by order: *subsections (5) to (7)*. The BBC must also pay to OFCOM such sums in respect of the carrying out of OFCOM's functions in relation to the BBC as may be agreed between the BBC and OFCOM (or, in the absence of agreement, set by the Secretary of State): *subsection (4)*.

Section 199: Functions of C4C

427.   The Channel Four Television Corporation are able to engage in activities which appear to them to be appropriate to carry on in association with their primary functions and to be connected (other than merely in financial terms) with activities undertaken by them for the carrying out of those functions.   Those functions are securing   the   continued   provision   of Channel 4   and   the   fulfilment   of   the

Channel's public service remit set out in section 265(3), as described in the notes to that section below. The Corporation may also do such things and enter into such transactions as appear to them incidental or conducive to the carrying out of their statutory functions.

428.   Under *subsection (3)* the Corporation will cease to have powers to establish or acquire interests in "qualifying companies" under section 24(5)(b) and (6) of the Broadcasting Act 1990.

429.   Schedule 9 provides a framework for the approval and enforcement of arrangements about the carrying out of the Corporation's activities.

430.   Paragraph 1 requires OFCOM to notify the Corporation that, within a period specified in the notification, the Corporation must submit to OFCOM proposals for arrangements that will apply to the relevant licence period. OFCOM must do this as soon as practicable after the commencement of this Schedule and as soon as practicable in the last twelve months preceding each date on which the Channel 4 licence would expire if not renewed.

431.   Where the Corporation have received a notification, they must submit proposals to OFCOM setting out the arrangements under which they are proposing to secure, so far as reasonably practicable, that all significant risks that their other activities will have an adverse effect on the carrying out of their primary functions (i.e. the provision of Channel 4 and the fulfilment of its public service remit) are identified, evaluated and properly managed. The proposals must include the arrangements that the Corporation consider appropriate for securing the transparency objectives set out in paragraph 2(4). They may relate in particular to the list of matters specified in paragraph 2(5), e.g. the management of new ventures, the assessment of risks.

432.   OFCOM must consider the proposed arrangements and approve them, approve them with modifications, or require the Corporation to submit revised proposals. OFCOM may review the arrangements once during each licence period, either as a single review of all of the arrangements or two separate reviews, one relating to the arrangements to secure the transparency objectives and one relating to other matters. OFCOM must also publish the arrangements.

433.   The Corporation must act in accordance with the approved arrangements. OFCOM have powers to enforce the arrangements and may impose a penalty, which may not exceed 3 per cent. of the Corporation's qualifying revenue, if they are contravened.

   *Qualifying revenue has the same meaning as in section 19(2) to (6) of and Part 1 of Schedule 7 to the Broadcasting Act 1990 with any necessary modifications.

434.   In carrying out their functions under Schedule 9, OFCOM must have regard to the need to secure, so far as reasonably practicable, that all significant risks that the

Corporation's other activities will have an adverse effect on the provision of Channel 4 or its public service remit are identified, evaluated and properly managed.

Section 200: Removal of members of C4C

435.   This section gives OFCOM the power, after consulting the Secretary of State, to remove members of the Channel Four Television Corporation appointed by them.

Section 201: Deficits and surpluses of C4C

436.   This section repeals sections 26 and 27 of the Broadcasting Act 1990 (revenue deficits and excesses of Channel Four Television Corporation to be met or distributed to providers of Channel 3 services) in respect of any year ending after the commencement of this section.

Section 202: Borrowing limit for C4C

437.   The Secretary of State may by order limit the amount of money that the Channel Four Television Corporation are permitted to borrow. Before making an order under this section, the Secretary of State must consult the Corporation and obtain the consent of the Treasury. The Corporation must not borrow money in excess of any limit set by the Secretary of State. The effect of this will be only to circumscribe new borrowing – the setting of a limit at a figure below that of the Corporation's actual outstanding borrowing would not require the Corporation to take positive steps to reduce their outstanding borrowing to a level which did not exceed the limit.

Section 203: Function of OFCOM in relation to the Welsh Authority

438.   OFCOM are to regulate the services provided by the Welsh Authority to the extent provided by Part 5 of the Broadcasting Act 1996 and the present Act.

Section 204: Welsh Authority's function of providing S4C and S4C Digital

439.   The Welsh Authority, as currently constituted, shall continue to exist. However, their functions as described under section 57 of the Broadcasting Act 1990, will be replaced with the function in *subsection (2)*, namely of providing high quality television programmes for reception in Wales. The Welsh Authority must continue to provide S4C and may continue to provide S4C Digital. However, under *subsections (8) and (9)*, the Secretary of State may by order require the Welsh Authority to provide S4C in digital rather than analogue form, to merge S4C and S4C Digital and/or to provide the whole or part of the merged service in both analogue and digital form for a period specified in the order.

440.   *Subsection (5)* imposes a duty on the Welsh Authority to ensure that S4C and S4C Digital are public services used for the dissemination of information, education and entertainment. The Welsh Authority may provide programming subtitles and

other ancillary services for their S4C programmes. They may also provide assistance
for disabled people and other ancillary services for their S4C Digital services.

Section 205: Powers to provide other services

441.   This section confers on the Welsh Authority the power to provide certain
services in addition to S4C and S4C Digital. *Subsection (1)* prohibits the Welsh
Authority from providing any television programme service (other than S4C and S4C
Digital) unless its provision is approved by an order made by the Secretary of State
and it is a public service of high quality used for the dissemination of information,
education or entertainment wholly or mainly to the Welsh public. Any television
programme services provided under this section must broaden the existing range of
public television programme services in Wales.

   *The meaning of a television programme service is given in section 362(1).

442.   *Subsection (2)* allows the Welsh Authority to provide services other than
television programme services or sound services, provided they are public services of
high quality used for the dissemination of information, education or entertainment
which will be made available wholly or mainly to the Welsh public, or for use in
Wales, and have been approved by the Secretary of State. Examples of the types of
service that the Welsh Authority may provide under this subsection include (but are
not limited to) an interactive service delivered via the Internet. Paragraph 27(1) of
Schedule 18 stipulates that the Welsh Authority are not required to obtain the
Secretary of State's approval for the continued provision of any service that they are
providing before section 205 comes into effect.

443.   In the course of providing a service approved by the Secretary of State under
section 205, the Welsh Authority may under *subsection (7)* also provide: assistance
for disabled people in relation to programmes included in the service, services
ancillary to programmes included in the service and related to their content, and other
types of ancillary services offered in a digital format.

444.   Any programme service approved by the Secretary of State under this section
must contain a substantial proportion of programmes in the Welsh language.

Section 206: Other activities of Welsh Authority

445.   This section enables the Welsh Authority to carry on activities appearing to
them to be activities which it is appropriate for them to carry on in association with
the function of providing S4C, S4C Digital and any other service approved by the
Secretary of State under section 205, or to be connected (other than merely in
financial terms) with that function. Prior to carrying out such activities, the Welsh
Authority must obtain the approval of the Secretary of State under *subsection (2)*. The
types of activities that may be approved by her under *subsection (2)* include those
needed to secure, and those provided in connection with, the provision of licensable
services by an S4C company (e.g. a company controlled by the Authority: see section

362(1)), such as the formation of a company to provide a programme service, but do not include the provision of a licensable service. *Subsection (6)* amends the provisions in the Broadcasting Act 1990 which govern the power of the Welsh Authority to do things incidental or conducive to the carrying out of their functions. Paragraph 27(2) and (3) of Schedule 18 provides that the Secretary of State's approval is not required for the continuation of activities undertaken by the Welsh Authority or an S4C company before this section comes into effect.

> *A *licensable service* is defined in *subsection (7)* as an independent television or independent radio service that would be regulated under section 211 or 245 if provided by an S4C company.

Section 207: Welsh Authority finances

446.   It is unlawful under *subsection (2)* for the Welsh Authority to charge people in Wales for the reception or use of any of their public services, any assistance provided to disabled persons for programmes included in their public services or any of the ancillary services that they provide in a digital format.

> * Under *subsection (9)*, the Welsh Authority's public services are S4C, S4C Digital and other services approved by the Secretary of State under section 205.

447.   *Subsection (3)* states that the power of the Welsh Authority to do anything that is conducive or incidental to the carrying out of their functions includes the power to borrow money. However, they may not do so without the approval of the Secretary of State and the consent of the Treasury. The Welsh Authority must also pay such fees towards the carrying out of OFCOM's functions as may be agreed between the Authority and OFCOM (or, in the absence of agreement, as are set by the Secretary of State).

448.   *Subsection (7)* amends section 61 of the Broadcasting Act 1990 so that the Secretary of State may increase the annual grant paid to the Welsh Authority if she is satisfied that additional funding is appropriate in light of the costs they incur in providing their public services and broadcasting or distributing such services.

449.   *Subsection (8)* amends section 61A of the Broadcasting Act 1990 so that the Welsh Authority must use the money in their public service fund only for the provision of television programme services that are "public services" as defined by *subsection (9)*. *Subsection (8)* also amends section 61A of the Broadcasting Act 1990 so that the first broadcast of any programme funded from the public service fund must be on one of the Authority's public television services.

Section 208: The Gaelic Media Service

450.   This section renames the Gaelic Broadcasting Committee (Comataidh Craolaidh Gàidhlig), originally the Gaelic Television Committee (Comataidh Telebhisein Gàidhlig) established under section 183 of the Broadcasting Act 1990, as the Gaelic Media Service (Seirbheis nam Meadhanan Gàidhlig). It also inserts new subsections (3B), (4), (4A) and (4B) into section 183. These set out the functions

and powers of the Gaelic Media Service who must secure that a wide and diverse range of high quality programmes in Gaelic are broadcast or otherwise transmitted so as to be available for reception in Scotland.

451.   The Gaelic Media Service may apply the Gaelic Broadcasting Fund for the purpose of, or any purpose connected with, the carrying out of their functions: new subsection (4).   In carrying out their functions, the Gaelic Media Service may finance, or engage in, the making of television and sound programmes in Gaelic to be broadcast or transmitted so as to be available for reception in Scotland, provide or arrange training in relation to programme-making and carry out research to discover the types of television and sound programmes that the Gaelic-speaking community would like to be broadcast. The Gaelic Media Service may not provide any of the services specified in subsection (4B).

452.   Paragraph 28 of Schedule 18 provides for transitional provisions in respect of the membership of the Comataidh Craolaidh Gàidhlig. Paragraph 29 of that Schedule provides for the continuation of the Multiplex Licence (Broadcasting of Programmes in Gaelic) Order 1996 (S.I. 1996/2758).

Section 209: Membership of the Service

453.   This section inserts a new section 183A into the Broadcasting Act 1990 that deals with the composition of the Gaelic Media Service. The Service must consist of no more than 12 members, each of whom must be appointed by OFCOM, having regard to the matters listed in *subsection (6)* of section 183A, and must be approved by the Secretary of State for Scotland. OFCOM must appoint one member as chairman. One member must be nominated, respectively, by the BBC, Highlands and Islands Enterprise and the Bòrd Gàidhlig na h-Alba (Gaelic Development Agency).

454.   OFCOM must also secure that the members of the Services are able adequately to represent the interests of (i) providers of regional Channel 3 services for areas wholly in Scotland or such other areas as are determined by OFCOM under section 184(4)(b) of the Broadcasting Act 1990; (ii) the independent radio and television production industries in Scotland; and (iii) other persons and bodies concerned with the promotion and use of the Gaelic language.

455.   Schedule 19 to the Broadcasting Act 1990 (Gaelic Broadcasting Committee: supplementary provisions) (as amended by section 210 and paragraph 73 of Schedule 15) also applies to the Gaelic Media Service.

Section 210: Supplementary provisions about the Service

456.   This section amends Schedule 19 (supplementary provisions) to the Broadcasting Act 1990.

Chapter 2: Regulatory Structure for Independent Television Services

457.   Paragraph 30 of Schedule 18 provides that, subject to any express provision of this Act, any pre-transfer Broadcasting Act licence shall continue to have effect on the same terms and conditions, and for the same period, as it would have done had this Act not been passed.

Section 211: Regulation of independent television services

458.   This section specifies the television services that OFCOM are required to regulate. The first group of services comprises television broadcasting services (other than those broadcast only from a satellite), restricted television services and additional television services broadcast or provided from places in the United Kingdom, and television licensable content services and digital television programme services provided by persons under United Kingdom jurisdiction for the purposes of the Television without Frontiers Directive (see below). OFCOM are not under this section to regulate these services where they are provided by the BBC or the Welsh Authority. The second group of services comprises television multiplex services provided from places in the United Kingdom and digital additional television services provided by persons under United Kingdom jurisdiction. OFCOM are not under this section to regulate these services where they are provided by the BBC.

"television broadcasting service" is defined in section 362 as a service (other than any text service) which consists in a service of television programmes provided with a view to its being broadcast (whether in digital or in analogue form), and which is provided so as to be available for reception by members of the general public. It does not include a restricted television service, a television multiplex service, a service provided under the authority of a licence to provide a television licensable content service, or a service provided under the authority of a licence to provide a digital television programme service.

"restricted television service" has the same meaning as in section 42A of the Broadcasting Act 1990 (as amended by Schedule 19 to this Act), namely a service which consists in the broadcasting of television programmes for a particular establishment or other defined location, or a particular event, in the United Kingdom. The label in the 1990 Act is simply a "restricted service": the word "television" has been added here, and also in relation to digital television programme services and digital additional television services, to distinguish them from radio-related services which, in the 1990 and 1996 Acts are given the same name.

*the meaning of *"television licensable content services"* is given in section 232 and is described in more detail in the notes to that section below.

* a *"digital additional television service"* is defined under section 24 of the Broadcasting Act 1996, which is amended by Schedule 15 to this Act, as being any service provided with a view to its being broadcast to the public in digital form by means of a television or general multiplex service, but not including a Channel 3 service, Channel 4, Channel 5, a public television service of the Welsh Authority, the digital public teletext service, a digital television programme service, a digital sound programme service, an ancillary service, or a technical service.

* a *"digital television programme service"* means any digital programme service within the meaning of section 1(4) of the Broadcasting Act 1996, namely a service consisting in the provision of television programmes (together with any ancillary services as defined by section 24(2) of that Act) with a view to its being broadcast in digital form so as to be available for reception by members of the public (see the amendment in paragraph 74 of Schedule 15). It does not include a teletext service, any service in the case of which the visual images to be broadcast do not consist wholly or mainly of images capable of being seen as moving pictures (except to the extent that either of these services are ancillary to the

television programme) or a qualifying service.

* persons under United Kingdom jurisdiction for the purposes of the Television without Frontiers Directive are primarily persons established in the United Kingdom. A provider is deemed to be established in the United Kingdom if its head office is located here and this is where editorial decisions are taken, or if a significant part of the workforce engaged in the television broadcasting activity operates in the United Kingdom, or if this is where the provider first began broadcasting, assuming that the provider still maintains a stable and effective link with the economy of the United Kingdom. If these tests are not met, persons established under UK jurisdiction may also, in descending order, be persons using a frequency granted by the United Kingdom, persons who use a satellite capacity appertaining to the United Kingdom, and persons who use a satellite up-link situated in the United Kingdom. References to the Television without Frontiers Directive are to Council Directive 89/552/EEC, as amended by Directive 97/36/EC.

* *"additional television service"* is defined in section 48 of the Broadcasting Act 1990 as any service which consists in the sending of electronic signals for transmission by wireless telegraphy by means of the use of spare capacity within the signals carrying any television broadcasting service.

**"qualifying service"* has the meaning given in section 2 of the Broadcasting Act 1996.

* an *"ancillary service"* is defined in section 24 of the Broadcasting Act 1996, as amended by paragraph 93(3) of Schedule 15 to this Act, and refers to assistance for disabled people in relation to some or all of the programmes included in a digital programme service or qualifying service provided by a licence-holder, a service (apart from advertising) that relates to the promotion or listing of programmes included in such a service or in a digital sound programme service so provided or any other service (apart from advertising) that is ancillary to one or more programmes so included, and relates directly to their contents.

*a *"technical service"* is a service provided for the encryption or decryption of digital programme services, digital sound programme services, or digital additional services and specified in an order made by the Secretary of State (see section 24(3) of the Broadcasting Act 1996, as amended by paragraph 93(4) of Schedule 15 to this Act).

Section 212: Abolition of function of assigning television frequencies

459.   The Secretary of State shall no longer have the power to assign television frequencies for independent television services which are licensable under Part 1 of the Broadcasting Act 1990, for S4C, or for television multiplex services which are licensable under Part 1 of the Broadcasting Act 1996. The function of managing radio spectrum (from which the function of assigning frequencies derives) is transferred by the Act to OFCOM.

Section 213: Abolition of licensing for local cable systems

460.   From the television transfer date the provision of a local delivery service shall no longer require a licence under Part 2 of the Broadcasting Act 1990.

*a *"local delivery service"* is defined in section 72 of the 1990 Act to mean (broadly) a service of a kind specified by the Secretary of State consisting in the use of a telecommunication system (whether run by the person providing the local delivery service or not) for the delivery of various television and radio services listed in section 72(2). Licences are awarded on a system of cash bids.

* *"television transfer date"* means the date on which the ITC's functions under the Broadcasting Acts of 1990 and 1996 are transferred to OFCOM.

Section 214: Digital Channel 3 and Channel 5 licences

461. Any Channel 3 or a Channel 5 licence granted after the television transfer date must provide for the licensed service to be broadcast digitally. Such a licence may also contain such conditions requiring the service also to be provided in analogue form as OFCOM consider appropriate. In such cases the programming (apart from advertisements) should replicate that of the digital service (see *subsection (4)*).

462. The conditions included in the licence must enable compliance with any directions given from time to time by the Secretary of State about the continuation of analogue services.

463. Any licence taking effect before "the initial expiry date"(which is 31st December 2014 or any later date set by the Secretary of State under section 224) must remain in force until the end of that day. Any licence taking effect thereafter must remain in force from the time when it takes effect until the end of the licensing period beginning or current at that time.

> * the meaning of *"the initial expiry date"* can be found in section 224. *Subsection (6)* of section 214 provides that a licensing period is the period beginning with the commencement of that section and ending with the initial expiry date, or any subsequent period of 10 years beginning with the end of the previous licensing period.

464. There can be no charge levied for the use of a licensed service or for any related assistance for disabled people or for ancillary services: *subsections (8) and (9)*.

Section 215: Replacement of existing Channel 3 and Channel 5 licences

465. As soon as practicable after the television transfer date OFCOM must offer persons who hold a Channel 3 or Channel 5 licence the opportunity to exchange that licence for a replacement licence, being a licence of the kind described in the notes to section 214 above. The replacement licence must provide for a service that is equivalent in all material respects to the present one, and for it to be provided for substantially the same area and times, although it does not have to be identical in all respects.

466. Any offer made by OFCOM to replace an existing licence must specify the terms of the proposed replacement licence, the conditions on which they propose to grant it, the time frame of their offer, the date on which the licence will be granted if the offer is accepted, the time from which the licence will take effect if the offer is accepted (which must fall within the period of twelve months after the television transfer date) and the time from which the licence will cease to have effect if the offer is rejected.

467. The financial terms of the offer must propose that the licensee will pay the same annual amount and percentage of qualifying revenue as would have been payable under the existing licence had it continued in force until the end of the period for which the replacement is granted.

468.   A licence holder refusing this offer will have his existing licence revoked on a date specified by OFCOM in the offer. This date must fall no later than eighteen months after the closing date for agreeing the offer.

Section 216: Renewal of Channel 3 and 5 licences

469.   This section permits the holders of a licence to provide a Channel 3 service or a licence to provide Channel 5 to apply to OFCOM for the renewal of his licence for the next licensing period.

470.   An application for renewal may only be made in the period beginning four years before the end of the current licensing period and ending three months before the day that OFCOM determine they would have to publish a tender notice if they were proposing to grant a fresh licence to take effect from the end of the current licensing period. Any determination of that date must be made at least one year before the date on which the tender notice would have to be published and must be notified to every person who is, at the time of the determination, a holder of a licence to provide a Channel 3 service or the Channel 5 licence.

471.   Unless the Secretary of State makes an order suspending the rights of renewal under section 230 (see *subsection (11)*), where OFCOM receive an application for the renewal of a licence, they must determine whether or not they will be renewing the licence and, if they will, the financial terms on which the licence will be renewed. They must also notify the applicant accordingly. *Subsections (6)* and *(7)* provide that OFCOM may determine that they will not renew a licence if:

- they are not satisfied that the applicant (if his licence were renewed) would provide a service complying with the requirements imposed under Chapter 4 of Part 3 of the Act relating to the public service remit for the licensed service, programming quotas, news and current affairs programmes or regional programming; or

- they propose to grant a fresh licence for a service replacing the licensed service which would differ from the licensed service in the areas where it would be provided or the times of the day, or days of the week, between or on which it would be provided.

472.   OFCOM must not grant a renewal under this section more than 18 months before the end of the current licensing period: *subsection (9)*.

473.   Where OFCOM determine that a licence should be renewed, they must renew it on the same terms and subject to the same conditions, with such modifications as are required to give effect to the requirements imposed under section 217(4) (*subsection (10)*).

Section 217: Financial terms of licence renewed under s.216

474.   Any offer made by OFCOM to renew an existing licence under section 216 must specify the amount that the licensee is required to pay during the first year of the replacement licence and the percentage of qualifying revenue to be paid for each accounting period of the applicant falling within the relevant licence period.

475.   The amount payable for the first year of the renewed licence must approximate to what OFCOM estimate would have been the cash bid of the licensee had the licence been offered by a notice requesting tenders under section 15 of the Broadcasting Act 1990. When determining the percentage of qualifying revenue, OFCOM may set different percentages (including nil percentages) for different accounting periods.

476.   OFCOM must include conditions in any replacement licence requiring payment of: the amount for the first calendar year of the licence, that amount increased by an appropriate percentage for each subsequent year and a specified percentage of the qualifying revenue attributable to a licence holder in each accounting period of the licence term. Payments required under these conditions are in addition to the fees required by OFCOM under section 4(1)(b) of the Broadcasting Act 1990.

Section 218: Duty to secure the provision of a public teletext service

477.   This section imposes a duty on OFCOM to secure (i) the provision of a single, nationwide, public teletext service in a digital format broadcast by way of a television multiplex service, and (ii) the provision of an analogue teletext service on the spare capacity available on Channels 3 and 4 and S4C until the first of these services ceases to transmit in analogue format. The licence holder will thereafter have the option of continuing to provide an analogue service.

> *Subsection (4)* specifies that the analogue teletext service is a single additional television service that uses the spare radio spectrum allocated to Channel 3 services, Channel 4 and S4C for the provision of additional television services.

478.   OFCOM must ensure that the analogue and digital teletext services are provided by the same person, although the content of the two services may differ and the licence holder may appoint third parties to provide the teletext services in accordance with section 220.

479.   OFCOM shall have regard to their duties under this section when making radio spectrum available to providers of Channel 3 services, Channel 4 and S4C and when making determinations of spare capacity under section 48(2)(b) of the Broadcasting Act 1990.

Section 219: Licensing of the public teletext service

480.　The public teletext service is to be licensed under Part 1 of the Broadcasting Act 1990, subject to the restrictions and conditions set out in this section. For example, *subsection (5)* specifies that OFCOM must include in the public teletext service licence a condition prohibiting the imposition of charges for the reception of the licensed service in the United Kingdom.

481.　Schedule 10 specifies the procedure with which OFCOM must comply when it seeks to award a licence to provide the public teletext service and the conditions to be included in the licence. It also gives OFCOM powers to enforce the conditions included in the public teletext service licence.

482.　When OFCOM propose to award a licence to provide a public teletext service, they must publish (along with general guidance) a notice that sets out the information listed in paragraph 1(2). OFCOM must include the additional information listed in paragraph 1(3) if the teletext service must be provided in analogue form.

483.　Any application made in response to a notice published by OFCOM must be accompanied by the appropriate fee and must also include the information listed in paragraph 3(1), e.g. a technical plan indicating the nature of the service proposed to be provided.　OFCOM may require the applicant to provide further information once they have received the application.　Following the closing date for applications, OFCOM must then publish the name of each applicant along with certain details of each application as described in paragraph 4(1).　OFCOM must also invite the public to make representations.

484.　Before OFCOM may consider whether to award a public teletext service licence to an applicant, they must find that: (i) the applicant's technical plan and its proposals relating to the fulfilment of the public service remit for the public teletext service, the inclusion and updating of news items and the inclusion of material of interest to different communities in the United Kingdom are acceptable to them; and (ii) the provision of the proposed services can be maintained during the licence term. OFCOM must then award the licence in accordance with sections 17 and 17A of the Broadcasting Act 1990 (as modified by this Schedule).

485.　Paragraph 6 permits OFCOM to revoke and re-award a public teletext service licence when the licensee indicates that he does not intend to provide the service or OFCOM have reasonable grounds to believe that the licensee will not provide the service. Before revoking a licence, OFCOM must serve a notice on the licensee and offer him a reasonable opportunity to submit representations.

486.　Paragraph 7 requires OFCOM to include in a public teletext service licence conditions requiring payment of the following determined in accordance with Schedule 10, during the licence term: an annual amount, increased by an appropriate percentage, and a specified percentage of the qualifying revenue for each accounting period of the licensee falling within the licence term. Payments required under these conditions are in addition to those required by OFCOM under section 4(1)(b) of the Broadcasting Act 1990.

*Appropriate percentage has the same meaning as in section 19 of the Broadcasting Act 1990 (i.e. it takes account of inflation).

487. OFCOM may also include conditions permitting them to estimate the amount of payments due from the licence holder during an accounting period and requiring him to make monthly interim payments. Conditions permitting OFCOM to revise their estimate and the monthly interim payments made by the licence holder and to make adjustments for any over- or under payment made may also be included.

488. Paragraph 8 provides that section 40 of the Broadcasting Act 1990 (power to direct correction or statement of findings) has effect in relation to the public teletext service.

489. Paragraphs 9 and 10 confer on OFCOM the power to enforce the conditions included in the public teletext service licence. Where OFCOM are satisfied that a licence holder has contravened a condition of the licence or has failed to comply with a direction given by OFCOM under the Broadcasting Acts 1990 or 1996 or Part 3 of this Act, they may impose a penalty and/or reduce the term of the licence by up to two years. Licences may also be revoked for contraventions of licence conditions or directions. Where OFCOM do not revoke the licence they may fine the offender up to 5 per cent of the qualifying revenue for its last complete accounting period.

490. Before imposing a penalty or reducing the term of the public teletext service licence, OFCOM must notify the licence holder and provide him with a reasonable opportunity to make representations. A licence may be revoked where OFCOM are satisfied that the conduct of the licence holder justifies its revocation.

491. Where OFCOM decide to revoke a public teletext service licence, they must also notify the former licence holder of the penalty that he must pay. A maximum fine (whichever is the greater) of either £500,000 or 7 per cent of either the estimated or actual qualifying revenue may be imposed. The Secretary of State can modify the amount of the maximum fine by order.

*"qualifying revenue" is defined for the purposes of this Schedule in paragraph 15.

Section 220: Delegation of provision of public teletext service

492. A licence for the provision of the public teletext service may enable the licence holder to subcontract the provision of all or part of the service to a third party, subject to and in accordance with the requirements of conditions set by OFCOM. Contravention by the relevant third party of a condition imposed under this section will be treated for the purposes of Chapter 2 of Part 3 and the Broadcasting Act 1990 as a contravention by the licensee.

Section 221: Replacement of existing public teletext provider's licence

493.   As soon as practicable after the television transfer date, OFCOM must offer the person who holds the existing licence to provide the public teletext service the opportunity to exchange that licence for a replacement licence. The replacement licence must provide for a service that is equivalent in all material respects both to the existing service and to the digital service that the licensee is required to provide under section 30 of the Broadcasting Act 1996. The replacement licence must be awarded in accordance with section 219 and Part 1 of the Broadcasting Act 1990. However, the procedure in Part 1 of Schedule 10 is not to apply to the replacement licence.

494.   The offer of the replacement licence must specify each of the following as determined by OFCOM: the conditions on which they propose to grant the replacement licence, the timeframe of their offer, the date on which the licence will take effect if the offer is accepted (which must fall within the period of twelve months after the television transfer date), and the time from which the licence will cease to have effect of the offer is rejected. The financial terms of the offer must propose that the licensee will pay the same annual amount and percentage of qualifying revenue as would have been payable under the existing licence had it continued in force until the end of the period for which the replacement is granted. A licence holder refusing this offer will have his existing licence revoked on a date specified by OFCOM in the offer. This date must fall no later than eighteen months after the closing date for agreeing the offer.

Section 222: Renewal of public teletext licence

495.   This section permits the holder of the licence to provide the public teletext service to apply to OFCOM for the renewal of his licence for the next licensing period.

> * *Subsection (12)* provides that a licensing period is the period beginning with the commencement of this section and ending with the initial expiry date (see section 224); or any subsequent period of 10 years beginning with the end of the previous licensing period.

496.   An application for renewal may only be made in the period beginning four years before the end of the current licensing period and ending three months before the day that OFCOM determine they would have to publish a tender notice if they were proposing to grant a fresh licence to take effect from the end of the current licensing period. Any determination of that date must be made at least one year before the date on which the tender notice would have to be published and must be notified to the person who is holding the public teletext licence at the time that the determination is made.

497.   Unless the Secretary of State makes an order suspending the rights of renewal under section 230, where OFCOM receive an application for the renewal of a licence they must determine whether or not they will renew the licence and, if they do intend to renew the licence, the financial terms on which they intend to do so. They must

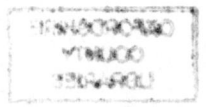

also notify the applicant accordingly. *Subsections (6) and (7)* provide that OFCOM may determine that they will not renew a licence if:

- they are not satisfied that the applicant (if his licence were renewed) would provide a service complying with the requirements imposed under Chapter 4 of Part 3 of the Act relating to the public service remit for the public teletext service, news programmes and regional matters; or

- they propose to grant a fresh licence for a service replacing the licensed service which would differ from the licensed service in any material respect.

498.   OFCOM must not grant a renewal under this section more than 18 months before the end of the current licensing period.

499.   Where OFCOM determine that a licence should be renewed, they must renew it on the same terms and conditions, subject only to such modifications as are required to give effect to the requirements imposed under paragraph 7 of Schedule 10 (payments to be made to OFCOM by the licence-holder).

Section 223: Financial terms of licence renewed under s. 222

500.   Any offer made by OFCOM to renew an existing licence under section 222 must include a determination of the amount that the licensee is required to pay during the first complete calendar year of the renewal period and the percentage of qualifying revenue to be paid for each accounting period of the applicant falling within the relevant renewal period. The amount for the first year of the replacement licence must approximate to what OFCOM estimate would have been the highest cash bid of the licensee had the licence been awarded under Part 1 of Schedule 10.   When determining the percentage of qualifying revenue, OFCOM may set different percentages (including nil percentages) for different accounting periods.

Section 224: Meaning of "initial expiry date"

501.   The initial expiry date for the purposes of Part 3 of the Act is 31st December 2014, unless it is postponed under this section.

502.   The Secretary of State may postpone the initial expiry date on one or more occasions. This is to ensure that the licences will not expire less than eighteen months after the date set for digital switchover. This power can only be exercised where switchover is later than 30th June 2013.

503.   *Subsections (4) and (5)* have the effect that the initial expiry date must always fall at least 18 months after digital switchover (so that the licences will continue for at least that long after switchover).

504.   The extended licence will be deemed to be granted on the same terms as the original one.

505.   "The date for digital switchover" is defined by *subsection (8)* as the date that appears to the Secretary of State to be the date after which Channel 3 and Channel 5 services are no longer to be broadcast to any significant extent in analogue form.

Section 225: Application for review of financial terms of replacement licences

506.   The holder of a licence granted under section 215 (Channel 3 or 5) or 221 (the public teletext service) may apply for a review of the financial terms of this licence, on one or more different occasions. The first one may happen at any time during the first review period, i.e. the period starting four years before the first notional expiry date (see below) and ending on a date fixed by OFCOM. The subsequent reviews may happen at any point during any subsequent review period, which begins four years before the relevant subsequent notional expiry date and ends on a date fixed by OFCOM.

507.   No such application may be made when an application for a review under section 226 is pending or less than twelve months after a determination of new financial terms has been made by OFCOM under that section.

508.   *Subsection (7)* defines the "first notional expiry date" as the date on which the existing licence would have expired if not renewed and "subsequent notional expiry date", in relation to a replacement licence, as either the tenth anniversary of the last notional expiry date, or, if the licensee has previously applied for a review under this section, the tenth anniversary of the date on which OFCOM's determination of that review was notified to the licensee.

Section 226: Application for review of financial terms in consequence of new obligations

509.   This section applies where a commencement order brings into force any of sections 272, 273 or 274 (must-offer in relation to networks and satellite services and must-provide). In that event a Channel 3 service provider or the provider of Channel 5 or of the public teletext service may apply for a review of the financial terms of his licence. Any application for a review must be made during the review period, namely the period running from the day on which the order is made until the coming in to force of the relevant section (or sections). Sections 272(10), 273(8) and 274(11) have the effect of ensuring that this period is at least six months long.

Section 227: Reviews under ss. 225 and 226

510.   A determination made by OFCOM under this section following an application for a review must include the amount to be paid for the first calendar year of the period under review (which must be what OFCOM think would have been the amount that the licensee would have bid if the licence were awarded in response to a notice under section 15 of the Broadcasting Act 1990) and the percentage of qualifying revenue to be used for each accounting period.

511.   When determining these new financial terms, OFCOM must have regard to any additional costs that are likely to be incurred by the licence holder as a consequence of the new conditions imposed following the commencement of sections 272, 273 and/or 274.

Section 228: Giving effect to reviews under ss. 225 and 226

512.   This section provides that, as soon as reasonably practicable after making a determination under section 227, OFCOM must send to the applicant a notification setting out this determination, the modifications required in the applicant's licence, a response date by which the applicant has to notify his acceptance to OFCOM, and an end date by which the licence will cease to have effect if he does not.

513.   *Subsection (5)* provides that the new licence conditions are to have effect when the applicant notifies OFCOM that he accepts the determination. If the applicant does not notify his acceptance before the response date set by OFCOM, his licence will cease to have effect on the end date set by OFCOM.

Section 229: Report in anticipation of new licensing round

514.   This section gives a duty to OFCOM, no later than 30 months before the end of each licensing period, to report to the Secretary of State on the effects of the conditions which would be included in the renewed licences on the capacity of the holders of Channel 3, 5 and public teletext service licences to contribute to the fulfilment of the public service remit at a cost that is commercially sustainable for them.

515.   Under *subsection (4)*, OFCOM will also include any recommendations that they consider appropriate to make as to the use by the Secretary of State of her powers under section 230 or under Chapter 4 of Part 3 of this Act.

516.   When the Secretary of State has made an order extending the licences under section 224, after the report was submitted, she has, under subsection (5), the power to require a supplementary report.

Section 230: Orders suspending rights of renewal

517.   This section applies when the Secretary of State receives a report made by OFCOM under section 229. If the report contains a recommendation to make an order under this section, or (in the absence of a recommendation) where the Secretary of State believes it is appropriate to do so, she may by order provide that specified licences are not to be renewed under section 216 or 222 from the end of the current licensing period.

518.   *Subsection (3)* provides that such an order must be made at least eighteen months before the end of the current licensing period.

519.   Under *subsection (4)*, the power to prevent the renewal of the licences from the end of the initial licensing period can be exercised only if a date for switchover has been fixed which falls before the end of that period. *Subsection (5)* provides that if the Secretary of State postpones the date for switchover after she has made an order preventing the renewal of licences, this order will not have effect if the new date for switchover falls after the end of that initial licensing period. However, in such a case, the Secretary of State will be able to make another order preventing the renewal of licences. But this power will be subject to the requirement, set by subsection 224(5), that she must postpone the initial expiry date of the licences when this date falls within the period of eighteen months after switchover.

520.   Under *subsection (7)*, an order with respect to Channel 3 licences must apply to all licences to provide a Channel 3 service, or to all licences to provide a national Channel 3 service, or to all licences to provide a regional Channel 3 service. Any order made by the Secretary of State will be subject to the affirmative resolution procedure.

Section 231: Replacement of Channel 4 licence

521.   When *subsection (1)* comes into force, Channel 4 shall be granted a new licence under this section. Its licence granted under section 24(3) of the Broadcasting Act 1990 shall no longer apply. In advance of this, OFCOM must prepare a draft replacement licence and consult the Channel Four Television Corporation on its contents. The replacement licence must provide for the service to be broadcast digitally and may provide that the service is also to be provided in analogue form until such time as is determined according to conditions in the licence giving effect to the Secretary of State's directions as to how long the service must continue to be provided in analogue form. The programming of the analogue service should replicate that of the digital service, or such part of it as is specified by the licence conditions included under *subsection (3)(b)*. There can be no charge levied for the use of such a service or for any assistance for disabled people or for other ancillary services included in the service.

522.   *Subsection (6)* provides that such a replacement licence must continue in force until the end of 2014. The licence may be renewed as OFCOM think fit.

Section 232: Meaning of "television licensable content service"

523.   A "television licensable content service" is defined in this section as any service (i) which is provided (whether in digital or analogue form) as a service to be made available for reception by members of the public (as defined in section 361) by being broadcast from a satellite, or distributed by an electronic communications network, and (ii) which consists of television programmes or electronic programme guides (or both). The service covered by a single licence will comprise not only what *subsection (3)* calls a "main service" (which could consist either of television programmes or of an electronic programme guide, or both) but also such

of the ancillary services and facilities provided with it as are "relevant ancillary services" and are not "two-way services". "Two way services" are defined in *subsection (5)* and encompass services such as video conferencing. The term "relevant ancillary services" encompasses both services that are actually provided by the provider of the "main service" and those facilities which are no more than links to services provided by others. It is not intended to encompass any apparatus (such as a television set, a PC, or a set-top box).

524.   A licensee is not held to be providing services which may be accessed from the "main service", unless he has general control over them (*subsection (4)*).

525.   Ancillary services that are not "relevant" ones are not to be covered by the licence for the main service (although some might be licensable in their own right, e.g. if they constitute a television licensable content service provided by someone other than the provider of the main service). To give some examples, say you are watching a wildlife programme on the "main service" i.e. a television channel in the conventional sense, albeit that it includes all the enhanced features to be expected from digital services. A menu might offer access to different camera angles: these would constitute "relevant ancillary services" which would be part of the licensed service. The menu might also give you access to additional factual information (provided within the broadcast stream) about the animals you are watching. That is expected to be within the scope of the licence too. But there might be a link (a "facility") which might take you to a website. The fact that the link is provided would be within the licence (and so OFCOM might require it to be removed if it led directly to unsuitable material), but the website at the end of the link would neither be regulated nor within the licence of the "main service" as it would not be a service made "available for reception by members of the public". Also outside the scope of the licence would be content that could be accessed from the "main service" but which is not under the general control of the provider of the "main service", such as a television service provided by someone else showing similar wildlife programmes. Other services, such as being able to order takeaway food, or engage in on-line banking, or participate in an on-line chatroom, would not be within the licence either. These are just examples, and the question of whether particular services fall within the scope of a person's television licensable content service licence would depend on the exact nature of the services and facilities offered and the circumstances in which they were offered.

*an electronic programme guide is defined in subsection (6) as a service which lists and/or promotes television programmes, including programmes of providers other than the provider of the guide. The service must also allow the user to access programmes contained in the guide.

Section 233: Services that are not television licensable content services

526.   This section sets out the services that are excluded from the definition of a television licensable content service in section 232. A service is not a television content service licence if it is broadcast by means of a multiplex service or to the extent that it consists of a service which is authorised by a licence to provide a

television broadcasting service, the licence to provide the public teletext service or a licence to provide additional television services. Nor does it meet the description of a television licensable content service if it forms part only of a service provided by means of an electronic communications service or is one of a number of services that may be accessed through such a service where the purpose of the service provided by these means is not wholly or mainly to make available television and/or radio programmes for reception by members of the public. A service is also excluded if it is a two-way service (as defined in the previous section). The aim of these provisions is, broadly, to maintain licensing obligations in respect of services which are or equate to broadcasting while excluding Internet services, such as web sites or web-casting, from OFCOM's regulatory powers. The effect of *subsection (3)* is to exclude not only any website material provided as part of another service (for example, a website which is accessed via an ISP which also provides its own in-house content) but also material provided from a stand alone site, whether it be text, web-cast or video images. *Subsection (6)* also excludes a service that is distributed to a single set of premises by an electronic communications network that is contained within the premises and is not connected to any external network. *Subsections (7) and (8)* exclude a service that is provided for the purpose only of being received by persons who have an interest in receiving the service for use in their business or employment, such as stockbrokers or bookmakers.

Section 234: Modification of ss. 232 and 233

527. The Secretary of State may modify sections 232 or 233 by order, if she considers it appropriate. In making any modification, she must have regard to the level of protection expected by the public as regards the content of television programmes and text services, taking into account the means of reception; the ability of the public – having been made aware of the contents of a forthcoming programme – to control what they watch; technical innovation; the financial consequences of modification; and the relative ease or difficulty of setting different levels of regulation for different services.

Section 235: Licensing of television licensable content services

528. A television licensable content service is required for the purposes of section 13 of the Broadcasting Act 1990 to have a licence under Part 1 of that Act awarded according to an application procedure that is set by OFCOM. OFCOM must approve the application unless they are not satisfied that the applicant is a fit and proper person to hold the licence, or if the person is disqualified from holding the licence by virtue of Part 2 of Schedule 2 of the Broadcasting Act 1990 or if there would be a contravention of Schedule 14 of this Act if he held the licence. OFCOM are entitled to refuse an application if satisfied that the service would be unlikely to comply with OFCOM's standards code or the code on fairness issued under Part 5 of the Broadcasting Act 1996.

529. *Subsection (4)* requires that a provider must seek a separate licence for every television licensable content service he proposes to offer. In other words, if a

provider is intending to offer three television licensable content services he must have three licences, one for each service. *Subsection (5)* provides that a single licence may authorise different programmes to be broadcast simultaneously, or virtually so, for example where a service provides a choice of programmes that may be viewed at any one time.

530.   Each licence for a television licensable content service will be valid until surrendered or revoked.

Section 236: Direction to licensee to take remedial action

531.   If the licence holder has breached a condition of his television licensable content service licence then, if this will sufficiently remedy the breach, OFCOM may, after giving him a chance to comment, require the licence holder to include a correction in the licensed service or broadcast a finding by OFCOM against the licence holder. The licence holder may announce that he is making a correction or a statement of findings because OFCOM have directed him to do so. OFCOM must send a copy of any direction given to a BBC company requiring the broadcasting of a correction and/or statement of findings and any representations received from that BBC company to the Secretary of State.

532.   OFCOM may direct a television licensable content service licence holder not to include a programme in the service on a future occasion if satisfied that the previous inclusion of that programme in the service involved a contravention of a licence condition.

Section 237: Penalties for contravention of licence condition or direction

533.   If OFCOM are satisfied that a television licensable content service licence holder has breached a condition of that licence, or has not complied with a direction given by OFCOM, they may serve a notice on that person imposing a fine. The maximum fine is the greater of £250,000 or 5 per cent of qualifying revenue within the relevant period. OFCOM may not impose a fine unless they have first given the licence holder the chance to comment. If OFCOM serve a notice on a BBC company, they must send a copy of that notice, and of any representations received from the company, to the Secretary of State. The Secretary of State may vary the amount of the maximum fine by order.

> * *"qualifying revenue"* is calculated in accordance with section 19(2) to (6) of the Broadcasting Act 1990 and Part 1 of Schedule 7 to that Act, with any necessary modifications.

Section 238: Revocation of television licensable content service licence

534.   If satisfied that a television licensable content service licence holder is in contravention of the terms of his licence, or is failing to comply with a direction, and that such a contravention or failure would, if not remedied, warrant revocation of the licence, OFCOM must serve a notice on the licence holder. The notice must specify

the nature of the contravention or failure and state that the licence will be revoked unless the licence holder takes specified steps within a specified period. If the licence holder does not comply within the specified period then OFCOM may, if satisfied that this is necessary in the public interest, revoke the licence. At each stage in the process, OFCOM shall first give the licence holder the chance to comment. The provisions in this section do not apply to the revocation of a licence under section 239 (see below).

535.   *Subsections (4)* and *(5)* provide that OFCOM may revoke a television licensable content service licence if satisfied that the licence holder is no longer providing the service, or that the licence holder provided false or misleading information in support of his licence application.

536.   If OFCOM serve a notice on a BBC company under this section, they must send a copy of that notice, and of any representations received from the company, to the Secretary of State.

Section 239: Action against licence holders who incite crime or disorder

537.   OFCOM must serve a notice under *subsection (2)* on a television licensable content service licence holder if satisfied that the service has included one or more programmes which contain material likely to encourage or to incite crime or disorder, that this has contravened a licence condition, and that the contravention warrants the revocation of that licence. A notice under subsection (2) must specify the nature of the contravention, state that the licence may be revoked at the end of 21 days beginning with the date of service of the notice, and inform the licence holder of his right to make representations. The effect of the notice is to suspend the licence until revocation, or until OFCOM decide not to revoke the licence. At the end of 21 days, and having considered any representations, OFCOM may, if satisfied that this is necessary in the public interest, serve on the licence holder a notice of revocation. This may not take effect less than 28 days after being served.

Section 240: Abolition of separate licences for certain television services

538.   This section abolishes the two forms of licence which the television licensable content services licence replaces, that is satellite television service and licensable programme service licences. It puts in place transitional provisions so that after the television transfer date, any person holding one of the abolished licence types is to be regulated by OFCOM as if he held a television licensable content services licence, unless the service is of a kind that falls outside the new definition and so no longer requires a licence at all. To the extent that any existing licence takes effect as a licence to provide a television licensable content service, OFCOM must use their power under section 3 of the Broadcasting Act 1990 to modify that licence if they feel that it is necessary to do so in order to comply with their duty under section 263 (see below).

Section 241: Television multiplex services

539.   References in Part 1 of the Broadcasting Act 1996 to a television multiplex service are references to a service (i) which is broadcast for general reception, otherwise than by satellite, so as to be available to members of the public and (ii) which provides, or is capable of providing, two or more services which include at least one "relevant television service" (as defined in *subsection (9)*) for simultaneous broadcast on the same frequency.

540.   *Subsection (3)* provides that it is not an offence to provide a television multiplex service that is not licensed under the Broadcasting Act 1996. Only where a wireless telegraphy licence provides that any television multiplex service being broadcast using the station or apparatus to which that licence relates must itself be licensed, shall that multiplex service require a licence. This will be assumed to be the case where the multiplex service is already licensed under the Broadcasting Act 1996 and the service is broadcast using a station or apparatus that is authorised by a wireless telegraphy licence. Where this assumption applies, and a person affected by it either ceases to be licensed under Part 1 of the Broadcasting Act 1996 or ceases to exist, OFCOM may revoke the wireless telegraphy licence relating to the provision by that person of the television multiplex service in question.

Section 242: Composition of services in television multiplexes

541.   This section amends section 12 of the Broadcasting Act 1996. OFCOM will now be able to include conditions in any multiplex licence granted under that Act to secure that: (i) all digital programme services and digital additional services provided by the BBC may be carried on that multiplex, (ii) the digital sound programme services broadcast under the licence are either provided by the BBC or licensed under section 60 of that Act and (iii) a licensee does not show undue discrimination either against or in favour of a digital sound programme service provider, or restrict that provider's ability to share any of his spare capacity (unless it is reasonable to do so in order to ensure the technical quality of the multiplex service).

542.   Currently, section 12(1)(h) requires that at least 90 per cent. of digital capacity on the frequency of the service to which the licence relates be available for broadcasting digital programmes and related services. *Subsection (1)(f)* amends the 90 per cent. threshold to 'the required percentage'. This figure, to be set by OFCOM as they think appropriate, must be 90 per cent or higher. The Secretary of State retains the power to amend the minimum percentage, by order. *Subsection (2)* adds digital programme services and digital sound programme services provided by the BBC to the services currently listed in section 12(1)(h). Digital sound programme services provided otherwise than by the BBC must be accommodated within the remaining capacity. *Subsection (3)* of this section makes a consequential change to the test that the Independent Television Commission currently apply where a multiplex licence holder applies for a variation of any condition imposed relating to the implementation of any proposals as to the characteristics of the digital programme services to be broadcast.

Section 243: Powers where frequencies reserved for qualifying services

543.   OFCOM, in fulfilling their spectrum management role, may require providers of television multiplex services to reserve digital capacity on their frequencies for the provision of certain types of service. The Secretary of State may by order provide that OFCOM must ensure that the holders of licences for multiplex services on these reserved frequencies enter into agreements with relevant public service broadcasters for the broadcasting of services provided by those broadcasters on the reserved digital capacity. An order under this section may also require OFCOM to include in the licence conditions requiring any such broadcaster to pay the licence holder for use of the reserved digital capacity. The amount paid is to be agreed between the broadcaster and the television multiplex licensee or (in the absence of any agreement) determined by OFCOM.

*a *"relevant public service broadcaster"* is defined in *subsection (7)* as a holder of a Channel 3 service licence, the C4 Corporation, the holder of a Channel 5 licence, the Welsh Authority or the public teletext provider. This definition excludes the BBC.

* *"public teletext provider"* is defined in section 362 as the person who holds the licence to provide that service awarded under section 217 (or, in relation to a time before such a licence is awarded, the holder of the additional services licence under the 1990 Act which relates to the public teletext service).

Section 244: Local digital television services

544.   The Secretary of State may, by order, apply (with modifications) the provisions of Part 3 of the Act (except for this section and any provisions relating exclusively to sound services), or any part of Part 1 of the Broadcasting Act 1990, or of Part 1 of the Broadcasting Act 1996, to make special provision for local digital television services of the type further described in *subsections (3) to (5)*. Such services should be provided with a view to including them in a television multiplex service. Such an order can be made only where the Secretary of State is satisfied that this will enhance the provision of such services. In turn, this should benefit the locality where the services are to be received, not least by broadening the range of programmes that can be received in that locality. The order may restrict advertising and programme sponsorship in the service.

Chapter 3: Regulatory Structure for Independent Radio Services

Section 245: Regulation of independent radio services

545.   This section sets out those independent radio services whose regulation is a function of OFCOM, as specified in *subsections (1) and (2)*. These are national, local or restricted sound broadcasting services (so long as not broadcast solely by satellite); radio licensable content services; additional radio services; radio multiplex services; digital sound programme services; and digital additional sound services. All of these must be broadcast from the United Kingdom and are not to be regulated under this section if they are broadcast by the BBC. OFCOM's regulatory function also extends to the types of service set out above provided from somewhere outside the

United Kingdom by a person (other than the BBC) whose principal place of business is in the United Kingdom.

* *"additional radio service"* has the meaning given to it by section 114(1) of the Broadcasting Act 1990, namely any radio service which consists in the sending of signals for transmission by wireless telegraphy using the spare capacity within signals carrying any sound broadcasting service.

* *"digital additional sound service"* means a digital additional service as defined by section 63 of the Broadcasting Act 1996, being any service which is provided for broadcast in digital form by means of a multiplex service, for reception by members of the public, but which is not a digital sound programme service, a simulcast radio service, an ancillary service or a technical service.

* an *"ancillary service"* refers to services that are ancillary to programmes and directly related to their contents, or which relate to the promotion or listing of such programmes. Such a service is provided by the holder of a digital sound programme licence or by an independent national (analogue radio) broadcaster.

*a *"technical service"* is a service provided for the encryption or decryption of digital programme services or digital additional services and specified in an order made by the Secretary of State (see section 63 of the 1996 Act).

* *"digital sound programme service"*, defined in section 40(5) of the Broadcasting Act 1996 (as amended by paragraph 101 of Schedule 15), means a service consisting in the provision of programmes consisting wholly of sound (together with any ancillary services), with a view to their being broadcast in digital form so as to be available for reception by members of the public (as defined in section 361 of this Act), but does not include a simulcast radio service or a service where the sounds are to be received through the use of coded reference to pre-defined phonetic elements of sounds.

* *"radio multiplex service"* is defined in section 40(1) of the Broadcasting Act 1996 (and see also section 258 of this Act, and paragraph 101(2) of Schedule 15) as a service provided by any person which consists in broadcasting, for general reception, two or more digital sound programme services, simulcast radio services or digital additional sound services, by combining the relevant information in digital form.

* *"radio licensable content service"* has the meaning given in section 247.

* *"simulcast radio service"* is defined in section 41(2) of the Broadcasting Act 1996 (as amended by section 256 of this Act) as a service which is provided by an independent national broadcaster for broadcasting in digital form, which corresponds to a national service provided in analogue form.

546.   *Subsections (5)* and *(6)* specify when services will be treated as if they are provided from the United Kingdom. Satellite radio services transmitted to the satellite from the UK are to be so treated, unless they are licensed or otherwise authorised under the laws of another EEA state.

Section 246: Abolition of function of assigning radio frequencies

547.   This section removes the Secretary of State's power to assign frequency for the purpose of the regulation of radio services, or the provision of any radio multiplex services.

Section 247: Meaning of "radio licensable content services"

548.   Broadly, subject to the following provisions of the Act, this term includes all sound programmes broadcast for reception by members of the public from a satellite, or through an electronic communications network, whether in analogue or digital form.

Section 248: Services that are not radio licensable content services

549.   Services that are not radio licensable content services include services comprised in television licensable content services, sound broadcasting services of the type regulated by OFCOM pursuant to section 245(3), and services provided with a view to their being broadcast by means of radio multiplex services. Nor does a service meet the description of a radio licensable content service if it is a two-way service (as defined in *subsection (4)*); or if it forms part only of a service provided by means of an electronic communications service or is one of a number of services that may be accessed through such a service where the purpose of the service provided by these means is not wholly or mainly to make available television and/or radio programmes for reception by members of the public; or if it is received only by people who have an interest in receiving the services for use in their business or employment. Finally, a service is not a radio licensable content service where it is distributed to a single set of premises by an electronic network which is contained within the premises and is not connected to any external network. These exclusions serve similar purposes to those in section 233 (television licensable content services).

Section 249: Modification of ss. 247 and 248

550.   The Secretary of State may modify sections 247 or 248 by order, if she considers it appropriate, taking into account the level of content protection expected by the public; technical innovation; the financial consequences of modification; and the relative ease or difficulty of setting different levels of regulation for different services. The Secretary of State may also provide that a particular service should not be treated as a radio licensable content service for such provisions of this Act as she specifies.

Section 250: Licensing of radio licensable content services

551.   An application for this type of licence under Part 3 of the Broadcasting Act 1990 must follow a procedure to be set by OFCOM. *Subsection (3)* applies sections 109 to 111A of the Broadcasting Act 1990 (powers to require broadcast of corrections, to impose penalties or shorten licence periods and to revoke licences) for the purposes of the enforcement of radio licensable content service licences.

Section 251: Abolition of separate licences for certain sound services

552.   This section abolishes the two forms of licence which the radio licensable content service licence replaces. It puts in place transitional provisions so that after the radio transfer date any persons holding one of the abolished licence types is to be regulated by OFCOM as if he held a radio licensable content service licence, unless the service is of a kind that falls outside the definition and so no longer requires a licence at all. To the extent that any existing licence takes effect as a licence to provide a radio licensable content service, OFCOM must use their power under section 86 of the Broadcasting Act 1990 to modify that licence if they feel that it is necessary to do so in order to comply with their duty under section 263 (see below).

Section 252: Extension of licence periods

553.   *Subsection (1)* amends section 86 of the Broadcasting Act 1990 by stating that licences shall continue in force until the earlier of their being surrendered or revoked, or the licences coming to the end of their terms. The exception is for radio licensable content services - they shall continue in force until the relevant licences are surrendered or revoked. Any licence to provide local, national or additional services must specify a maximum licence period of twelve years (*subsection (2)*).

Section 253: Extension and modification of existing licences

554.   Previously, a newly granted licence to provide a local, national or additional service could not continue in force for more than eight years. This has now been extended to twelve years. To ensure that holders of pre-transfer national or local licences are not disadvantaged, holders of such licences can make an application for a four-year extension to that licence, and OFCOM shall grant the extension if satisfied as to the ability of the licence holder to maintain the service and the likelihood of a contravention by that licence holder of any condition imposed as to the character of the service by virtue of section 106 of the Broadcasting Act 1990, or the making of payments to OFCOM (see *subsection (8)*). On extending the licence, OFCOM may modify the licence as they think fit, by extending the period for which the licence is to be in force and making any other modifications necessaryto make the licence correspond with licences granted after the radio transfer date. In the case of national licence, OFCOM must also modify the sums to be paid to OFCOM under the licence.

555.   The period within which an application may be made begins no sooner than three years before the date the licence would otherwise expire and ends three months before the day that OFCOM would need to publish a notice inviting applications if they were proposing to grant a fresh licence.

> *a *"pre-transfer licence"* is defined in *subsection (13)* as a licence granted under the Broadcasting Act 1990 prior to the radio transfer date that has not been modified under section 253 or renewed any time on or after that date.

Section 254: Renewal of local licences

556.   This section amends section 104A(5) of the Broadcasting Act 1990 (conditions of renewal of local licences). When a renewal application has been made, OFCOM will be required to grant the licence provided the following criteria are met: (i) they are satisfied that the applicant would, if the licence were renewed, provide a local service complying with any conditions imposed to secure the character of the licensed service (ii) the nominated local digital sound programme service the applicant provides is being broadcast by means of a nominated local radio multiplex services; and (iii) they are satisfied that the period and times at which the nominated local digital sound programme service will be available under the renewed licence will not be significantly different, week by week, from those for and at which the licensed local service will be broadcast. This third criterion is added by this section.

Section 255: Extension of special application procedure for local licences

557.   This section extends to all local licences the special "fast-track" application procedure for local licences under section 104B of the Broadcasting Act 1990. This allows the expedited award of a new licence to the existing licence holder if no declarations of intent to apply for the new licence are received from a person other than the licence-holder.

Section 256: Definition of simulcast radio services

558.   This section amends the definition of simulcast radio services found in section 41 of the Broadcasting Act 1996.   Broadly, they are services provided for broadcasting in digital form and which correspond to national services, as defined by section 245(4)(a) of this Act.

Section 257: Promotion of simulcast radio services

559.   This section amends Chapter 2 of Part 3 of the Broadcasting Act 1990 (sound broadcasting services) so that OFCOM promotes the provision of simulcast radio services.   When OFCOM propose to award a national service licence, they must indicate the amount of digital capacity that national radio multiplex licensees will have available for the broadcasting of simulcast radio services.

> * A *"national radio multiplex licence"* has the same meaning as in Part 2 of the Broadcasting Act 1996 (digital terrestrial sound broadcasting).

560.   An application for a national service licence must contain the applicant's proposals (if any) for providing a digital simulcast of their national analogue radio services. When determining the recipient of a national service licence, OFCOM may disregard the requirement under section 100 of the Broadcasting Act 1990 to award the licence to the absolute highest bidder and award the licence instead to the highest bidder amongst those applicants who propose to provide simulcast radio services. In the event of a tie between the highest bidders, OFCOM shall also have the power to exclude applicants who do not propose to provide simulcast radio services.

561.   *Subsection (6)* confers on OFCOM the duty to impose conditions in a national service licence requiring a licensee to provide simulcast radio services where his application included proposals to provide such services.

Section 258: Radio multiplex services

562.   Where a radio multiplex service is referred to in Part 2 of the Broadcasting Act 1996, it means a service (i) which is broadcast otherwise than by satellite so as to be available to members of the public and (ii) which provides, or is capable of providing, two or more digital sound services for simultaneous broadcast on the same frequency.

563.   *Subsection (3)* provides that it will not be an offence to provide a radio

multiplex service that is not licensed under the Broadcasting Act 1996. Only where a wireless telegraphy licence provides that any radio multiplex service being broadcast using the station or apparatus to which that licence relates must itself be licensed, shall that radio multiplex service require a licence. This will be assumed to be the case where the multiplex service is provided under a licence under the Broadcasting Act 1996 that was in force immediately before this section comes into force and the service is broadcast using a station or apparatus that is authorised by a wireless telegraphy licence.

Section 259: Composition of services in radio multiplexes

564.   This section makes changes to section 54 of the 1996 Act (conditions attached to radio multiplex licences) to allow OFCOM, rather than the Secretary of State, to increase (on a licence-by-licence basis) the minimum percentage of radio multiplex capacity that must be devoted to broadcasting services.

565.   The Secretary of State retains the power to vary the lowest percentage that could be specified by OFCOM in a licence (currently 80%) (see *subsections (5) and (6)*).

Section 260: Digital sound services for inclusion in non-radio multiplexes

566.   This section amends the definition of national digital sound programme services in section 60 of the Broadcasting Act 1996. Such services may now be carried by a national radio multiplex service, a television multiplex service, or even a general multiplex service.

567.   *Subsection (2)* amends the definition of digital additional sound services, in section 63 of the same Act, to encompass such services whether provided by means of a radio multiplex service or a general multiplex service.

568.   *Subsection (4)* amends section 72 of that Act to define a general multiplex service by reference to Part 3 of this Act. A general multiplex service is a multiplex service that is neither a television multiplex service nor a radio multiplex service: see section 362 of this Act.

Section 261: Renewal of radio multiplex licences

569.   This section amends section 58 of the 1996 Act. Under that section, radio multiplex licences granted within 6 years of commencement of that section may be renewed for 12 years. This section extends the period during which an extension can be made from 6 to 10 years, and reduces the length of an extension made more than 6 years after commencement from 12 to 8 years.

Section 262: Community radio

570.   The Secretary of State may by order modify the Act and the Broadcasting Acts to make special provision for radio services broadcast mainly for the benefit of the public (or members of a particular community) rather than for commercial reasons. The services should confer significant benefits on the public for which they are provided.   The order may restrict advertising and programme sponsorship in the service.

Chapter 4: Regulatory Provisions

Section 263: Application of regulatory regimes

571.   OFCOM must use their Broadcasting Act powers, and their powers under this Act, to implement and enforce the regulatory regime for each licensed service. The Secretary of State has the power to remove any condition from the regulatory regime.

Section 264: OFCOM reports on the fulfilment of the public service remit

572.   OFCOM are to prepare - twelve months after commencement of this section, and thereafter no less frequently than every five years - a report on the current state of public service television broadcasting, documenting the extent to which broadcasters have together satisfied the requirements of the public service television broadcasting remit set out in this section. In essence, the remit involves the provision of a balanced diversity of high-quality programming, which meets the needs and interests of different audiences (*subsection (4)*).

573.   OFCOM are also to have regard to the more detailed obligations listed in *subsection (6)*. These include obligations relating to culture, news and current affairs, sport, education, entertainment, religion and other beliefs, science, social issues, matters of international significance, programming for children, and local programming.   OFCOM are also required to have regard to the number of programmes within the services which are made outside the M25 area. In addition, OFCOM must consider the costs to the broadcasters of fulfilling their public service television remit and their available resources.

> * the *public service broadcasters* listed in *subsection (12)* are the BBC, the Welsh Authority, the public teletext provider and the providers of licensed public service channels, namely the providers of Channel 3 services, Channel 4 or Channel 5 (see section 362).

Section 265: Public service remits of licensed providers

574.   A public service remit applies to each licensed public service channel. For Channel 3 services, and Channel 5, the remit is to provide a range of high quality and diverse programming. For Channel 4, the remit specifically includes the need for programming to be innovative, creative and distinctive, for it to take account of cultural diversity and to make a significant contribution to meeting the need for

licensed public service channels to include educational programmes. For the public teletext service (transmitted in both analogue and digital form) the remit is to provide a range of high quality and diverse text material. Licences relating to each of these must include a condition requiring that the public service remit be satisfied.

Section 266: Statements of programme policy

575. The provider of a licensed public service channel must publish an annual statement of programme policy, and must review its performance against this statement. The statement must demonstrate how, in the coming year, the broadcaster will satisfy its public service remit, as well as those more specific programming obligations under sections 277 to 296 of the Act, and report on how successful it was in doing so in the previous year.

576. *Subsection (4)* provides that the statement should take account of OFCOM's guidance on its preparation, and should have regard to the reports of OFCOM as described in the notes to section 264 above and section 358 below. Particular regard should be had to the latest such report. *Subsection (7)* states that licences for public service channels may include conditions relating to the treatment of any "previous statement of policy" made by the licensee. However, *subsection (9)* provides that such conditions may not postpone the time at which the licensee is required to make his first statement of programme policy under this section.

577. The first statement should be published as soon as possible after this section comes into force. The term "previous statement of policy" is defined in *subsection (8)*.

Section 267: Changes of programme policy

578. The statement described in the notes to section 266 above must not contain proposals for what is to be regarded (taking account of OFCOM's guidance) as a material change in the character of the channel, unless OFCOM have been consulted and the provider of the channel has taken account of OFCOM's views. If this process has not been followed, OFCOM may insist that the provider publish a revised statement that has been approved by OFCOM. In determining what constitutes a material change, regard is to be had to OFCOM's guidance and to the time over which the change (and any related change) will take effect. OFCOM are obliged to review their guidance from time to time and amend it as appropriate.

Section 268: Statements of service policy by the public teletext provider

579. This section sets out similar requirements to section 266. The provider of the public teletext service must publish an annual statement of policy, and must review its performance against this statement. The statement must demonstrate how, in the coming year, the provider will satisfy its public service remit and report on how successful it was in doing so in the previous year. The statement must also address, where relevant, both analogue and digital teletext services.

580.   *Subsection (5)* provides that the statement should take account of OFCOM's guidance on its preparation, and should have regard to the reports of OFCOM as described in the notes to section 264 above and section 358 below. Particular regard should be had to the latest such report. *Subsection (8)* states that licences for the public teletext provider may include conditions relating to the treatment of any "previous statement of policy" made by the licensee. However, *subsection (10)* provides that such conditions may not postpone the time at which the licensee is required to make his first statement of programme policy under this section.

581.   The first statement should be published as soon as possible after this section comes into force. The term "previous statement of policy" is defined in *subsection (9)*.

Section 269: Changes of service policy

582.   This section mirrors section 267. The statement described in the notes on section 268 above must not contain proposals for what is to be regarded (taking account of OFCOM's guidance) as a material change in the character of the service unless OFCOM have been consulted and the service provider has taken account of OFCOM's views. If this process has not been followed, OFCOM may insist that the provider publish a revised statement that has been approved by OFCOM.

Section 270: Enforcement of public service remits

583.   This section provides for the case where OFCOM conclude that a provider of a licensed public service channel or the public teletext provider has failed to fulfil its public service remit, or has not contributed adequately to the general requirements for public service broadcasting. If OFCOM are of the opinion that this failure is serious, and cannot be excused by reference to economic or market conditions, OFCOM may exercise their powers under this section. Before doing so, OFCOM must also consider the factors set out in *subsection (3)* regarding the provider's remit and more general performance.

584.   OFCOM may have recourse to a number of powers. *Subsection (4)* provides that OFCOM may direct that the provider amend his policy statement as directed, and may direct that the provider remedy its failure to fulfil satisfactorily its public service obligations. Such directions are to be accompanied by a reasonable timetable for compliance and guidance as to how OFCOM will decide whether the failure has been remedied and whether they will exercise their powers under subsection (6).

585.   If OFCOM are satisfied that their directions have not been complied with, that the provider is still failing its public service remit, and that this reasonably merits variation of the provider's licence, they may replace the self-regulatory regime described in the notes above with more detailed regulation (*subsection (6)*). In other words, the conditions set under sections 265 to 269 would be replaced by specific conditions set by OFCOM in order to ensure that the provider fulfils its public service remit.

586.   One of the general objectives of the Act is that OFCOM be required to review continually the need for regulation in the sector, ensuring that unnecessary regulatory burdens are neither imposed nor maintained. In accordance with this de-regulatory approach, *subsection (8)* gives OFCOM the power, having previously exercised their powers in accordance with *subsection (6)*, to vary again a provider's licence in order to reinstate the conditions imposed under sections 265 to 269, and to remove or amend any specific conditions that were inserted in their place.

587.   Before giving any direction, or exercising any of their powers, under this section, OFCOM shall consult the provider affected.

Section 271: Power to amend public service remits

588.   This section provides the Secretary of State with the power to make an order amending the public service remits under section 261 for any licensed public service channel or the public teletext service, the list of public service television broadcasting purposes set out at section 264(4), and the list of more detailed matters set out at subsections (5) and (6) of section 264. No such order may be made unless OFCOM have recommended it in a report under section 229 or 264, unless *subsection (3)* applies. Before recommending the making of an order under this provision OFCOM will be under an obligation to consult members of the public, such public service broadcasters (including the public teletext service provider if appropriate) as are likely to be affected by the proposed change and other providers of television and radio services as appropriate. Before making an order the Secretary of State must consult OFCOM, the public service broadcasters likely to be affected and other relevant providers. Any order made by the Secretary of State will be subject to the affirmative resolution procedure.

Section 272: Must-offer obligations in relation to networks

589.   This section requires OFCOM to include in the licences for every licensed public service channel, the public teletext service and every licensed television service added to the list of must-carry services under section 64 conditions which they consider appropriate for securing the three following objectives:

- that digital channels or services on the list of must-carry services under section 64 are offered for broadcasting and distribution over every appropriate network;

- that each provider of those channels or services enters into arrangements which ensure that their digital channels or services and any ancillary services are broadcast or distributed on appropriate networks so that those channels and services are made available for reception by as many members of the intended audience (as defined in *subsection (7)*) for a given service as possible; and

- that such arrangements prohibit the provider of the network from charging for reception of the channels or services.

* An *"appropriate network"* is defined in *subsection (7)* as a network used to provide public electronic communications services to a significant number of end-users as their principal means of receiving television programmes.

Section 273: Must-offer obligations in relation to satellite services

590.   This section requires OFCOM to include in the licences for every licensed public service channel, the public teletext service and every other licensed television service specified by the Secretary of State conditions which they consider appropriate for securing the following three objectives:

- that digital channels or services to which this section applies are offered as available for broadcast by means of every satellite television service available for reception in the whole or a part of the United Kingdom;

- that each provider of those channels or services enters into arrangements which ensure that its digital channels or services and any related ancillary services are broadcast by means of satellite television services, such that they are available for reception by as many members of the intended audience (as defined in *subsection (7)*) for a given service as possible; and

- that such arrangements prohibit a charge being imposed for the reception of the channel or service.

* A *"satellite television service"* is defined in *subsection (7)* as a service which consists of broadcasting television programme services from a satellite and is used by a significant number of persons as their principal means of receiving television programmes.

591.   These objectives apply to a service or channel only whilst its digital form is included in the list of "must-provide" services for the purpose of section 274 (see below).

Section 274: Securing reception of must-provide services in certain areas

592.   This section requires OFCOM to include in the licences for every licensed public service channel, the public teletext service and every licensed television service added to the list of must-provide services under section 275 conditions which secure the reception of those services. Such conditions may provide that where persons required to provide must-provide services fail to enter into or maintain arrangements that meet the requirements of *subsection (3)*, OFCOM may impose such arrangements. Before doing so, OFCOM must consult all persons who provide must-provide services. The arrangements that may be entered into by, or imposed upon, providers of must-provide services must secure that, where necessary, any member of the intended audience (as defined in *subsection (10)*) for a given service, who has bought the relevant equipment (for instance a dish and a digital satellite decoder), has available to them a facility for receiving the must-provide services (including any that are broadcast by satellite) and that this is made available free of charge. This applies only where that person could not otherwise (e.g. by digital terrestrial broadcasting) receive the service to an acceptable technical standard. The effect of the arrangements

currently, for example, would be to require the relevant broadcasters to supply "smart" cards for the operation of receiving equipment that will permit reception of the free-to-view services ("solus cards"). The broadcasters must share the costs involved. They must also establish complaints procedures and ensure that these procedures are publicised in accordance with OFCOM's guidance. Any such arrangements will only take effect if approved by OFCOM.

593. *Subsections (6) and (7)* clarify when reception of a service is to be regarded as being free of charge. *Subsection (8)* provides that OFCOM shall determine the quality of reception required before someone can be treated for the purpose of this section as receiving a service in an intelligible form.

Section 275: Must-provide services for the purposes of s.274

594. This section provides that the list of must-provide services for the purposes of section 274 includes the following: every service of digital television programmes provided by the BBC and in relation to which OFCOM have functions; the Channel 3 services, Channel 4 and Channel 5 services, so far as any of them are provided in digital form; S4C Digital; and the digital public teletext service. The Secretary of State may by order amend the list of must-provide services. In exercising this power, she must have regard to the public benefit to be secured by the modification, the likely financial effects of the proposed modification on the affected parties and the proportionality of these effects when set against the public benefit secured.

Section 276: Co-operation with the public teletext provider

595. OFCOM are to include, in each licence to provide a Channel 3 service or Channel 4, conditions that secure that the public teletext provider and any person authorised by him under section 220 have access to such of the facilities of the relevant provider as are needed in order to provide the public teletext service. A provider of a Channel 3 service or Channel 4 may require the public teletext provider and authorised persons to pay a reasonable charge for such access. Similar provisions apply to the Welsh Authority: see paragraph 11 of Schedule 12.

Section 277: Programming quotas for independent productions

596. OFCOM are to include conditions in the licences of all licensed public service channels in order to secure that at least 25 per cent (or such other figure as is substituted by the Secretary of State by order) of the time allocated to the broadcasting of qualifying programmes on that channel is allocated to the broadcasting of a range and diversity (judged both in terms of the types of programmes involved and of the cost of their acquisition) of independent productions.

* *"qualifying programmes"* are defined in *subsection (2)(a)* as programmes of such a description as the Secretary of State may by order specify as qualifying programmes. Paragraph 34 of Schedule 18 provides that any order under the Broadcasting Act 1990 as to the definition of qualifying programmes shall continue to be effective after the commencement of sections 277 and 309 of the Act and paragraphs 1 and 7 of Schedule 12 to the Act.

* *"independent productions"* are defined in *subsection (2)(b)* as programmes of such a description as the Secretary of State may by order specify as independent productions. Paragraph 34 of Schedule 18 provides that any order under the Broadcasting Act 1990 as to the definition of independent productions shall continue to be effective after the commencement of the Act as specified above.

* *"licensed public service channels"* are defined in section 362 as meaning any of the following services (whether provided for broadcasting in digital or in analogue form): any Channel 3 service, Channel 4 and Channel 5.

597. OFCOM may give directions to the providers of the licensed public service channels for the purpose of carrying over to one or more subsequent years any shortfall for any year in meeting the independent productions quota.

598. The Secretary of State may also provide, by order, that OFCOM include conditions in the licences of the licensed public service channels in order to secure that, in each year, not less than a specified percentage of the programming budget for that channel is applied in the acquisition of independent productions. These conditions may apply as well as, or instead of, the requirement to allocate 25% of airtime to independent productions.

* *"programming budget"* is defined in *subsection (13)* as the budget for the production and acquisition of qualifying programmes.

Section 278: Programming quotas for original productions

599. OFCOM are to include conditions in the licences of all licensed public service channels in order to secure that an appropriate amount of airtime is allocated to original productions and that the time allocated is divided as may be appropriate between peak viewing times and other times. OFCOM may also include conditions excluding specified descriptions of programmes from the calculation of the necessary proportion of original productions. Before including such a condition, OFCOM must consult the licence holder on whom it is to be imposed.

*References to original productions in section 278 are to programmes of such description as the Secretary of State may by order specify as original productions. The Secretary of State may confer such discretions on OFCOM as she sees fit for the purposes of the order. The Secretary of State must consult OFCOM, the BBC and the Welsh Authority before making any order under this section.

* *"Peak viewing time"* is defined in *subsection (10)* as such time as appears to OFCOM to be – actually or potentially - a peak viewing time for any given public service channel.

Section 279: News and current affairs programmes

600. OFCOM are to include conditions in the licences of all public service channels in order to secure that the programmes included on those channels include news and current affairs programmes and that the time allocated to the broadcasting of news and current affairs programmes is an appropriate proportion of the total time allocated to the broadcasting of all other programmes. Such programmes are to be of a high standard, and are to cover both national and international matters. News programmes should be broadcast at intervals throughout the day, and the times at which both news and current affairs programmes are to be broadcast should include an appropriate

amount of peak viewing times. OFCOM must consult with the channel provider before determining the proportion of broadcasting time to be allocated to news and current affairs programmes and what constitutes a peak viewing time.

> * *"peak viewing time"* is defined in *subsection (5)* as such time as appears to OFCOM to be – actually or potentially – a peak viewing time for that channel.

Section 280: Appointed news providers for Channel 3

601.   OFCOM are to include in every regional Channel 3 licence conditions to secure nationwide broadcasting of news programmes that are able to compete with other television news programmes broadcast nationwide in the United Kingdom. Such conditions must require that all holders of regional Channel 3 licences maintain arrangements for the appointment of a single body corporate as the appointed news provider and that at all times when a licensee is providing a regional Channel 3 service there is a news provider appointed under those arrangements.

602.   *Subsection (3)* provides that OFCOM must approve the terms of appointment, to ensure that the finances of the appointed person are adequate to meet news obligations throughout the period of appointment. Holders of the regional Channel 3 licences and the body which is the appointed news provider are required to provide OFCOM with all such information as they may need to ensure that the necessary arrangements are in place and working effectively.

603.   *Subsection (5)* provides that news programmes must always be provided by the person who is the appointed news provider, and must be broadcast simultaneously with the broadcasting of news programmes included in other regional Channel 3 services.

Section 281: Disqualification from appointment as news provider

604.   OFCOM may impose conditions to ensure that a body does not become or remain the appointed news provider (i) if it is a disqualified person under Part 2 of Schedule 2 to the 1990 Act in relation to a Channel 3 licence (such as a local authority, a political body, the BBC, the Welsh Authority or a Channel 4 company) or (ii) if there would be a contravention of Part 1 of Schedule 14 to this Act if that body held a licence to provide a Channel 3 service, (e.g. because the body has interests in national or local newspapers).

Section 282: Power to repeal or modify Channel 3 news provider provisions

605.   This section allows the Secretary of State, by an affirmative procedure order, to repeal or modify the provisions of section 280 or 281. Unless simply giving effect to recommendations made by OFCOM, the Secretary of State must consult OFCOM before making an order under this section.

Section 283: News providers for Channel 5

606.   The Secretary of State may by order impose requirements for the provision of Channel 5 news programmes that correspond to the news provider provisions for Channel 3 services, with such modifications as the Secretary of State sees fit.   An order may only be made on OFCOM's recommendation or after consulting OFCOM. Before the Channel 5 licence is varied, the licence-holder must be given an opportunity to make representations to OFCOM.

607.   The Secretary of State is prohibited from imposing new obligations in relation to Channel 5 unless she is satisfied that Channel 5's share of the audience is broadly equivalent to that for the services comprising Channel 3.

Section 284: News provision on the public teletext service

608.   OFCOM are to include in the licence of the public teletext provider conditions that secure that news items are included in public teletext services, and that they are up-to-date and regularly revised.

Section 285: Code relating to programme commissioning

609.   OFCOM are to include conditions in the licences of every licensed public service channel in order to secure that the channel provider draws up, from time to time revises and complies with a code of practice setting out the principles he will apply when agreeing terms for the commissioning of independent productions.   The code must be submitted to OFCOM for approval and will have effect only if approved by OFCOM.

610.   OFCOM must issue general guidance setting out the procedure for drawing up and revising the code and the matters to be covered.   OFCOM's guidance may not however specify particular terms to be included in agreements to which the guidance relates. OFCOM must ensure that there is always published guidance for the purposes of this section in force and must consult the providers of the licensed public service channels, persons who make independent productions (or persons appearing to OFCOM to represent them), the BBC and the Welsh Authority before issuing or revising the guidance.

    *an "independent production" has the same meaning as in section 277.

Section 286: Regional programme-making for Channels 3 and 5

611.   OFCOM may include in every licence for a Channel 3 service conditions to secure that, where Channel 3 programmes are broadcast in more than one Channel 3 area, a suitable proportion of those programmes that are made in the United Kingdom are made outside the area enclosed by the M25.   Such programmes should make up a suitable range of programmes.   An associated requirement is that Channel 3 providers invest sufficiently in programme production at a suitable range of production centres

in different parts of the United Kingdom outside the area enclosed by the M25. None of these requirements need be included as a licence condition for a national Channel 3 service, unless OFCOM consider this to be appropriate having regard to the nature of the service. OFCOM must consult the licence holder on whom conditions under this section are to be imposed before imposing the conditions.

> *a "national Channel 3 service" is defined in section 362 as a Channel 3 service provided between particular times of the day for more than one area for which regional Channel 3 services are provided.

612.   OFCOM are also to include conditions in the licence for Channel 5 in order to ensure that a suitable proportion of Channel 5 programmes that are made in the United Kingdom are made outside the area enclosed by the M25. Such programmes should comprise a suitable range of programmes. The Channel 5 provider must also invest sufficiently in programme production at a suitable range of production centres in different parts of the United Kingdom outside the area enclosed by the M25.

Section 287: Regional programmes on Channel 3

613.   OFCOM are to include in national, regional and local Channel 3 licences conditions to secure that the areas served by the licensee are provided with programmes appropriate to the area concerned. In relation to regional and national services, the objectives to be secured are set out in *subsections (1) and (4)*, respectively, and include ensuring that a sufficient amount of time is given in the service to regional programmes, including news programmes, which are of high quality, that a suitable proportion of regional programmes included in the service consists of programmes made in the relevant regional area and that a sufficient proportion of such programmes are broadcast at or around peak time.

> * "regional programme" is defined in *subsection (8)* as - in relation to a regional Channel 3 service – a programme included in that service as being of particular interest to persons within the area covered by the service or - in relation to a national Channel 3 service – as being of particular interest to persons within a particular area of the United Kingdom.

614.   In this section, a Channel 3 service is a local service if it is required to provide programmes for specific areas or specific communities within that region (*subsection (7)*). In the case of a local service, OFCOM may include conditions requiring that a sufficient amount of time is given in the service to an appropriate range of local programmes, including news programmes, which are of high quality; that a sufficient proportion of such programmes are broadcast at or around peak time; and that an adequate proportion of such programmes have been produced in the relevant locality.

> * "local programme" is defined in *subsection (7)* as a programme included in a regional Channel 3 service for part of an area, or for a particular community.

615.   Before including a licence condition in this respect OFCOM must consult the licence holder on whom it is to be imposed.

Section 288: Regional programme-making for Channel 4

616.   OFCOM are to include in the Channel 4 licence conditions providing that a suitable proportion of the programmes to be broadcast on Channel 4 that are made in the United Kingdom are made outside the area enclosed by the M25.   Such programmes should comprise a suitable range of programmes.   The Channel Four Television Corporation must also invest sufficiently in programme production at a suitable range of production centres in different parts of the United Kingdom outside the area enclosed by the M25.   Before imposing a condition under this section, OFCOM must consult the Corporation.

Section 289: Regional matters in the public teletext service

617.   OFCOM must include, in the public teletext service licence, conditions which ensure that an appropriate proportion of material reflecting the interests of the different regions of the United Kingdom is included in the analogue and digital teletext services.

Section 290: Proposals for arrangements

618.   Any application for a regional Channel 3 licence must include the applicant's proposals for participating in networking arrangements. OFCOM may publish guidance for applicants on the kinds of proposals which they are likely to consider satisfactory.

> *For the purposes of Part 3, arrangements are networking arrangements if they: (1) apply to all holders of regional Channel 3 licences; (2) allow programmes made, commissioned or acquired by a Channel 3 licensee to be made available to all other regional Channel 3 licensees for broadcasting; and (3) enable regional Channel 3 services (taken as a whole) to compete effectively with other television programme services provided in the United Kingdom.

Section 291: Obligation as to making and continuance of approved arrangements
619.   OFCOM are to include in every regional Channel 3 licence conditions to secure that, where no arrangements imposed by OFCOM under section 292 are in force, the licensee has entered into and given effect to networking arrangements (including any modification thereto) that are approved by OFCOM in accordance with Schedule 11. The Chapter I prohibition of the Competition Act 1998 does not apply to any networking arrangements that have been approved by OFCOM in accordance with any licence condition imposed by them under this section or that have been considered and approved under Schedule 4 to the Broadcasting Act 1990 (*subsection (3)*).

620.   Under paragraph 36 of Schedule 18, networking arrangements that are in force immediately before the commencement of this section and have been approved under section 39 of the Broadcasting Act 1990 will be treated as if approved by OFCOM under this section.

Section 292: OFCOM's power to impose arrangements

621. Any notice published by OFCOM stating that they propose to award one or more regional Channel 3 licences must specify a date by which networking arrangements must be entered into if they are to be effective before the new Channel 3 licensees start to provide their licensed services. If suitable networking arrangements do not exist by that date or subsequently cease to apply, OFCOM may impose appropriate networking arrangements on all regional Channel 3 providers, including the new licensee. *Subsection (7)* allows OFCOM to set licence conditions appropriate for securing that regional Channel 3 providers comply with networking arrangements imposed under this section. The imposed networking arrangements will cease to have effect if the licence holders bound by those arrangements enter into alternative networking arrangements which are approved by OFCOM.

Section 293: Review of approved networking arrangements etc.

622. This section imposes a duty on OFCOM to carry out general reviews of the networking arrangements approved under section 291 or imposed under section 292. The first review must be carried out no more than six months after the last closure date for an offer of a replacement regional Channel 3 licence, made under section 215. Reviews must be undertaken yearly thereafter. OFCOM may also, at any other time, carry out a review of whether the networking arrangements continue to satisfy one of the two competition tests set out in paragraph 6 of Schedule 11 (approval, imposition and modification of networking arrangements).

* The first competition test is that the networking arrangements do not have the object or effect of preventing, restricting or distorting competition within the United Kingdom. The second competition test is that the networking arrangements do have such an object or effect but would satisfy the criteria set out in section 9 of the Competition Act 1998 (agreements contributing to improving the production or distribution of goods or to promoting technical or economic progress).

623. Where, following a review, OFCOM are satisfied that modifications to the networking arrangements are required, they may require regional Channel 3 licensees to give effect to those modifications or, in the case of arrangements imposed under section 292, make those modifications themselves. OFCOM may not require modifications to be made to approved networking arrangements already in force without conducting a review under section 293 unless they have the consent of the Channel 3 licensees affected by the modification.

624. *Subsection (7)* allows OFCOM to set licence conditions that secure that Channel 3 licensees give effect to any modifications of the networking arrangements proposed by OFCOM.

Section 294: Supplemental provision about networking arrangements

625. Schedule 11 sets out the procedures to be followed by OFCOM when approving, imposing or modifying networking arrangements under sections 291 to 293.

626.   Where networking arrangements (and modifications thereto) are submitted to OFCOM for their approval, OFCOM must publish a description of those arrangements and allow third parties a reasonable period of time to comment on them. OFCOM may then approve, or conditionally approve, or reject the arrangements (or modifications to them). Before deciding to give a conditional approval requiring changes to the arrangements, OFCOM must consult each holder of a regional Channel 3 licence about the changes. OFCOM must then, subject to confidentiality, publish their decision and their reasons for it. Once arrangements have been approved by OFCOM they are not to be modified without OFCOM's approval.

627.   Paragraph 5 requires OFCOM to publish, subject to confidentiality, reports explaining any networking arrangements that they impose under section 292 and the outcome of any reviews carried out under section 293.

628.   Under paragraphs 6 and 7, OFCOM must not approve, impose or modify any networking arrangements under sections 291 to 293 unless:

- they are satisfied that the arrangements satisfy the first or second competition tests (as described in the note to section 293 above); and

- they consider that the networking arrangements represent a satisfactory means of achieving the purpose of enabling regional Channel 3 services (taken as a whole) to compete effectively with other television programme services provided in the United Kingdom. OFCOM must also take into consideration the likely effect of the arrangements on the ability of regional Channel 3 licensees to maintain the quality and range of their regional programmes and the regional character of their services.

629.   Under paragraph 8, OFCOM may not approve, impose or modify any networking arrangements where it appears to them that they are likely to prejudice the ability of regional Channel 3 licensees to comply with their public service remits or conditions imposed under sections 286, 287 or 352.

630.   Paragraph 9 confers a right of appeal against OFCOM's decisions concerning the competition aspects of networking arrangements. The right of appeal extends to any holder of a regional Channel 3 licence. An appeal may be brought only by sending a notice of appeal to the Competition Appeal Tribunal (CAT) and on the grounds listed in sub-paragraph (4). A Channel 3 licensee is not required to comply with OFCOM's decision, pending the outcome of the appeal.

631.   The CAT is to decide the appeal on the merits. The CAT is to decide whether OFCOM's decision was appropriate and may confirm OFCOM's decision or issue any directions it considers are necessary to give effect to its decision. OFCOM must comply with any such directions. A decision of the CAT may be appealed under paragraph 11 on a point of law to the Court of Appeal or, in Scotland, to the Court of Session. Such an appeal may, with the permission of the CAT or the appellate court, be brought by a party to the original CAT proceedings.

632.   Paragraph 12 allows OFCOM to require any person to provide them with information necessary to enable OFCOM to carry out their functions under section 293 or Schedule 11. *Sub-paragraph (4)* limits the types of document that OFCOM may demand. The High Court, the Court of Session or, in Northern Ireland, the High Court or a judge of the High Court may, on an application made by OFCOM, enquire into whether a person has refused or otherwise failed (without reasonable excuse) to comply with a request from OFCOM. If the court is satisfied that that is the case, the person concerned may be punished as if he had been held in contempt of court (paragraph 13).

633.   A person is guilty of an offence under paragraph 13 if he:

- intentionally alters, suppresses or destroys a document requested by OFCOM; or

- knowingly or recklessly provides OFCOM with false or misleading information himself or knowingly or recklessly provides false or misleading information to a third person which he knows will be provided to OFCOM.

634.   The penalties to which any person found guilty of committing an offence will be liable are set out in sub-paragraph (11).

Section 295: Involvement of C4 Corporation in programme-making

635.   OFCOM are to include in the Channel 4 licence a condition prohibiting the Channel Four Television Corporation from being involved in making programmes to be aired on Channel 4, except as permitted by OFCOM.

Section 296: Schools programmes on Channel 4

636.   OFCOM are to include in the Channel 4 licence any conditions necessary to ensure that Channel 4 broadcasts a sufficient proportion of schools programmes. This may be achieved by setting a minimum number of hours (in term time or within normal school hours) that must be dedicated to schools programming. The Corporation may also be required to finance the production of schools programmes, to acquire such programmes from others and/or to produce any materials that may be necessary to ensure the effective use of such programmes. The programming should be of a high standard and, in producing their schools programmes, the Corporation should consult such persons concerned with schools or schools programmes as OFCOM direct. OFCOM must consult the Corporation before imposing any conditions under this section.

> **schools programmes* are defined in *subsection (12)* as programmes which are intended for use in schools.

637.   *Subsection (11)* provides that the requirement in section 34 of the Broadcasting Act 1990, that a suitable proportion of the programmes which are included in Channel 3 services and Channel 4 and 5 (taken as a whole) are

schools programmes, shall no longer apply.

Section 297: Channel 4 contribution towards national television archive

638.   This section amends section 185 of the Broadcasting Act 1990 to allow OFCOM to determine the amount of money that the holder of the Channel 4 licence must contribute after the television transfer date towards the expenses of maintaining a television archive for the United Kingdom.

639.   Section 185 already requires such contributions from holders of Channel 3 and 5 licences and similar arrangements apply to the BBC under the BBC Agreement.

Section 298: Conditions prohibiting interference with other services

640.   OFCOM must include in the licence for the public teletext service conditions that prohibit the public teletext service provider from causing interference with any television broadcasting service on whose frequency it is provided or any other wireless telegraphy transmissions.

Section 299: Categorisation of listed events

641.   This section amends section 97 of the Broadcasting Act 1996 to provide for the existing concept of 'listed events' to be divided into two categories, called 'group A' and 'group B'. Listed events are sporting or other events of national interest, which the Secretary of State has listed for the purpose of attracting the legal consequences provided for by Part 4 of the 1996 Act. The amendment requires all listed events to be allocated to one of these groups. When an event is listed, the Secretary of State will allocate it to a group, and she may decide to move a listed event from one group to another, subject to the same consultation requirements that already apply to a decision to list an event. The existing requirement to consult the ITC is replaced by one to consult OFCOM.

Section 300: Effects of categorisation of listed events

642.   *Subsection (1)* amends section 99(1) of the Broadcasting Act 1996 so that it applies only to Group A listed events. Section 99(1) makes a contract void if it purports to grant exclusive rights to televise a listed event live for reception in the UK. It will, therefore, become possible for valid contracts to be made granting such exclusive rights in relation to group B events.

643.   *Subsection (2)* amends section 101 of the Broadcasting Act 1996. That section currently prohibits a television service provider who provides, for reception in the UK, a service falling within either of the categories set out in section 98(1) of the 1996 Act from including in that service live coverage of the whole or any part of a listed event unless either the live rights have also been acquired by another person providing a service in the other of those two categories, or the ITC has given its consent. As well as replacing references to the ITC with references to OFCOM, the

amendment introduces a new ground on which live coverage can be included without satisfying either of those existing grounds. The new ground applies only to group B events, and requires that rights to provide adequate alternative coverage have been acquired by one or more persons, other than the person proposing to include the live coverage in his service, who satisfy the requirements of regulations made under section 104ZA of the 1996 Act (which is inserted by section 302 of this Act). The amendments also make minor drafting improvements.

Section 301: Code relating to listed events

644.   This section amends section 104 of the Broadcasting Act 1996, which makes provision for an ITC Code for various purposes of Part 4 of that Act. The amendment transfers responsibility to OFCOM and repeals one of the Code's existing functions, that of specifying the circumstances in which the televising of listed events is, or is not, to be treated as live for various purposes of Part 4 (which becomes instead a function of regulations under section 104A, which is inserted by section 302 of this Act).

645.   Paragraph 51 of Schedule 18 provides that until OFCOM draw up a code under this clause, the code drawn up by the ITC under section 104 of the Broadcasting Act 1996 shall have effect.

Section 302: Regulations about coverage of listed events

646.   This section inserts a new section 104ZA into the Broadcasting Act 1996 enabling OFCOM to make regulations for determining, for the purposes of Part IV of that Act, first, the circumstances in which the televising of listed events is, or is not, to be treated as live and, secondly, what is to be taken to represent the provision of adequate alternative coverage (the first function was formerly one of the Code drawn up under section 104, and the second is relevant to the amendment of section 101 made by section 300 of this Act).

Section 303: Code relating to provision for deaf and visually impaired

647.   This section provides that OFCOM are to draw up, publish and maintain a code giving guidance as to the extent to which the services to which the section applies should promote their understanding and enjoyment by persons who are deaf or hard of hearing, persons who are blind or partially-sighted and persons with a dual sensory impairment. *Subsections (4)* and *(5)* set out obligations on the services set out at *subsection (12)* that must, from the fifth and tenth anniversaries respectively of the 'relevant date' (which is defined in section 305), be fulfilled. *Subsection (4)* sets out targets in respect of subtitling, and *subsection (5)* sets out targets in respect of subtitling, audio-description and sign language. The total of programmes from which that proportion is set shall exclude such programmes as OFCOM consider should be excluded under *subsection (7)* having regard to the factors set out in *subsection (8)*. OFCOM may also set interim targets and exclude different descriptions of programmes in relation to different services. Where OFCOM are satisfied that

a service is a special case they may exclude all the programmes in that service.

Section 304: Procedure for issuing and revising code under s. 303

648.   Before drawing up the code described in the notes to section 303 above, OFCOM shall, as they see fit, consult with representatives of the deaf or hard of hearing, blind or partially-sighted, and dual sensory impaired, as well as with those providing the relevant services. When the code is published it shall be in a form easily accessed by those who are deaf or hard of hearing, those who are blind or partially-sighted, and those with a dual sensory impairment.

Section 305: Meaning of "relevant date" in s. 303

649.   This section defines "relevant date" for the purposes of section 303. The definition varies according to the service in question, and when provision of that service commenced.

Section 306: Power to modify targets in s. 303

650.   The Secretary of State, following consultation with OFCOM, may by order increase the target percentages set out in *subsection (4)* of section 303, or substitute a different anniversary, where it appears that the obligation set out in that subsection has been or is likely to be fulfilled before the specified anniversary. She may also substitute a later anniversary for the one specified in *subsection (5)* or substitute a higher percentage.

Section 307: Observance of code under s. 303

651.   OFCOM are to include in the licence for every service to which this section applies (namely, any of the services listed in section 303(12)) conditions requiring that the code provided for in section 303 is observed.

Section 308: Assistance for the visually impaired with the public teletext service

652.   OFCOM are to include in the licence for the public teletext service conditions to secure, so far as is reasonable and practicable, that the service includes features enabling persons with disabilities affecting their sight to use the service.

Section 309: Quotas for independent programmes

653.   OFCOM are to include in every licence for a digital television programme service that is not comprised in a licensed public service channel conditions to secure that at least 10 per cent of the time allocated to the broadcasting of qualifying programmes in the service is allocated to the broadcasting of a range and diversity (judged both in terms of the types of programmes involved and of the cost of their acquisition) of independent productions. The Secretary of State may, by order, and having consulted OFCOM, vary this percentage and determine what are to be

considered "qualifying programmes" and "independent productions".

Section 310: Code of practice for electronic programme guides

654.   OFCOM must draft and maintain a code of practice for the provision of electronic programme guides (EPGs). This must ensure that EPG providers give the listing and/or promotion of the programmes on public service channels an appropriate degree of prominence, as determined by OFCOM. This obligation also applies to the means of selecting and accessing the programmes on these channels from an EPG.

655.   These obligations are expressed by reference to "intended audience" (defined in *subsection (7)*). This has the effect that, where the provider of a public service channel provides the channel in regional versions, in any given region the channel's most prominent EPG listing will be occupied by the programmes provided for that region. Programmes on the other regional versions of that channel will usually be found listed further down the EPG.

> * an *"electronic programme guide"* is defined, for the purposes of this section, in *subsection (8)* as a service which comprises (i) the listing and/or promotion of some or all of the programmes included in any one or more programme services the providers of which are, or include, persons other than the provider of the guide and (ii) a facility for obtaining access, in whole or in part, to the programme service so far as it is promoted or listed in the guide. As at the date of Royal Assent, the only EPGs available are principally visual services. However, the Act has been drafted to provide for EPGs whether their features are wholly visual, or a combination of sound and vision, or even (if they are developed) EPGs that operate wholly in sound.

656.   The code must also ensure that providers of guides comply with any decision of OFCOM that specified features should be incorporated in the guides in order to (i) help people who have disabilities affecting their sight and/or hearing to use the guides for the same purposes as they are used by those without such disabilities and (ii) ensure that such people are informed about and are able to use any assistance provided for them in relation to the programmes listed and/or promoted.

657.   For the purposes of these provisions the public service channels are the BBC's television services in digital form, any Channel 3 service in digital form, Channel 4 in digital form, Channel 5 in digital form, S4C Digital, and the digital public teletext service. *Subsection (5)* provides the Secretary of State with a power to amend this list by order, though she must not do so without consulting OFCOM (*subsection (6)*).

Section 311: Conditions to comply with code under s. 310

658.   OFCOM are to include in every licence for a service which comprises or includes the provision of an electronic programme guide conditions to secure the observation of the code provided for in section 310.

Section 312: Character and coverage of sound broadcasting services

659.   This section amends section 106 of the Broadcasting Act 1990 dealing with

the character and coverage of radio services. Broadly, OFCOM are to set such conditions as are necessary for maintaining the character of the service. The character of the service includes the music and spoken material selected for inclusion in that service. The conditions may provide that OFCOM may only consent to a departure from the original character if such a departure would not substantially change that character, if the departure would not narrow the range of relevant independent radio services available in the area covered by the service, if, in the case of local licences, there is user demand for the changes that the departure would effect or if the departure would be in the interests of competition.

> **"Relevant independent radio services"* consist of sound broadcasting services, radio licensable content services and additional radio services that fall within the scope of OFCOM's regulatory functions under section 245.

660.   OFCOM may allow a local licence holder to extend the area to which he broadcasts, but only if such an extension is not significant and is justified by exceptional circumstances.

Section 313: Consultation about change of character of local service

661.   This section adds a new section 106A to the Broadcasting Act 1990. It requires OFCOM, before agreeing to a substantial departure from the character of a local or national analogue service, to publish a notice specifying the proposed departure and the period within which representations may be made to OFCOM (normally not less than 28 days). The notice must be published in a manner in which appears to OFCOM appropriate for bringing it to the intention of those likely to be affected by such a departure. OFCOM do not have to consult if they are satisfied that the departure would not substantially alter the character of the service.

662.   OFCOM also do not have to consult, or can shorten the consultation period, if they consider that to do so would result in a delay which would be likely prejudicially to affect the licence holder (for example, where they might go out of business). OFCOM are not required to publish confidential material.

Section 314: Local content and character of local sound broadcasting services

663.   *Subsection (1)* imposes a duty on OFCOM to ensure that local sound broadcasting services contain local material, to the extent (if any) that OFCOM consider appropriate in that case, and include locally-made programmes. OFCOM are required to draft, publish and maintain guidance setting out when local sound broadcasting services satisfy the requirements of *subsection (1)* and to have regard to that guidance when carrying out their functions in relation to local sound broadcasting services. OFCOM's guidance may extend to such issues as providing descriptions of local material and locally-made programmes. *Subsection (5)* requires OFCOM to consult with persons having an interest in local sound broadcasting services before drafting or revising the guidance. OFCOM's duties under this section do not extend to local advertising.

Section 315: Variations of radio multiplex licences affecting service characteristics

664.   This section replaces subsection (6) of section 54 of the Broadcasting Act 1996 with subsections (6) to (6B). Upon the request of a radio multiplex licensee to vary a licence condition implementing a proposal submitted in his original application under section 46(4) or 50(4) of the Broadcasting Act 1996 relating to the number of digital sound programme services and the characteristics of each service to be broadcast, the timetable for the launch for those services, the broadcasting of digital additional services or the promotion of the acquisition of digital receivers by the listening public, OFCOM must vary the licence as requested, subject to the tests set out in subsections (6A) and (6B).

665.   Section 54(6A) provides that OFCOM may not vary a national radio multiplex licence where it appears that, if the requested amendment were made, the capacity of the digital sound programme services broadcast under the licence to appeal to a variety of tastes and interests would be unacceptably diminished.

666.   Section 54(6B) stipulates that OFCOM may vary a local radio multiplex licence only where they are satisfied that:

- the variation would not unacceptably narrow the range of programmes available to people living in the areas where the multiplex service is provided;

- the variation is in the interests of competition; or

- there is user demand for the changes to the services.

Section 316: Conditions relating to competition matters

667.   Section 316 makes specific provision for OFCOM to have powers, in addition to concurrent powers under the Competition Act, to use licence conditions to ensure fair and effective competition in the provision of licensed services and connected services. This gives OFCOM competition powers specific to the broadcasting sector. *Subsection (3)* provides that, in order to ensure fair and effective competition between licence holders, OFCOM can require licence holders to comply with a code approved by OFCOM on the specifics of how they should comply with the licence conditions and that they can also issue directions to individual licensees for that purpose.

licenced service means a service licensed by a Broadcasting Act licence.

Section 317: Exercise of Broadcasting Act powers for a competition purpose

668.   This section applies to OFCOM's Broadcasting Act powers, as defined in *subsection (1)*. The effect of *subsections (2) and (3)* is that OFCOM are not to use Broadcasting Act powers for a competition purpose (as defined in *subsection (9)*), where they consider that a more appropriate way of proceeding would be through the

use of their general competition powers under the Competition Act 1998.

> *OFCOM's *Broadcasting Act powers* are their powers under Part 3 of this Act and under the Broadcasting Acts to impose or vary licence conditions, their powers to give approvals or directions for the purposes of such conditions and their powers to enforce such conditions.

669.   *Subsections (4) and (5)* require that where OFCOM decide to exercise their Broadcasting Act powers for a competition purpose, they must notify that decision to persons likely to be affected by it, and the notification must include a description of the rights of appeal that apply. *Subsection (6)* provides that where OFCOM have considered that the exercise of their Broadcasting Act powers for a competition purpose is the more appropriate way to proceed, the route of appeal for any person affected by any decisions under these powers shall be to the Competition Appeal Tribunal. *Subsection (8)* limits the jurisdiction of the Tribunal in any such appeal, so as to exclude questions as to whether OFCOM have complied with subsections (2) and (3): those questions can, though, be challenged by way of judicial review. *Subsection (10)* provides that this section does not apply to the exercise by OFCOM of their powers in relation to Channel 3 networking arrangements under sections 290 to 294 and Schedule 11.

Section 318: Review of powers exercised for competition purposes

670.   This section provides for OFCOM periodically to review any guidance or codes or directions that they issue in respect of their Broadcasting Act powers and which has effect for a competition purpose. OFCOM must consult on any changes they propose to make.

Section 319: OFCOM's standards code

671.   *Subsection (1)* places OFCOM under a duty to set standards for the content of television and radio services, which shall be contained in a code or codes.

672.   These codes must secure the objectives set out in *subsection (2)*. Those objectives relate to the protection of minors; the prohibition of material likely to encourage crime or disorder; the impartiality of television and radio services; the accuracy of the news; the content of religious programmes; the protection of the public from offensive and harmful material; the exclusion of advertising which contravenes the ban on political advertising set out in section 321(2); the prevention of misleading, harmful or offensive advertising and unsuitable sponsorship; compliance with the United Kingdom's international obligations with respect to advertsing; the prevention of undue discrimination between advertisers; and the prohibition of broadcasts of subliminal material.

673.   A particular standards objective relates to responsible religious broadcasting. *Subsection (6)* expands upon this to safeguard against the improper exploitation of any susceptibilities of the audience or the abusive treatment of the religious views and beliefs of those belonging to a particular religion or denomination.

674.   *Subsection (5)* makes clear that, while minimum standards will be of general application, OFCOM are also under a duty to set standards for particular types of programme or service (for example, children's programmes) where OFCOM consider that such standards are appropriate to achieve the objectives contained in *subsection (2)*.

675.   In setting the standards, OFCOM are under a duty to have regard to the factors set out in *subsection (4)* so far as they are relevant. These concern the degree of harm or offence likely to be caused by the content of programmes; the probable size and composition of the audience; the expectation of the audience as to the nature of a programme's content and the extent to which it can be brought to their attention; the danger of accidental exposure of a person to content, the nature of which they were unaware; the desirability of indicating when there is a change affecting the nature of the service being watched or listened to; and the desirability of maintaining independent editorial control over the content of a programme.

676.   Paragraph 43 of Schedule 18 provides that any code drawn up under section 6, 7, 9, 90, 91 or 93 of the Broadcasting Act 1990 or section 108 of the Broadcasting Act 1996 shall have effect as if it were a code issued by OFCOM for the purpose of this section. However, codes drawn up under the Broadcasting Act 1990 shall only apply to services authorised by licences under that Act and, in the case of codes under section 6, 7 and 9 of that Act, S4C. As regards codes drawn up under section 108 of the Broadcasting Act 1996, these will only have effect for services provided by the BBC or the Welsh Authority and then only to the extent that the codes contain provisions applying to those services and, in the case of the Welsh Authority, which relate to matters other than advertising and impartiality.

Section 320: Special impartiality requirements

677.   The standards objectives referred to in section 319 include the objective that the impartiality requirements set out in this section are observed. This section specifies particular requirements, some of which are to be further expanded upon by rules in OFCOM's standards code, placed upon service providers to ensure that programme services are free from undue bias. The matters to which the requirements apply are matters of political or industrial controversy, and matters relating to current public policy. The requirements are:

- the service provider must not air its own views on such matters (unless they concern the provision of television or radio programme services); as in the 1990 Act, this restriction does not apply to providers of radio restricted services.

- as regards every television programme service, teletext service, national radio service and national digital sound programme service, the service provider must preserve due impartiality about such matters. The relevant rules in OFCOM's standards code must particularly take account of the need to preserve impartiality for major matters of political or industrial controversy or relating to current public policy. Fulfilment of this requirement need not necessarily be measured programme by programme, but on balance over all programmes included in the relevant service; and

- as regards local radio services, local digital sound programme services, and radio licensable content services, the service provider must ensure that undue prominence is not given to any particular viewpoint about such matters. This need be satisfied only by considering the entire service, rather than programme by programme, or even series by series.

Section 321: Objectives for advertisements and sponsorship

678.   This section specifies standards objectiveswhich must include general provisions about the required standards in advertising and sponsorship and permits OFCOM to prohibit advertisements and methods of advertising and sponsorship.

679.   *Subsection (2)* imposes on OFCOM a duty to secure in the broadcast media a general prohibition on political advertising and advertising related to industrial disputes. This reproduces the duty imposed under the Broadcasting Act 1990 on the ITC and the Radio Authority to secure a similar prohibition. *Subsection (7)* specifies that an advertisement of a public service nature which is inserted by or on behalf of a government department, and a party political or referendum campaign broadcast required by a condition imposed under section 333 or by paragraph 18 of Schedule 12, may nonetheless be broadcast. The Act sets out in *subsection (3)* the matters which are included in the reference in *subsection (2)* to "objects of a political nature" and "political ends", so as to make clear the scope of the prohibition. These include each of the following: influencing the outcome of elections or referendums in the UK or elsewhere; bringing about changes in the law or otherwise influencing the legislative process in the UK or elsewhere; influencing the policies or decisions of local, regional or national governments in the UK or elsewhere; influencing the policies or decisions of persons on whom public functions are conferred by or under the law of the UK or of a country or territory outside the UK; influencing the policy or decisions of persons on whom functions are conferred by or under international agreements; influencing public opinion on a matter which in the UK is a matter of public controversy; and promoting the interests of a party or other group of persons organised in the UK or elsewhere for political ends.

680.   It is because of the ban that this section (in conjunction with section 319(2)(g)) would impose on political advertising that, in the light of the decision of the European Court of Human Rights in the case of <u>Vgt Verein gegen Tierfabriken v Switzerland</u>, the Minister in charge of the Bill was unable to make a statement of compatibility under section 19(1)(a) of the Human Rights Act 1998. The fact that the Minister made a statement under section 19(1)(b) of that Act does not, however, mean that the Government believes the ban would necessarily be found to be incompatible if the ban were to be challenged in the United Kingdom courts or to be considered by the European Court of Human Rights.

681.   More generally, *subsections (5) and (6)* provide for consultation by OFCOM with the Secretary of State regarding the descriptions of advertisements that should not be included in programme services; and the forms and methods of advertising and sponsorship that should not be used. In addition, the Secretary of State has a power to issue directions (with which OFCOM must comply) on any of those matters.

Section 322: Supplementary powers relating to advertising

682.   This section requires all licences related to the provision of programme services, the public teletext service and other teletext services (either additional television services or digital additional television services) to include a condition that the licence holder must comply with OFCOM's directions on the maximum time to be given to advertisements in any given time period, the minimum interval that must elapse between two periods of advertisements, the number of advertisement slots that are allowed in any programme or hour or day, and the exclusion of any advertisement from a specified part of a service.

Section 323: Modification of matters to be taken into account under s. 319

683.   This section provides that the Secretary of State, following consultation with OFCOM, may by order modify the factors set out in section 319(4) to be considered by OFCOM when setting or amending standards codes.

Section 324: Setting and publication of standards

684.   This section concerns the procedures for setting the codes containing the standards for the content of television, radio and teletext services. *Subsections (1) to (5)* deal with the consultation process that OFCOM must enter into prior to setting or revising these standards. Different provision is made regarding the persons to be consulted depending on the relevance of the code to their interests.

685.   Following this process, OFCOM may modify their proposed standards code as they see fit in light of the consultation, and must then publish the code. If new standards are being set, or old standards being revised, OFCOM must bring them to the attention of those whom the standards are likely to affect and send a copy to the Secretary of State, the BBC (unless it is a code containing only standards for advertising or sponsorship) and, if the code relates to television programme services, the Welsh Authority.

Section 325: Observance of standards code

686.   OFCOM are to include in every Broadcasting Act licence for a programme service such conditions as they deem to be suitable in order to safeguard the standards listed in section 319. OFCOM must also implement procedures for hearing complaints in connection with the non-observance of such standards. OFCOM may report to the Secretary of State periodically regarding issues relating to OFCOM's standards code that appear to raise questions of general broadcasting policy.

687.   Regarding advertising and sponsorship, OFCOM must include a further licence condition obliging the licence holder for a programme service to comply with any direction from OFCOM on the matters set out in *subsection (5)*, all of which relate to the exclusion of certain advertisements or sponsorship.

Section 326: Duty to observe fairness code

688.   This section requires OFCOM to include in each Broadcasting Act licence for a programme service such conditions as they consider appropriate for securing observance, in connection with the provision of that service and in relation to programmes included in that service, of the fairness code for the time being in force under section 107 of the Broadcasting Act 1996.

Section 327: Standards with respect to fairness

689.   This section relates to the exercise by OFCOM of functions relating to the consideration of complaints regarding fairness and privacy which were formerly exercised by the Broadcasting Standards Commission under Part 5 of the Broadcasting Act 1996.

690.   A standards complaint under Part 5 of that Act may not be made after the commencement of this section. This section amends the provisions in sections 115, 119 and 120 of the 1996 Act relating to the consideration of fairness complaints.

> *a standards complaint* is defined in section 110(4) of the Broadcasting Act 1996 as a complaint made to the Broadcasting Standards Commission which relates to the portrayal of violence or sexual conduct or to standards of taste and decency.

Section 328: Duty to publicise OFCOM's functions in relation to complaints

691.   OFCOM are to include in a licence for every service to which this section applies conditions to ensure that procedures for handling and resolving complaints about observance of standards, including OFCOM's functions under Part 5 of the Broadcasting Act 1996, are publicised. This section applies to every programme service licensed by a Broadcasting Act licence

Section 329: Proscription orders

692.   Where OFCOM have notified the Secretary of State that a foreign television or sound service repeatedly contains programmes with content that offends taste or decency, is likely to incite crime or disorder or is likely to be offensive to public feeling, she may issue a proscription order where she is satisfied that to do so is in the public interest and compatible with the international obligations of the United Kingdom. *Subsection (6)* sets out the services to which this section applies.

> *The meaning of a foreign service is given in *subsection (7)* and broadly encompasses those services which do not need to be licensed under the Broadcasting Acts 1990 and 1996 but would be if they were provided in the United Kingdom or the provider fell within the jurisdiction of the

United Kingdom for the purposes of the Television without Frontiers Directive.

Section 330: Effect of proscription order

693.   No service proscribed by the Secretary of State in an order made under section 329 can be included in any multiplex service or any cable package service (as defined in *subsections (3) and (4)* respectively).   The effect of *subsection (5)* is that the provision of radio and/or television (or similar) services via the Internet will not constitute the provision of a cable package service.

Section 331: Notification for enforcing proscription

694.   Where OFCOM have reasonable grounds to believe that a service proscribed by an order made under section 329 is included in a multiplex service or cable package, they may notify the multiplex service provider or cable packager accordingly and require that person to cease including the proscribed service. OFCOM must give the notified provider 7 days to comply with their request, although he must cease to include the service in less than 7 days if reasonably practicable.   A notified provider has a statutory duty to comply with OFCOM's request, failure to comply with which is enforceable in civil proceedings by OFCOM.

Section 332: Penalties for contravention of notification under s.331

695.   OFCOM may impose a penalty on any multiplex service provider or cable packager who contravenes a requirement notified by OFCOM under section 331. Before imposing a penalty, OFCOM must give a multiplex service provider or cable packager a reasonable opportunity to make representations. Any penalty imposed must be appropriate and proportionate to the contravention, and in any case may not exceed £5,000 per day for each day (or part thereof) that a multiplex service provider or cable packager includes a proscribed service in contravention of a notification made under section 331. The Secretary of State may, by order, amend the maximum penalty set out in *subsection (3)*.

Section 333: Party political broadcasts

696.   OFCOM must include in the licence for every licensed public service channel and every national radio service conditions requiring the licensee to broadcast party political broadcasts and referendum campaign broadcasts and to observe associated rules set by OFCOM.   These rules may include provision for determining which political parties and designated organisations may make broadcasts, and how long and frequent these broadcasts may be.   OFCOM are subject in this respect to the Political Parties, Elections and Referendums Act 2000 (c.41) and shall have regard to the views of the Electoral Commission.   Paragraph 38 of Schedule 18 provides that any rules made by the ITC under section 38 of the Broadcasting Act 1990 or by the Radio Authority under section 107 of that Act, which are in force immediately before the commencement of this section, shall have effect as rules made by OFCOM under this section.

Section 334: Retention and production of recordings

697.   OFCOM are to include in the licence for every programme service licensed under the Broadcasting Acts conditions requiring the licensee to record every programme that they broadcast, and to keep each recording for a specified period (which for radio programmes shall be no longer than 42 days and for television programmes shall be no longer than 90 days) and, at OFCOM's request, to provide them with any such recording as well as any script or transcript of the relevant programme that the licensee is able to produce. Under *subsection (3)*, OFCOM may themselves make and use recordings of programmes for the purposes of supervision. However, *subsection (4)* makes it clear that they are not required to vet programmes in advance of their being broadcast.

Section 335: Conditions securing compliance with international obligations

698.   OFCOM are to include in the licence for every service of the types listed in *subsection (3)* conditions to secure compliance with such of the United Kingdom's international obligations as have been notified to OFCOM by the Secretary of State.

Section 336: Government requirements for licensed services

699.   The Secretary of State, or any other Minister of the Crown, has the power by notice to require OFCOM to issue a direction to licence holders to include a particular announcement in their service at specified times. The Secretary of State alone may require OFCOM to direct licence holders to refrain from including any particular matter in their services.

> **Subsection (9)* makes clear that *Minister of the Crown* includes the Treasury.

700.   Where a licence holder is obliged to make a particular announcement, they may make clear in their service that this is being carried out further to a direction given by OFCOM. Similarly, where a licence holder has been obliged to refrain from including a particular matter in their service, the licence holder may announce in the service that this is the case, and may also announce when that obligation has come to an end.

701.   The purpose of these provisions is principally to allow Ministers to address matters of national security or major public interest, and to do so in such a way that the affected broadcasters are not required to take editorial responsibility for the content of the announcements.

Section 337: Promotion of equal opportunities and training

702.   OFCOM are to include in the licence for every service to which this section applies (as defined in *subsections (6) to (8)*) conditions to promote equality of opportunity in relation to employment with the licence holder. The conditions must promote equality between men and women and between different races. Licensees

must also be required to promote the equalisation of opportunities for disabled persons.

703.   OFCOM must also impose on licensees any conditions necessary to ensure that licensees make such arrangements for the training and retraining of their employees (employed both in the provision of the service and in the making of programmes to be included in the service) as OFCOM consider appropriate.

704.   The conditions imposed by OFCOM must require licensees to ensure that the arrangements put in place by the licensees to meet equal opportunities and training requirements are notified to those affected by them. Also the licensee must review the arrangements from time to time and publish annually his observations on their operation.

705.   Those licensees that employ no more than 20 people, or broadcast for no more than 31 days per year, are not covered by these provisions, though OFCOM are able to aggregate the numbers of staff employed across a group of companies or a range of services under the provisions in *subsections (7)* and *(10)* and the definition of "licensed service" in *subsection (9)*.

Section 338: Corresponding rules for the BBC and the Welsh Authority

706.   This section provides that Schedule 12 shall have effect. Schedule 12 provides for the imposition on the BBC and the Welsh Authority of obligations that correspond to those described above in the regulatory regime for licensed providers and it is explained in more detail below.

Section 339: Review of fulfilment by Welsh Authority of public service remits

707.   The Welsh Authority is under a duty to ensure that S4C, S4C Digital and services approved by the Secretary of State under section 205 fulfil their public service remits. The Secretary of State may review the Welsh Authority's performance in this regard, but not within five years of the passage of the Act. Any subsequent review must not be undertaken within a further five-year period. The Secretary of State must consult the National Assembly for Wales and the Welsh Authority on the matters under review, must have regard to their opinions when reaching her conclusions and must publish a report of those conclusions after each review.

Section 340: Directions to Welsh Authority to take remedial action

708.   If the review described in the notes to section 339 above reveals that, without reasonable excuse, the Welsh Authority have not properly performed their duty to fulfil their public service remits, the Secretary of State may, having consulted the Welsh Authority, direct the Welsh Authority to take remedial action. Any such direction must first be approved, in draft, by both Houses of Parliament.

Section 341: Imposition of penalties on the Welsh Authority

709. This section gives OFCOM the power to fine the Welsh Authority where they are satisfied that a contravention of any requirement listed in *subsection (1)* has occurred. Broadly, these include obligations relating to programme quotas, news and current affairs, programming standards, advertising or sponsorship, complaints procedure publicity, international obligations, assistance for disabled people and fairness. The maximum fine is £250,000. Under *subsection (6)*, the Secretary of State may vary the maximum penalty by order. *Subsection (4)* states that OFCOM may not fine the Welsh Authority without giving them a chance to make representations in its defence. *Subsection (5)* makes clear that the imposition of a fine would not prevent OFCOM from issuing a direction to the Welsh Authority, under paragraph 15 of Schedule 12, to broadcast a correction or a finding by OFCOM of a breach of the standards code issued under section 319.

Section 342: Contraventions recorded in Welsh Authority's annual report

710. This section amends Schedule 6 to the Broadcasting Act 1990 to ensure that any notifications given to the Welsh Authority by OFCOM about contraventions by the Authority of either the Broadcasting Acts or Part 3 of this Act are recorded in the Welsh Authority's annual report.

Section 343: Provision of information by Welsh Authority

711. This section imposes a duty on the Welsh Authority to provide such information as OFCOM reasonably request in order that OFCOM may fulfil their functions, under this Act and the Broadcasting Acts, as regards the Welsh Authority.

Section 344: Transmission of statement of findings

712. This section amends sections 40 and 109 of the Broadcasting Act 1990 (power to direct licensee to broadcast correction or apology). As amended, these sections provide that OFCOM may direct the broadcast of a correction or a statement of OFCOM's findings in relation to a contravention of licence conditions, for example a failure to comply with OFCOM's standards code. This change arises from a recommendation of the Joint Committee on Human Rights.

Section 345: Financial penalties imposable on licence holders

713. Schedule 13, which modifies the maximum penalties that may be imposed on the holders of Broadcasting Act licences, shall have effect. Further detail on this Schedule is set out below.

Section 346: Recovery of fees and penalties

714. Where a payment of a kind listed in *subsection (1)* is payable to OFCOM, it is recoverable by them as a debt due from the person who must pay it. Those

payments include amounts paid under licences granted under the Broadcasting Acts 1990 and 1996 and penalties imposed by OFCOM under those Acts.

Section 347: Statement of charging principles

715.   This section provides that OFCOM must not fix a tariff under section 4(3) or 87(3) of the Broadcasting Act 1990 or under section 4(3) or 43(3) of the Broadcasting Act 1996 unless at the time they do so there is in force a statement of the principles they propose to apply in fixing that tariff. Any tariff must be fixed in accordance with those principles.

716.   The principles set out in any statement must be likely to secure, on the basis of such estimates of the likely costs as it is practicable for OFCOM to make, that the aggregate amount of the Broadcasting Act licence fees required to be paid to OFCOM during a financial year is sufficient to enable them to meet, but does not exceed, the annual costs of the carrying out during that year of their functions relating to the regulation of broadcasting; that tariffs are justifiable and proportionate to the matters in respect of which they are imposed; and that the relationship between meeting the cost of carrying out those functions and the tariffs applied to such fees is transparent.

> * *"Broadcasting Act licence fee"* means a fee required to be paid to OFCOM in pursuance of conditions included in a Broadcasting Act licence under any of the following provisions –
>
>> (a) section 4(1)(b) or 87(1)(c) of the Broadcasting Act 1990; or
>>
>> (b) section 4(1)(b) or 43(1)(c) of the Broadcasting Act 1996.
>
> *Financial year* means a period of 12 months ending with 31st March.

717.   *Subsection (3)* requires that, before making or revising a statement of principles, OFCOM must consult such persons as they consider likely to be affected by those principles as they think fit. Under *subsection (4)*, the making or revision of a statement of principles is by the publication of the statement, or revised statement, in such manner as OFCOM consider appropriate to bring it to the attention of those likely, in OFCOM's opinion, to be affected by it.

718.   Under *subsections (5) and (6)*, OFCOM must publish a statement as soon as practicable after the end of each financial year, setting out the aggregate amount of Broadcasting Act licence fees received by them which were required to be paid during that year; the aggregate amount of Broadcasting Act licence fees remaining outstanding and likely to be paid or recovered; and, the costs to OFCOM of carrying out their functions in relation to the regulation of broadcasting during that year. Any deficit or surplus must be carried forward by OFCOM and taken into account in determining the amount required in relation to the following year.

719.   References to OFCOM's functions in relation to the regulation of broadcasting do not include any of their functions in relation to the BBC or Welsh Authority.

Chapter 5: Media Ownership and Control

Section 348: Modification of disqualification provisions

720.   This section amends Part 2 of Schedule 2 to the Broadcasting Act 1990. Under *subsection (1)* persons not resident or established in the EEA are no longer disqualified from holding Broadcasting Act licences. *Subsections (2) and (3)* amend paragraph 2 of that Part, disqualifying religious bodies from holding the following licences granted under the Broadcasting Acts 1990 and 1996:

- A Channel 3 licence;

- A Channel 5 licence;

- A national sound broadcasting licence;

- A public teletext licence;

- An additional television service licence;

- A television multiplex licence; and

- A radio multiplex licence.

This needs to be read with paragraph 15 in Part 4 of Schedule 14 to the Act. In the case of licences that are not in this list, a religious body may apply for a licence and OFCOM may grant the licence if they make a determination in the case of that organisation; and they may make such a determination if (and only if) they consider it appropriate for that body to hold a licence of that description. This applies to-

- restricted service licences;

- digital television programme licences;

- digital additional television services licences;

- licences to provide television licensable content services;

- licences under Part 3 of the 1990 Act (other than a national licence) - meaning local analogue radio licences, licences to provide radio licensable content services, and licences to provide (analogue) additional services;

- national and local digital sound programme licences;

- digital additional sound services licences.

721.   OFCOM are required to publish guidance for persons wishing to make such applications.

722.   *Subsections (5), (6) and (7)* allow the Secretary of State, following consultation with OFCOM and with Parliament's approval, to make an order amending or repealing the provisions of paragraph 2 of Part 2 of Schedule 2 to the 1990 Act . Paragraph 16 of Schedule 14 gives a similar power to repeal or

otherwise modify the restrictions set out in Part 4 of that Schedule.

Section 349: Licence holding by local authorities

723.   This section inserts a new provision into Part 2 of Schedule 2 to the Broadcasting Act 1990, the effect of which is that local authorities will no longer be disqualified from holding a licence where the service in question is provided solely in pursuance of the functions of local authorities under section 142 of the Local Government Act 1972.

724.   Section 142 relates to the provision by a local authority of information concerning their functions and the services available within their area.. *Subsection (2)* of section 349 inserts into section 142 provisions allowing a local authority to provide an electronic communications network or electronic communications service for the purpose of broadcasting or distributing information generally relating to the functions of the authority or about services available within their area that are provided by them or by another local authority or by an authority, board or committee with similar functions, or to arrange for the broadcasting or distribution of such information by means of an electronic communications network or electronic communications service provided by someone else.

> *   *"electronic communications network"* and *"electronic communications service"* are defined in section 32.

725.   *Subsection (3)* amends section 2(1) of the Local Government Act 1986 in order to widen the prohibition on a local authority from publishing any material which appears to be designed to affect public support for a political party, to a local authority arranging for such a publication.

Section 350: Relaxation of licence-holding restrictions

726.   *Subsection (1)* repeals the rules in Parts 3, 4 and 5 of Schedule 2 to the Broadcasting Act 1990 relating to restrictions on accumulations of interests and on licence holding by newspapers and telecommunications providers, some of which are replaced by Schedule 14 to this Act.   Rules relating to licences for local sound broadcasting and local digital sound programme service licences are to be replaced by provision made by order under paragraphs 11 and 12 of Schedule 14. *Subsections (4), (5) and (6)* ensure that these rules will not lapse before the relevant orders come into force.

727.   Part 1 of Schedule 14 establishes the new rules relating to the ownership of television services, replacing the rules repealed by section 350. These apply only to Channel 3 services and not, as before, to Channel 5.

728.   Paragraph 1 sets out the circumstances in which a person may not hold a licence for a Channel 3 service. A person may not hold any such licence if he runs national newspapers with more than 20 per cent of the total national market. No one

may own a regional Channel 3 licence if he runs local newspapers which together have more than 20 per cent of the local market in the coverage area of the service. For these purposes, a licence to provide a Channel 3 service is to be treated as held by the actual licence holder and every person connected with him.

*the expression "connected person" is defined for these purposes by paragraph 3 of Part 1 of Schedule 2 to the 1990 Act. For example, a company ("A") is connected with any person that controls A (e.g. a holding company), with any company controlled by A, and with another company ("B") if someone else controls both A and B. Separate rules apply for determining who is "connected with" an individual. For example, an individual is connected with certain of his relations, with business partners and with companies of which he is a director.

729.   Paragraph 2 establishes further restrictions on participation in companies holding Channel 3 licences. No one may hold more than a 20 per cent share in such a company if he is the proprietor of national newspapers with more than a 20 per cent share of the total national market. No licence-holder may own more than a 20 per cent share of any such national newspaper proprietor. A company in which such a newspaper proprietor holds more than a 20 per cent share cannot be a participant with more than a 20 per cent share of a company that holds a licence. These rules apply as much to participation in a company that controls the holder of a Channel 3 licence as they do to participation in the actual holder of the licence, and restrictions applicable to a proprietor or licence holder apply as if he and every person connected with him were one person.

* "control" is defined in paragraph 1(3) of Part 1 of Schedule 2 to the 1990 Act, as amended by section 357 of this Act.

730.   Paragraph 3 explains how 'national newspaper', 'local newspaper' and 'market share' are to be defined for the purposes of the above rules. References to national or local newspapers are references to newspapers that circulate wholly or mainly in the United Kingdom (national) or in a part of the United Kingdom (local). Where there is any difficulty with this definition (for example if a newspaper is published in different regional editions) OFCOM have the power to define whether the newspaper in question is national, local or both. Market share is defined as the percentage of total newspaper sales in the relevant area (either the UK or a Channel 3 licence region) represented by sales of the newspaper in question over the previous six months. If a newspaper is distributed free of charge, 'sales' are taken to include the number of copies distributed.

731.   Paragraph 4 identifies a person as running a newspaper if he is either the proprietor of the newspaper or controls a body which is the proprietor. The definition of 'control' is that in the Broadcasting Act 1990, Schedule 2, Part 1, paragraph 1(3).

732.   Paragraph 6 gives the Secretary of State power to repeal or modify any of the rules in Part 1 by order. Before making any such order (unless it is confined to giving effect to recommendations made by OFCOM under section 391), the Secretary of State must consult OFCOM; and no such order may be made unless it has been approved in draft by both Houses of Parliament: see paragraph 17.

733.   Part 2 of Schedule 14 establishes the rules relating to the ownership of radio multiplex licences, again replacing the rules repealed by section 350. Paragraph 7 prevents one person from owning more than one national radio multiplex licence at the same time.

734.   Paragraph 8 deals with the ownership of local radio multiplex licences. It establishes a limit of one multiplex licence per owner in areas where there is overlap of services so that the potential audience of one service includes at least half the potential audience of another. OFCOM are to lay down the technical standards by which 'coverage area' can be determined. If a person is in contravention of this rule when it is enacted, but is not in contravention of the existing rules on multiplex ownership, the contravention will be ignored and no divestment will be required until another person becomes the holder of the licences in question.

735.   Paragraph 9 provides that a radio multiplex licence is to be treated for the purposes of this Part of this Schedule as if it were held by the actual licence holder and any person connected with him.

736.   Under paragraph 10, the Secretary of State is given power to repeal or modify any of the rules in Part 2 by order.

737.   Part 3 of Schedule 14 contains a power for the Secretary of State to impose by order new rules on the holding of local sound broadcasting licences and the provision of local digital sound programme services. Such rules would replace those repealed by section 350.

738.   That Part allows the Secretary of State to impose limits on the number of licences that any person owns, or to prevent a person owning any licences at all in certain circumstances. The circumstances that could be specified in establishing rules of this sort include:

- the degree of overlap of the different services involved;
- the size of the potential audience for those services and the times when they would be made available;
- the extent to which there would be other persons with licences to broadcast to the same potential audience, the number of those persons and the audience size and coverage area of their stations;
- whether the person who holds (or wants to hold) the licence runs national newspapers, and the national market share of those newspapers;
- whether that person runs local newspapers that serve any part of the coverage area for which they would hold a radio licence, and the newspapers' local market share;
- whether and to what extent the coverage area of the licence in question overlaps with the coverage area of a regional Channel 3 service for which he also owns the licence.

739.   Paragraph 12 gives the Secretary of State similar powers to impose limits on the provision of local digital sound programme services, with the exception that the newspaper and Channel 3 assets held by a person are not included in the list of factors that may be considered when establishing rules.

740.   Paragraph 13 explains that definitions of the different forms of licence-holding, and of national and local newspapers and their market share, may be made under the order-making powers in paragraphs 11 and 12, and makes other supplemental provision. Paragraph 14 contains transitional provisions for orders made under paragraphs 11 and 12. If a person is in contravention of any rule established by such an order when it is enacted, but is not in contravention of the rules that preceded it, then the contravention will be ignored and no divestment will be required until there is a relevant change of circumstances in the licence-holding arrangements.

741.   Part 4 of this Schedule is concerned with the ownership of broadcasting licences by religious bodies, and the details are covered under section 348 above.

742.   Part 5 of Schedule 14 contains supplementary provisions relating to its implementation and interpretation. There is a requirement for the Secretary of State to consult OFCOM before making an order under any provision in the Schedule. There is also a stipulation that Part 1 of Schedule 2 to the 1990 Act should apply to Schedule 14 in the same way as it does to Part 2 of that Schedule. An overlapping area is defined as including any area that is the same as, or lies wholly inside, another area.

Section 351: Changes of control of Channel 3 services

743.   OFCOM are to include in the licence for every Channel 3 service conditions to ensure that any body corporate holding such a licence notifies OFCOM in advance of any proposals that may result in a change of control of the licensee, or of a person connected with the licensee who is, actually or potentially, involved to a substantial extent in providing programmes for inclusion in the licensed service.

744.   Where such a change of control may result, or has resulted, over a body corporate holding a Channel 3 licence, OFCOM must review and publish a report on the effects or likely effects, and their proposed response. OFCOM must review the impact of the change of control on the quality and range of regional programmes and the effect on the regional character of the service (*subsection (6)*), as well as the amount of time given in the service to regional programmes, the proportion of regional programmes made in the relevant region and the extent to which persons are employed in and decisions are made in the relevant region in connection with the service (*subsection (7)*). They must also review the effect on the time allocated in the service to original productions and news and current affairs programmes (*subsection (4)*); and the extent to which Channel 3 programmes in the service are made in the UK outside the M25 area, the range of such programmes, the extent to which expenditure by the Channel 3 provider on Channel 3 programmes is referable to programme production at different production centres outside the M25, and the range of such

production centres to which the expenditure is referable (*subsection (5)*).

745.   In the case of a national Channel 3 service, OFCOM will only review the effect on programme production and production expenditure outside the M25 area where a national Channel 3 service is subject to relevant conditions under section 286 (programme production) or OFCOM otherwise consider it would be appropriate.

Section 352: Action following review under s. 351

746.   If, following a review under section 351, OFCOM consider that the effect of the change of control is prejudicial to any of the matters they have reviewed, then under section 352 they must vary the licence, the only exception being where the matter in issue relates to subsection (7) of section 351, in which case they have a discretion whether to vary the licence. Any such variation may lead to the inclusion in the licence of conditions that are more burdensome than those included prior to the variation.   However, they must be conditions that would have been fulfilled throughout the twelve months immediately before the relevant change of control.

747.   The licensee must be given a reasonable opportunity to comment on the report before OFCOM vary the licence. The variation shall not be effective until the change of control actually occurs.

Section 353: Changes of control of Channel 5

748.   OFCOM are to include in the licence for Channel 5 conditions to ensure that any body corporate holding such a licence notifies OFCOM in advance of any proposals that may result in a change of control of the licensee, or of a person connected with the licensee who is, actually or potentially, involved to a substantial extent in providing programmes for inclusion in the licensed service.

749.   Where such a change of control may result, or has resulted, over a body corporate holding the Channel 5 licence, OFCOM shall review and publish a report on the effects or likely effects, and their proposed response. OFCOM must review the effect of the change of control on the time allocated in the service to original productions and news and current affairs programmes; and the extent to which Channel 5 programmes in the service are made in the UK outside the M25 area, the range of such programmes, the extent to which expenditure by the Channel 5 provider on Channel 5 programmes is referable to programme production at different production centres outside the M25, and the range of such production centres to which the expenditure is referable.

Section 354: Action following review under s. 353

750.   If, following a review under section 353, OFCOM consider that the effect of the change of control is prejudicial to any of the matters they have reviewed, then under section 354 they must vary the licence. Any such variation may lead to the inclusion in the licence of conditions that are more burdensome than those included

prior to the variation. However, they must be conditions that would have been fulfilled throughout the twelve months immediately before the relevant change of control.

751. The licensee must be given a reasonable opportunity to comment on the report before OFCOM vary the licence. The variation shall not be effective until the change of control actually occurs.

Section 355: Variation of local licence following change of control

752. OFCOM are to include in the licence for every local sound broadcasting service conditions to ensure that any body corporate holding such a licence notifies OFCOM in advance of any proposals that may result in a change of control of the licensee, or of a person connected with the licensee who is, actually or potentially, involved to a substantial extent in providing programmes for inclusion in the licensed service. Where such a change of control may result, or has resulted, over a body corporate holding a relevant licence, OFCOM shall review the effects, or likely effects, of the change. The review will consider the possible impact of such a change on: the quality and range of programmes; the character of the service; OFCOM's duty in respect of the local content and character of services (set out in section 314). The character of the service includes the music and spoken material selected for inclusion on that service. OFCOM must publish a report of their review setting out its conclusions and any proposed action.

Section 356: Action following review under section 353

753. If, following a review under section 353, OFCOM consider that the effect of the relevant change of control is prejudicial to the matters set out in section 353(4), they must vary the relevant licence. Any such variation may lead to the inclusion in the licence of conditions that are more burdensome than those included prior to the variation. However, they must be conditions that would have been fulfilled during the three months prior to the change of control or, if those three months were atypical of the licensee's performance during the previous year, another three-month period during the preceding year. The licensee must always be given the opportunity to comment on the report before OFCOM vary the licence. The variation shall not be effective until the change of control actually occurs.

Section 357: Meaning of "control"

754. This section amends the provisions relating to the control of a body corporate set out in paragraph 1 of Schedule 2 to the Broadcasting Act 1990 (circumstances where there is deemed to be control even though the person in question does not have a 50 per cent, or greater, interest in a company):

- It provides that a person will be treated as having de facto control of such a body if he would (if he chose to) be able in most cases or in significant respects to ensure that affairs of the company are conducted in accordance with his wishes.

- OFCOM will be required to publish and update guidance on some, but not necessarily all, of the factors they will take into account when determining whether a person has "control" of a body, within the meaning of paragraph 1(3)(b) of Part 1 of Schedule 2 to the 1990 Act.

Chapter 6: Other provisions about television and radio services

Section 358: Annual factual and statistical report

755. OFCOM are under a duty to carry out a review of the provision of the television and radio programmes in the United Kingdom and to prepare and publish a factual and statistical report setting out their findings twelve months after the commencement of this section and annually thereafter. In carrying out the review, OFCOM must consider each of the matters listed in *subsection (3)*. These include: the extent to which television and radio programmes are representative of the principal genres of such programmes; the extent to which OFCOM's codes relating to, for example, provision for the deaf and visually impaired, listed events and fairness have been complied with; trends in audience behaviour; the financial condition of the television and radio programme market(s); the operation of the independent productions quota in section 277 and paragraphs 1 and 7 of Schedule 12; relevant intellectual property matters that have been significant during the period; technological developments; the availability of people with skills used to provide television and radio services and programmes; and the availability of facilities for the provision of and training in such skills. OFCOM's duty under this section is in addition to their duty to prepare a report on the current state of public service television broadcasting under section 264.

Section 359: Grants to providers

756. OFCOM may make such grants as they consider appropriate to the providers of community radio (seethe notes to section 262 above). Under *subsection (2)*, the Secretary of State may by order provide that OFCOM may also give grants to providers of local digital television services (see the notes to section 244 above). The terms and conditions of such grants are at the discretion of OFCOM, but neither the bestowing of a grant upon any person, nor the terms on which this is done, shall make that person a disqualified person under Schedule 2 to the Broadcasting Act 1990 in relation to a community radio or local digital television licence.

Section 360: Amendments of 1990 and 1996 Acts

757. This section amends the definition of programme services in the 1990 Act so as to correspond to the language of the Act. The 1990 Act definition will continue to include a broader range of services than is licensable under the Communications Act, including on-demand and Internet services. Separate definitions are needed for this

Act and the 1990 Act because various outlying statutory provisions will continue to rely on the broader 1990 Act definition to control activities that go beyond what is licensable. For example, provisions in the Children Act 1989 seek to protect the privacy of children involved in certain legal proceedings, and the effectiveness of that restriction would be lessened if it did not extend beyond broadcast material. This section also introduces Schedule 15, which makes amendments to the 1990 and 1996 Acts. Most of these amendments are consequential on the Act. They are described in more detail in the notes for Schedule 15.

Section 361: Meaning of "available for reception by members of the public"

758.   This section defines "available for reception by members of the public" in such a way as to exclude 'one to one' services made available on cable, satellite or by means of a multiplex service. Examples of such services include internet and video-on-demand services where an individual viewer requests an individual library item such as a film. However, any television service that is designed to be broadcast or distributed simultaneously, or virtually simultaneously, to its audience will be held to be "available for reception by members of the public", even where the technical means of distribution is on a one to one basis.

759.   The Secretary of State may by order modify section 361 having regard to: the public's expectations of protection as regards the contents of television programmes; the extent to which members of the public are able to make use of facilities for exercising control over the programmes accessed; the practicability of applying different levels of regulation for different services; the financial impact of any proposed modifications on service providers; and technological developments.

Section 362: Interpretation of Part 3

760.   This section provides for the interpretation of defined terms used in Part 3.

PART 4: LICENSING OF TV RECEPTION

761.   The requirement to hold a licence for the use of a television receiver is currently contained in the Wireless Telegraphy Act 1949, as amended by the Broadcasting Act 1990. The 1990 Act made the BBC (rather than the Secretary of State) responsible for TV licence administration. Part 4 of the Act consolidates the existing provisions relating to the administration and enforcement of TV licences, with amendments, and separates them from provisions relating to other wireless telegraphy licences.

Section 363: Licence required for use of TV receiver

762.   This section prohibits the installation or use of a television receiver without a TV licence issued by the BBC, and makes it an offence, punishable by a fine, for any person to:

- install or use a television receiver without a TV licence; or

- have a television receiver in his possession or under his control, intending to install or use it without a TV licence, or knowing (or having reasonable grounds for believing) that another person intends to install or use it without a TV licence.

763.   *Subsection (5)* exempts from the requirement to hold a TV licence any person who, in the course of business as a dealer, delivers, installs on delivery, demonstrates, tests or repairs television receivers.   *Subsection (6)* gives the Secretary of State the power to make regulations creating further categories of exemptions from the requirement to hold a TV licence for prescribed equipment, persons, circumstances or purposes.

764.   Paragraph 55 of Schedule 18 provides that any television licence granted under the Wireless Telegraphy Act 1949 before the coming into effect of this section shall have effect after its coming into force as a licence for the purposes of this section.

Section 364: TV licences

765.   This section provides for the issuing by the BBC of TV licences. The BBC may include in TV licences such conditions and restrictions as they think fit. They must attach such conditions and restrictions as the Secretary of State directs, and may not attach any conditions expressly prohibited by a direction issued by the Secretary of State. They are also precluded from including any provision conferring a power of entry to any premises.

766.   *Subsection (2)* gives a non-exhaustive list of the type of conditions that might be included in a TV licence, including provisions relating to the type of television receiver covered by the licence, the persons authorised to install or use a television receiver under the licence, and the purpose for which the receiver may be installed or used.

767.   *Subsection (5)* gives the BBC the power to revoke or modify a TV licence either by notice to the licensee or by a general notice published in a manner as specified in the licence. The BBC must modify the conditions or restrictions in a TV licence if directed by the Secretary of State to do so. Otherwise the licence continues for the period specified in the licence.

Section 365: TV licence fees

768.   This section allows the Secretary of State – subject to obtaining the consent of the Treasury - to make regulations setting the fees payable by licensees to the BBC (i) on the issue or renewal of a TV licence; and (ii) in such other circumstances as the Secretary of State provides for in the regulations. Regulations may also allow for concessions, and provide for payment of the licence fee by instalments.

Section 366: Powers to enforce TV licensing

769.   This section sets out procedures for the issue and use of search warrants for the purpose of investigating offences under section 363. *Subsections (1)* and *(2)* provide that a justice of the peace in England or Wales, a sheriff in Scotland, or a lay magistrate in Northern Ireland, may grant a search warrant to one or more persons authorised by the BBC or OFCOM where he is satisfied by information provided under oath that there are reasonable grounds for suspecting (i) that an offence under section 363 has been or is being committed; (ii) that evidence related to such an offence is likely to be on premises or in any vehicle specified in the warrant; and (iii) that one or more of the conditions set out in *subsection (3)* are satisfied.   Those conditions are: that it is impracticable to communicate with any person who may grant entry to the relevant premises or vehicle; that there is no one with whom it is practicable to communicate who is entitled to grant access to the evidence; that entry will not be granted unless a warrant is produced; or that the purpose of the search may be frustrated or seriously prejudiced unless carried out immediately on arrival at the relevant premises or vehicle.

   *vehicle is defined in *subsection (10)* as including any vessel, aircraft or hovercraft.

770.   A warrant granted under this section will be valid for one month after the day of grant. It may grant powers to enter and search specified premises or vehicles and to examine and test any television receiver found there. A warrant issued to a person authorised by OFCOM may only be used to investigate breaches of TV licence conditions relating to radio interference. Persons acting under a warrant may use reasonable force in the exercise of these powers.

771.   *Subsection (7)* imposes a duty on any person who is on the premises specified in the warrant, or who is in, in charge of, or present at the vehicle specified in the warrant, to provide any assistance necessary to enable any person acting under the warrant to examine or test any television receiver found there.

772.   *Subsection (8)* makes it an offence intentionally to obstruct the exercise of any powers granted under a warrant under this section or to fail (without reasonable excuse) to provide any assistance required under *subsection (7)*. A person guilty of such an offence is liable to a fine.

Section 367: Interpretation of provisions about dealer notification

773.   This section replaces the definitions of "television dealer", "television programme" and "television set" in section 6 of the Wireless Telegraphy Act 1967, enabling the Secretary of State, by regulations, to define a television dealer and a television set for the purposes of the dealer notification requirements of the Wireless Telegraphy Act 1967. The apparatus specified in regulations defining television sets may include software used in association with it.

Section 368: Meaning of "television receiver" and "use"

774.   This section defines a television receiver as apparatus of a description defined by the Secretary of State, by order, as a television receiver. The apparatus specified in an order may include software used in association with it.

PART 5: COMPETITION IN COMMUNICATIONS MARKETS

Chapter 1: Functions of OFCOM under Competition Legislation

775.   Chapter 1 of Part 5 of the Act allows OFCOM to exercise concurrent powers with the Office of Fair Trading (OFT) under Part 1 of the Competition Act 1998 and Part 4 of the Enterprise Act 2002.   Currently, the Director General of Telecommunications has concurrent jurisdiction with the OFT to exercise functions under these Acts in so far as they relate to "commercial activities connected with telecommunications" (see section 50 of the Telecommunications Act 1984, as amended by Part 2 of Schedule 9 to the Enterprise Act 2002).   Chapter 1 of Part 5 will give OFCOM concurrent powers in relation to a wider range of activities including broadcasting and related matters.

Section 369: Matters in relation to which OFCOM have competition functions

776.   This section explains the expression "communications matters" as it is used throughout this Chapter.   "Communications matters" include any one or more of the following:

- the provision of electronic communications networks;

- the provision of electronic communications services;

- the making available of services or facilities in association with an electronic communications network or service or for facilitating the use of a network or service;

- apparatus used for any of the above; and

- broadcasting and related matters.

777.   *Subsection (2)* gives the Secretary of State a power by order to amend this definition.   No such order is, however, to be made unless a draft of it has been laid before Parliament and approved by a resolution of each House.

Section 370: OFCOM's functions under Part 4 of the Enterprise Act 2002

778.   This section gives OFCOM current jurisdiction with the OFT to apply and enforce the provisions of Part 4 of the Enterprise Act 2002 (market investigations), with certain limited exceptions, in relation to commercial activities connected with communications matters.

* Under *subsection (4)*, the expression *activities connected with communications matters* includes the supply and export of apparatus used for providing or making available electronic communications networks or services and the production or acquisition of any such apparatus for supply or export.

779.   Part 4 of the Enterprise Act 2002 will replace the monopoly provisions of the Fair Trading Act 1973 with a new regime of "market investigations".   These are designed to complement the Competition Act 1998 by providing a means of addressing problems in markets where competition does not appear to be working well, but where there is no apparent breach of existing competition law.   An example of the sort of circumstances in which a market investigation might take place would be a situation where a few large firms supplied almost the whole of the market and, without there being any agreement between them, they all tended to follow parallel courses of conduct, while new competitors faced significant barriers to entry into the market, and there was little or no evidence of vigorous competition between the existing players (i.e. a non-collusive, uncompetitive oligopoly).   The OFT is able to make a reference to the Competition Commission where it has reasonable grounds to suspect that the structure of a market in or including the UK, or the conduct of persons supplying or acquiring goods, or of their customers, prevents, restricts or distorts competition in connection with the supply or acquisition of goods or services in the UK.   Where the Competition Commission finds that such an adverse effect on competition exists, it is under a duty to take such remedial action within its powers as it considers reasonable and practicable.   A number of sectoral regulators have concurrent powers with the OFT to make market investigation references in respect of markets which fall within their areas of responsibility. The Communications Act will give concurrent powers to OFCOM to exercise the OFT's functions under Part 4 of the Enterprise Act 2002 in relation to commercial activities connected with communications, except that, unlike the OFT, OFCOM will neither be obliged to keep a register of undertakings accepted and orders made under Part 4 (under section 166 of the Enterprise Act 2002) nor will they be obliged to issue guidance on the making of market references (under section 177 of that Act).

780.   *Subsections (5)* and *(6)* are designed to prevent the simultaneous exercise by both OFCOM and the OFT of their powers under Part 4 of the Enterprise Act 2002 in relation to the same matter.   These subsections place those bodies under a duty to consult with each other before exercising any of the concurrent powers under this section and prohibit them from exercising these powers in a case where the other has already done so.

781.   *Subsection (7)* places OFCOM under a duty, where they have referred a matter to the Competition Commission under the provisions of Part 4 of the Enterprise Act 2002, to provide the Competition Commission with any relevant information relevant to the investigation in their possession and with any other assistance that is within their power to give.

782.   *Subsection (8)* gives the Secretary of State the power to conclusively determine any question that arises as to whether OFCOM may carry out any particular function under this section.   However, *subsection (9)* also makes clear that no action

taken by OFCOM under Part 4 of the Enterprise Act 2002 is open to challenge on the grounds that such action should have been taken by the OFT.

783.   *Subsection (10)* applies section 117 of the Enterprise Act 2002 to the carrying out by OFCOM of functions under this section. Section 117 makes it an offence for a person knowingly or recklessly to supply materially false or misleading information to the Secretary of State, the OFT, the Competition Commission or to another person who he knows will use the information for the purpose of providing information to the Secretary of State, the OFT or the Competition Commission.

Section 371: OFCOM's functions under the Competition Act 1998

784.   This section is analogous to the existing provisions of the Competition Act 1998 giving concurrent jurisdiction to other sectoral regulators such as the Director General of Telecommunications. This section gives OFCOM concurrent jurisdiction with the OFT to apply and enforce Part 1 of the Competition Act 1998, with the exception of section 38 (1) to (6) and section 51. This means that OFCOM will be able to exercise almost all of the functions of the OFT under Part 1 of the 1998 Act in so far as they relate to activities connected with communications matters. *Subsection (8)* gives OFCOM concurrent jurisdiction with the OFT with respect to certain transitional provisions of the 1998 Act.

> *Section 38 of the Competition Act 1998 requires the OFT to prepare and publish guidance as to the appropriate amount of any penalty under Part 1 of the Act. Section 51 allows the OFT to make rules (currently in the form of the Competition Act 1998 (Director's Rules) Order 2000, SI 2000 No. 293) setting out the procedures to be followed by the OFT, the sectoral regulators and third parties under Part 1 of the Act.

> *Under *subsection (4)*, the expression *activities connected with communications matters* includes the supply and export of apparatus used for providing or making available electronic communications networks or services and the production or acquisition of any such apparatus for supply or export.

785.   The 1998 Act is based on Articles 81 and 82 of the EC Treaty. It contains two prohibitions: first, of agreements which prevent, restrict or distort competition and which may affect trade within the United Kingdom ('the Chapter I prohibition'); secondly, of conduct which amounts to an abuse of a dominant position in a market which may affect trade within the United Kingdom ('the Chapter II prohibition'). The 1998 Act is generally applied and enforced by the OFT. However, in a number of regulated industries such as telecommunications, gas, electricity, water and sewerage and railway services, functions under the Act are carried out by the sectoral regulator concurrently with the OFT. Examples of the functions in respect of which OFCOM will have concurrent jurisdiction include:

- to investigate possible infringements of the Chapter I or Chapter II prohibitions, either on their own initiative or in response to complaints;

- to impose financial penalties and/or to give directions to bring an infringement of either of the prohibitions to an end; and

- to issue general advice and information on how the Act applies to the communications sector.

786.   OFCOM and the OFT will consult with each other before a decision is made as to who will deal with a case in respect of which there is concurrent jurisdiction. Formal arrangements for consultation are set out in regulations made under the Competition Act 1998. In general, anti-competitive agreements or abusive conduct that relate to activities connected with communications matters will be dealt with by OFCOM (unless the OFT is better placed to do so). Where it is unclear which regulator has jurisdiction, the matter will be referred to, and determined by, the Secretary of State. However, no objection may be made against anything done by OFCOM on the grounds that it should have been done by the OFT.

> *Further provision for the co-ordination of the performance by the OFT and sectoral regulators of concurrent functions in contained in the Competition Act 1998 (Concurrency) Regulations 2000 (SI 2000 No. 260). The OFT and each regulator are also represented on the Concurrency Working Party which was formed in 1997 to ensure full co-ordination between regulators and the OFT and to ensure consistency of approach to casework.

787.   Section 44 of the Competition Act 1998 makes it an offence, directly or indirectly, to provide false or misleading information to the OFT. As *subsection (3)* of this section provides that references to the OFT in Chapter 1 of the Competition Act 1998 are generally to be read as including OFCOM, section 44 of the Competition Act 1998 will also apply in relation to information provided to OFCOM in connection with their exercise of concurrent jurisdiction under that Act.

Section 372: Application of the Competition Act 1998 to news provision

788.   This section amends section 194A of the Broadcasting Act 1990. Under that section, the Secretary of State may declare that any provisions in agreements between regional Channel 3 licence holders for the appointment of the Channel 3 news provider are either not anti-competitive or, if anti-competitive, are proportionate to the objectives being achieved. The effect of such a declaration is that the Chapter I prohibition in the Competition Act 1998 (referred to above) does not apply to those provisions and the OFT cannot use its powers under Chapter 3 of Part 1 of that Act to investigate the agreement. The Secretary of State is obliged to consult the OFT before making such declarations and to notify the OFT after making such declarations.

789.   This section amends the references in section 194A of the Broadcasting Act 1990 to the OFT to refer to both the OFT and to OFCOM. This reflects the concurrent jurisdiction of the OFT and OFCOM under Part 1 of the Competition Act 1998 in relation to communications matters.

790.   Paragraphs 56 and 57 of Schedule 18 (transitional provisions) provide that from the date on which sections 370 and 371 come into force, anything done by the Director General of Telecommunications under the Enterprise Act 2002 or the Competition Act 1998 which OFCOM would, under those provisions, have the power to do in the future, will be taken to have been done by OFCOM. Anything else will, from the date of entry into force, be taken to have been done by the OFT.

Chapter 2: Media mergers

791.   The Enterprise Act 2002 (EA 2002) repealed the majority of the merger provisions of the Fair Trading Act 1973 (FTA 1973) and created a new merger control regime.   However, the special newspaper merger regime contained in sections 57 to 62 FTA 1973 remained intact.   Under the special newspaper regime, a transfer of a newspaper or newspaper assets to a newspaper proprietor requires the prior written consent of the Secretary of State where the newspapers of the proprietor to whom the transfer is made (including the titles being acquired) have an average paid for circulation of 500,000 copies or more per day.   Subject to certain statutory exceptions, the Secretary of State cannot give this consent until the Competition Commission have reported on the matter.   If consent is not obtained when required, the transaction will be unlawful and void.

792.   Consideration of reform of this aspect of the merger control system was deferred so that it could be considered as part of the overall reform of media ownership rules in this Act.   Chapter 2 of Part 5 of this Act makes provision for the repeal of the existing newspaper merger regime provisions and the integration of newspaper mergers into the overall structure of the EA 2002 merger regime. Newspaper mergers will no longer be subject to mandatory pre-notification requirements and the criminal sanctions, which underpin the current regime, will not be continued.

793.   The EA 2002 provides for decisions on the majority of non-newspaper mergers to be taken by the independent competition authorities (the OFT and the Competition Commission) against a new competition-based test of whether they result in a substantial lessening of competition.   This replaces the broader public interest test used in the FTA 1973.   However, the EA 2002 also provides a mechanism whereby the Secretary of State can intervene and decide on particular mergers that raise specified public interest considerations, by the serving of an intervention notice. National security is the only public interest consideration currently specified in section 58 EA 2002, although there is a mechanism in the EA 2002 that enables the Secretary of State to add a new public interest consideration or remove or amend an existing public interest consideration.   The Secretary of State can serve an intervention notice in relation to any transaction that qualifies for consideration by the competition authorities because it is a "relevant merger situation" (see section 23 EA 2002).   She can also serve a "special intervention notice" in relation to mergers involving government defence contractors where the standard qualifying thresholds (i.e. 25% share of supply or UK turnover of company being acquired exceeds £70 million) are not satisfied (i.e. where there is a "special merger situation" - see section 59 EA 2002), allowing these to be examined by reference to the specified public interest consideration(s), but not on competition grounds.

794.   Chapter 2 of Part 5 of the Act integrates treatment of newspaper mergers with the merger regime of the EA 2002.   However, as newspaper mergers can potentially raise public interest concerns beyond the substantial lessening of competition test, provision is also made for public interest considerations relating to newspapers (the

need for accurate presentation of news and free expression of opinion in newspapers, and the need for, to the extent that is reasonable and practicable, a sufficient plurality of views in newspapers) to be specified in section 58 EA 2002 so that the Secretary of State can specify these in an intervention notice or special intervention notice under the EA 2002. Similarly, as media mergers can potentially raise public interest concerns beyond the substantial lessening of competition test, provision is also made for public interest considerations relating to media mergers and cross-media mergers (the need for plurality of persons with control of media enterprises, the need for the availability of a wide range of broadcasting and the need for persons carrying on such enterprises to have a genuine commitment to the broadcasting standards objectives) to be specified in section 58 EA 2002, allowing the Secretary of State to intervene on these grounds. Together, these are referred to as the "media public interest considerations". Provision is also made for OFCOM to have an additional advisory role where the Secretary of State intervenes in a case on media public interest grounds.

Section 373: Repeal of existing newspaper merger regime

795.   This section repeals sections 57 to 62 FTA 1973, which give effect to the existing special newspaper merger regime.

Section 374: Repeal of exclusion for newspaper mergers from general merger controls

796.   This section repeals section 69 EA 2002, which prevents a case from being referred to the Competition Commission under both the special newspaper merger regime in the FTA 1973 and the general merger regime in the EA 2002. With the repeal of sections 57 to 62 FTA 1973 (see section 373) this provision is no longer necessary.

Section 375: Media public interest considerations

797.   Under the EA 2002, the Secretary of State can only intervene in mergers which satisfy the jurisdictional criteria (i.e. where there is a "relevant merger situation" pursuant to section 23 EA 2002 or a "special merger situation" pursuant to section 59 EA 2002) if she believes that a public interest consideration specified in section 58 EA 2002 is relevant.

798.   Currently, only national security is a specified consideration in section 58 EA 2002. This section inserts new sections 58(2A) to (2C) into the EA 2002, which provide for media public interest considerations to be specified in section 58 of that Act, thus giving the Secretary of State the power to intervene in a merger which satisfies the jurisdictional criteria where any of these media public interest considerations are relevant. It also inserts a new section 58A into the EA 2002 for the purposes of construing new section 58(2C).

799.   New subsection (2A) specifies the need for accurate presentation of news and free expression of opinion in newspapers. This carries forward (albeit in a slightly different context) the specific reference to these two factors in the public interest test that is currently applied by the Competition Commission when considering newspaper transfers under the special newspaper merger regime of the FTA 1973 (see section 59(3) FTA 1973).

800.   New subsection (2B) specifies the need for a sufficient plurality of views in newspapers. This is intended to enable a number of plurality issues going beyond free expression or accurate presentation of news to be taken into account, in particular the structural impact of a transaction on the overall range of views and distribution of voice within the market. The test of a sufficient plurality of views is intended to enable regard to be had not only to the need for a sufficient number of views to be expressed, but also to the need for variety in those views, and for there to be a variety of outlets and publications in which they can be expressed. There is a qualitative element to the plurality assessment that requires account to be taken of the context in which titles circulate and the nature of those titles – for example, one title in a particular area may be of greater significance for plurality purposes than another.

801.   The newspaper plurality consideration in subsection (2B) is qualified by the reference to reasonableness and practicability of securing a sufficient plurality of views. This reflects the fact that although plurality in each and every market (which may be different to the economic market used for competition assessment) is the ideal goal of the regime, it may not be reasonable to seek to achieve this in relation to a particular part of the market – for example, because of the associated costs. Moreover, the level of plurality that may be considered reasonable in a large urban area may be different to that which is practicable in a small rural community. In making this assessment the Competition Commission will be able to take into account all relevant circumstances. It will be able to consider, for example, the size and location of the relevant area, and the extent to which other newspapers in the same area contribute to the level of plurality.

802.   New subsection (2C) has three elements: (a) the need in relation to every different audience in the UK or in a particular area or locality of the UK, for there to be a sufficient plurality of persons with control of the media enterprises serving that audience; (b) the need for the availability throughout the UK of a wide range of broadcasting which (taken as a whole) is both of high quality and calculated to appeal to a wide variety of tastes and interests; and (c) the need for persons carrying on media enterprises, and for those with control of such enterprises, to have a genuine commitment to the attainment in relation to broadcasting of the standards objectives set out in the Communications Act 2003. The first limb of this subsection is concerned primarily with ensuring that ownership of media enterprises is not overly concentrated in the hands of a limited number of persons. The second and third limbs of the test look at the content of the media enterprises involved and the extent to which media owners demonstrate a genuine commitment to complying with the standards objectives – i.e. complying with the spirit and not just the letter of the objectives.

803.   Section 375 also inserts a new section 58A into the EA 2002. New section 58A contains provisions relating to the operation of the public interest considerations set out in new section 58(2C). Section 58A(1) states that for the purposes of section 58, a media enterprise is one that consists in or involves broadcasting. Section 58A(2) provides that a newspaper enterprise may also be a media enterprise for the purposes of section 58 if it is involved in a merger with a broadcast media enterprise. This enables cross media mergers involving newspaper enterprises to be assessed against the public interest considerations specified in subsection (2C). Section 58A(3) clarifies that a newspaper enterprise is one consisting in or involving the supply of newspapers.

804.   New section 58A(4) makes clear that where a merger situation (i.e. a relevant merger situation or a special merger situation) involves two media enterprises serving the same audience, then there is deemed to be a reduction in the number of such media enterprises for the purposes of the plurality assessment in subsection (2C)(a). This means that all such mergers, including those involving an increase in levels of control of such media enterprises, may be scrutinised for the purposes of subsection (2C)(a), even though the number of enterprises may in fact be unchanged.

805.   New section 58A(5) ensures that the authorities can look at the substance of who controls media enterprises when carrying out a plurality assessment.

806.   New section 58A(5)(a) provides that, for the purposes of section 58, where a number of media enterprises would fall to be treated as under common ownership or common control for the purposes of section 26 of the EA 2002, they are treated as being controlled by one person. This is because, in assessing the effect of a merger on the sufficiency of plurality of persons with control of media enterprises, the decision-making authorities need to assess the total number of persons with control of media enterprises and what effect the merger will have on the plurality of media as a whole. Apart from the merging media enterprises, in order to get an accurate picture of who has control of the remaining media enterprises, it is important to be able to look not just at the owners of those entities, but at the persons with ultimate control of those entities.

807.   New section 58A(5)(b) provides that where a number of media enterprises are otherwise under the same ownership or control, they are treated as being controlled by one person. This is intended to cover any situation where the other media players may have never been "brought" under common ownership or control at any point in the section 26 EA 2002 sense.

808.   New section 58A(6) gives the decision-making authorities discretion to determine what is meant by the "audience" of a media enterprise for the purposes of subsection (2C) and section 58A in whichever of the ways specified in subsection (6) they considers appropriate. This enables the decision-making authority to treat different audiences as separate or to group them, or any of them, together. This is modelled on the discretion given to the decision-making authorities in assessing whether the share of supply threshold under the standard merger regime is

satisfied. Subsection (7) builds on this by making clear that the criteria for deciding the composition of an audience shall be such as the decision-making authority considers appropriate and may include potential members of that audience.

809.   New section 58A(8) clarifies that audience includes readership. This will be relevant in the context of cross media mergers involving a newspaper enterprise.

810.   New section 58A(9) extends the power in section 58(3) to modify the public interest considerations specified in section 58 so that modifications can also be made to the provisions of section 58A which construe section 58(2C). Any order made pursuant to section 58(3) to add, remove or amend a public interest consideration in that section is subject to the affirmative resolution procedure (see section 124 EA 2002).

811.   Section 375(3) amends section 127(1) of the EA 2002 so that, when determining whether enterprises are under common control for the purposes of new section 58(2C), associated persons are treated as one person. This provision enables interests held by family members, business partners etc to be aggregated.

Section 376: Adaptation of role of OFT in initial investigations and reports

812.   Under the public interest regime of the EA 2002, where the Secretary of State has intervened in a merger, the OFT is obliged to prepare a report for the Secretary of State under section 44 EA 2002. This section amends section 44 EA 2002 to adapt the role of the OFT in relation to mergers where a media public interest consideration has been specified in an intervention notice.

813.   *Subsection (1)* makes amendments to section 44(3)(b) EA 2002 to provide that the OFT's duty to provide the Secretary of State with a summary of relevant representations received in relation to public interest considerations mentioned in the intervention notice does not extend to representations received in relation to media public interest considerations. This is to avoid duplication, as OFCOM will have this duty where a media public interest consideration has been specified in the intervention notice (see section 377).

814.   *Subsection (2)* adds a new section 44(5A) EA 2002 that ensures that the OFT nonetheless has the power to include such a summary of representations. Such a power might be used, for example, if the OFT received representations after OFCOM had delivered its report, in order to ensure that representations were drawn to the Secretary of State's attention. It also clarifies that the OFT is not required to artificially separate out plurality and competition issues where this is unhelpful to the overall purpose of advising the Secretary of State.

815.   *Subsection (3)* inserts new sections 44(8) to (10) into the EA 2002. Sections 44(8), (9) and (10) contain the definitions of "media public interest consideration", "broadcasting" and "newspaper". The definition of "media public interest consideration" encompasses the considerations in new section 58(2A) to

(2C) EA 2002 that are inserted by section 375 of this Act or any other public interest consideration concerning broadcasting or newspapers that the Secretary of State thinks should be specified in section 58 EA 2002. This latter aspect could encompass, for example, any changes to the existing media public interest considerations that the Secretary of State thinks ought to be made. The definition of "broadcasting" covers the provision of services, the provision of which is required to be licensed under Part 1 or 3 of the Broadcasting Act 1990 or Part 1 or 2 of the Broadcasting Act 1996, or which would be required to be so licensed if provided by a person subject to licensing under the Part in question. The latter part of the definition is intended to capture services provided by the BBC or the Welsh Authority, or by broadcasters established abroad and broadcasting into the UK under EC licences. Although neither the BBC nor the Welsh Authority could be involved in a merger situation, this broad definition allows the Secretary of State to take account of the existence of their services when carrying out an assessment of the sufficiency of plurality of controllers of media enterprises for the purposes of new section 58(2C)(a). The definition of "newspaper" is the same as that currently used for the purposes of the special newspaper regime in the FTA 1973. This covers daily and Sunday newspapers (whether national or local) and local periodical newspapers.

816.   New section 44(11) EA 2002 sets out a power for the Secretary of State to amend the definition of "newspaper" or of "broadcasting" by statutory instrument. This power is designed to deal with future developments in the nature of the newspaper or broadcasting markets that might mean that the scope of the media public interest consideration should be redefined (for example, in relation to newspapers, if it became more common for newspaper titles to circulate across national boundaries such that important UK titles did not necessarily circulate "wholly or mainly" in the UK). An order under new section 44(11) can only be made after a draft has been laid before, and approved by a resolution of, each House of Parliament (see paragraph 24 of Schedule 16, which amends section 124 EA 2002).

Section 377: Additional investigation and report by OFCOM

817.   This section inserts a new section 44A in the EA 2002, which sets out OFCOM's reporting and related investigatory duties where an intervention notice has been served specifying any media public interest consideration.

818.   New section 44A(2) provides that OFCOM are obliged to report to the Secretary of State within a deadline specified by the Secretary of State. There is nothing to prevent the Secretary of State from altering the deadline if the circumstances so require. New section 44A(3) ensures that the Secretary of State will receive information in the report on at least two areas:

- OFCOM's advice and recommendations on any media public interest consideration mentioned in the intervention notice; and

- OFCOM's summary of the relevant representations that it has received in relation to any such media public interest consideration.

Section 378: Extension of special public interest regime for certain media mergers

819.   This section amends section 59 EA 2002, which currently makes provision for the Secretary of State to intervene and serve a "special intervention notice" in relation to an exceptional category of mergers involving government defence contractors. These may be referred for investigation, on specified public interest grounds only, even though they do not meet the normal qualifying thresholds (i.e. 25% share of supply or UK turnover of the company being acquired exceeds £70 million, as set out in section 23 EA 2002).

820.   *Subsection (1)* replaces sections 59(3) and (4) EA 2002 with new sections 59(3) to (3D). These incorporate the existing criteria set out in section 59 EA 2002 for establishing a "special merger situation" in cases involving government defence contractors, together with new provisions providing that a special merger situation also arises where:

- all of the criteria for a relevant merger situation within section 23 EA 2002 have been met except for the share of supply or turnover thresholds in sections 23(1)(b) and (2)(b) EA 2002 – that is, where two or more enterprises have ceased to be distinct within the relevant time limits (see sections 24-27 EA 2002); and

- at least 25% of the supply of newspapers of any description in the UK, or in a substantial part of the UK, was supplied by persons carrying on one of the enterprises concerned in the merger (unlike the general jurisdiction test in section 23(2)-(4) EA 2002, there is no requirement that the share of supply is created or enhanced by the merger); or

- at least 25% of the provision of broadcasting of any description, provided in the UK or a substantial part of the UK was provided by the person who carried on one of the enterprises involved in the merger. (As in the case of extended jurisdiction for newspapers, there is no requirement that this 25% share is created or enhanced).

821.   Intervention in relation to cases that fall within the special public interest regime is limited to the public interest grounds specified in section 58 EA 2002. They cannot be scrutinised on competition grounds.

822.   *Subsection (2)* inserts new subsection (6A) in section 59 EA 2002. Subsection (6A) gives the Secretary of State a power to amend the share of supply conditions relating to the broadcasting and newspaper extended jurisdiction. In particular, this will ensure that in the event that the Secretary of State exercises her powers in section 123 EA 2002 in order to amend the share of supply test in section 23 EA 2002, the changes can be carried across to section 59 EA 2002, such that the share of supply test remains consistent throughout Part 3 EA 2002.

823.   *Subsection (3)* inserts new section 59A into the EA 2002. This replicates for

the new newspaper and broadcasting share of supply provisions in the special public interest regime the provisions on the calculation of share of supply already included for the standard regime in section 23 EA 2002. New section 59A(1) makes it clear that, for the purposes of applying the newspaper share of supply test in new section 59(3C) or the broadcasting share of supply test in section 59(3D) the authorities can apply such criteria (such as value, cost, quantity etc.) as they consider appropriate to determine whether the 25% threshold is satisfied. New section 59A(2) allows the authorities to consider whether goods or services taken on their own, or with others or in groups, make up this proportion. Sections 59A(3), 59A(4) and 59A(5) give the competition authorities the discretion to decide when goods or services are the subject of different forms of supply.

Section 379: Adaptation of role of OFT in special public interest regime

824.   Under the special public interest regime of the EA 2002, where the Secretary of State has intervened in a merger under this regime, the OFT is obliged to prepare a report for the Secretary of State under section 61 of that Act. This section amends section 61 EA 2002 to adapt the role of the OFT in relation to mergers under the special public interest regime where a media public interest consideration has been specified in a special intervention notice.

825.   *Subsection (2)* makes amendments to section 61(3)(b) EA 2002 to provide that the OFT's duty to provide the Secretary of State with a summary of relevant representations received in relation to public interest considerations mentioned in the special intervention notice does not extend to representations about media public interest considerations. This is to avoid duplication, as OFCOM will have this duty (see section 380) where a media public interest consideration, which is specified in section 58 at the time, has been mentioned in the special intervention notice. The amendments made by this section refer only to considerations specified in sections 58(2A), (2B) and (2C) at the time of the notice, because the special public interest regime has no equivalent to the provisions in the standard public interest regime by which the Secretary of State can intervene on the basis of a new public interest consideration which has not been specified in section 58 (see section 42(3) EA 2002).

826.   *Subsection (4)* adds a new section 61(4A) EA 2002 to ensure that the OFT nonetheless has the power to include such a summary of representations. Such a power might be used, for example, if the OFT received representations after OFCOM had delivered its report, in order to ensure that representations were drawn to the Secretary of State's attention.

Section 380: Additional investigation and report by OFCOM: special public interest cases

827.   This section inserts a new section 61A in the EA 2002, which sets out OFCOM's reporting and related investigatory duties where a special intervention notice has been served mentioning any of the media public interest considerations that are specified in section 58(2A), (2B) or (2C) EA 2002. The new section refers

only to considerations specified in section 58(2A), (2B) or (2C) at the time of the giving of the special intervention notice because the special public interest regime has no equivalent to the provisions in the standard public interest regime by which the Secretary of State can intervene on the basis of a new public interest consideration which has not been specified in section 58 (see section 42(3) EA 2002).

828. New section 61A(2) provides that OFCOM is obliged to report to the Secretary of State within a deadline specified by the Secretary of State. There is nothing to prevent the Secretary of State from altering the deadline if the circumstances so require. New section 61A(3) ensures that the Secretary of State will receive information in the report on at least two areas:

- OFCOM's advice and recommendations on any media public interest considerations specified in section 58(2A), (2B) or (2C) and mentioned in the special intervention notice; and

- OFCOM's summary of the relevant representations that it has received in relation to any such media public interest consideration.

Section 381: Public consultation in relation to media mergers

829. This section introduces a new section 104A EA 2002, which applies only to references to the Competition Commission that specify a media public interest consideration. In conducting its inquiry into such cases the Competition Commission is specifically required, so far as it is practicable, to have regard to the need to consult the sections of the public that may be affected by the merger. The duty can be discharged by consulting such representative sample of the public as the Commission considers to be appropriate for this purpose. This duty applies in addition to the Commission's normal duties of investigation in relation to merger references in public interest cases (see sections 50(3) and 65(4) EA 2002).

Section 382: General information duties in relation to media mergers

830. This section amends section 105 EA 2002 to ensure that, where a media public interest consideration is invoked, OFCOM, as well as the OFT and the Competition Commission, will have general information duties vis-à-vis those that might be affected by the merger, each other and the Secretary of State.

831. *Subsection (2)* inserts a new section 105(1A) EA 2002 to ensure that where OFCOM are required to produce a report on any media public interest consideration, they will act, if practicable, to bring cases that they are investigating to the attention of those that might be affected by the transaction. The effect of the amendment to section 105(2) in *subsection (3)* is that this duty does not apply to merger notice cases, which carry their own publicity requirements (see section 99 EA 2002).

832. *Subsections (4) and (6)* amend section 105(3) and 105(4) EA 2002 to ensure that OFT has the same obligations to give relevant information to OFCOM as it

already has for the Competition Commission.

833.   *Subsections (5) and (7)* insert new sections 105(3A) and (4A) EA 2002 to provide that OFCOM will give relevant information to the OFT and the Competition Commission.

834.   *Subsections (8) and (9)* amend sections 105(5) and (6) EA 2002 to ensure that OFCOM have the same obligations as the OFT and the Competition Commission to give information and assistance to the Secretary of State in order to enable her to carry out her functions in relation to cases that raise public interest considerations.

835.   *Subsection (10)* amends section 105(7) EA 2002 to extend the duties of the Competition Commission and the Secretary of State to have regard to information given to them under sections 105(3) to (6) so as to encompass information supplied to them under those sections by OFCOM.

836.   *Subsection (11)* inserts a new section 105(7A) EA 2002, which provides that OFCOM must have regard to any information given to it by the OFT under sections 105(3) or (4) EA 2002 and that the OFT must have regard to any information given to it by OFCOM under new sections 105(3A) or 105(4A).

Section 383: Advice and information in relation to media mergers

837.   This section inserts a new section 106A EA 2002, which provides that the Secretary of State may publish advice and information to explain the media public interest considerations specified in sections 58(2A), (2B) and (2C) EA 2002 and to indicate how the Secretary of State expects the merger provisions of the EA 2002 to operate in relation to them. If the Secretary of State chooses to publish such advice she will be required, in preparing the advice, to consult the OFT, OFCOM, the Commission and such other persons as she considers appropriate.

Section 384: General advisory functions of OFCOM in relation to media mergers

838.   This section inserts a new section 106B EA 2002 setting out the general advisory functions of OFCOM.   In any case where a media public interest consideration has been invoked, OFCOM may give advice to the Secretary of State on any report by the Competition Commission on the case and the taking of enforcement action by the Secretary of State.

839.   There is also a general power for OFCOM to give advice where the Secretary of State has requested this in connection with any case on which they are required to report. This could be used, for example, in the event that the Secretary of State required supplementary advice on a particular aspect of a case. Except for the specific cases mentioned in new section 106B(1), this section does not empower OFCOM to give advice unless the Secretary of State has requested it.

840.   Any advice that is given will be published (subject to compliance with the

provisions of Part 9 EA 2002 relating to disclosure of information, in particular section 244 EA 2002), but not before the publication of the Competition Commission's report on the case.

Section 385: Other general functions of OFCOM in relation to media mergers

841.   This section inserts a new section 119A EA 2002 that gives OFCOM the function of obtaining and reviewing information relating to any of its functions in relation to the media public interest considerations. This information-gathering role, which may involve research, is with a view to OFCOM having the information it needs to make decisions and carry out its functions under Part 3 EA 2002.

842.   Subsection (4) of new section 119A EA 2002 provides that the general duties of OFCOM under section 3 of this Act do not apply when OFCOM are exercising their functions under the media merger provisions of the EA 2002 (see also section 3(7) of this Act). In practice the media merger provisions will operate as part of the EA 2002, and this Act has its own provisions setting out the functions and responsibilities of the different authorities.

Section 386: Monitoring role for OFT in relation to media mergers

843.   This section inserts a new section 119B EA 2002, which gives the OFT the function of obtaining and reviewing information that may be relevant to the Secretary of State's decision on whether or not to intervene on the basis of the media public interest considerations set out in section 58(2A), (2B) or (2C) EA 2002. In particular, the OFT in carrying out this function will ensure that the Secretary of State is made aware of cases where (in the OFT's opinion) she may wish to consider issuing a special intervention notice. The OFT will not be under any obligation to carry out a detailed analysis of any media public interest consideration that may be relevant.

844.   This section only applies to such cases where they may fall within the special public interest consideration regime in relation to a media public interest consideration. The OFT's duties in relation to public interest cases falling within the standard regime are already fully set out in the EA 2002 (see section 5 and Chapter 2 of Part 3 EA 2002).

Section 387: Enforcement powers in relation to newspaper and other media mergers

845.   This section inserts a new paragraph 20A in Schedule 8 EA 2002, which contains the list of matters that can be included in final orders for the purpose of remedying, mitigating or preventing any adverse public interest effects which have resulted, or may be expected to result, from a merger involving a newspaper enterprise. Remedies to an adverse finding on the basis of the media public interest consideration may be different in character to the remedies directed at competition detriments with which Schedule 8 is principally concerned. Accordingly, paragraph 20A allows the Secretary of State to make such provision, in relation to these cases,

as she considers appropriate in all the circumstances. Sub-paragraph (4) sets out a non-exhaustive list of the type of steps that might be taken in exercise of this power. These are remedies that experience in dealing with newspaper transfers under the FTA 1973 has shown it would be useful to be able to call upon.

846.   This provision applies only to orders made in cases where (i) any of the newspaper public interest considerations were specified in the intervention/special intervention notice and remain relevant at the point of a decision on remedies, or (ii) where a consideration in section 58(2C) has been specified, provided that the relevant merger situation or special merger situation in question is one where one of the enterprises ceasing to be distinct is a newspaper enterprise.

847.   New sub-paragraph (5) sets out the definition of a "newspaper public interest consideration". This is defined as a media public interest consideration other than one which is set out in section 58(2C) or which is a consideration concerned with broadcasting which the Secretary of State thought ought to have been specified in section 58.

Section 388: Alterations to newspaper panel of Competition Commission

848.   This section amends the definition of "newspaper merger reference" in paragraph 1 of Schedule 7 to the Competition Act 1998. Schedule 7 to that Act makes provision about the Competition Commission and includes provisions on the appointment of newspaper panel members to the group selected to carry out an inquiry following a reference. The effect of this amendment is that the provisions on the appointment of newspaper panel members to any constituted group will only apply where a merger reference is made specifying a newspaper public interest consideration.

Section 389: Further provision in connection with media mergers

849.   *Subsection (1)* of this section gives effect to Schedule 16, which contains further amendments in connection with media mergers.

850.   *Subsection (2)* extends to the provisions of this Chapter of the Act and its related repeals the provisions of sections 276(2) and (3) and 277 EA 2002, which gives the Secretary of State the power to make by order supplementary, incidental or consequential provisions for the purposes of, or in consequence of, or for giving full effect to, the EA 2002. *Subsection (3)* clarifies, for the avoidance of doubt, that this includes the power to modify the EA 2002.

PART 6: MISCELLANEOUS AND SUPPLEMENTAL

Section 390: Annual report on the Secretary of State's functions

851.   This section requires the Secretary of State to prepare and lay before Parliament annual reports about the performance of her functions under the

following legislation: this Act, the enactments relating to the management of the radio spectrum which are not part of this Act, the Office of Communications Act 2002 and the Broadcasting Acts 1990 and 1996. The first report must be prepared as soon as reasonably practicable after the first anniversary of the first order under section 2 transferring functions to OFCOM. The enactments relating to the management of the radio spectrum, in addition to Chapter 2 of Part 2 of the Act, are the Wireless Telegraphy Acts 1949, 1967 and 1998, the Marine, &c., Broadcasting (Offences) Act 1967 and Part 6 of the Telecommunications Act 1984 (see section 405).

Section 391: Review of media ownership

852.   OFCOM are required to carry out regular reviews of the operation of all media ownership and news provider provisions. OFCOM will provide a report on every review to the Secretary of State, including recommendations on whether the Secretary of State should exercise the powers available to modify, repeal or revoke rules contained in enactments and secondary legislation. OFCOM must publish every report in such a manner that it is brought to the attention of those persons whom OFCOM feel are likely to be affected by it. The first review must be carried out no more than 3 years after the commencement of this section, and subsequent reviews must be carried out at least every 3 years.

Section 392: Penalties imposed by OFCOM

853.   This section requires OFCOM to prepare, publish and keep up-to-date guidelines for determining the penalties to be imposed by them under the Act (including any that the BBC may be liable to pay) or under any other enactment, except the Competition Act 1998. Before publishing any guidelines, OFCOM must consult the Secretary of State and other appropriate persons. When determining the amount of any penalty to be imposed OFCOM must have regard to their published guidelines.

Section 393: General restrictions on disclosure of information

854.   With the exception of information obtained in accordance with section 196 of the Broadcasting Act 1990 (powers of entry and search, under which stricter rules apply), this section imposes limits on the disclosure of information relating to the affairs of any particular business obtained under this Act, the other enactments relating to the management of the radio spectrum and the Broadcasting Acts 1990 and 1996. *Subsection (1)* prohibits the disclosure of such information while the business in question is still being carried on, unless consent has been obtained from the person carrying on that business.

855.   *Subsections (2)* to *(5)* provide for a limited number of exemptions from this prohibition where the disclosure satisfies certain criteria. Examples of exempt disclosures include those required to facilitate the carrying out by OFCOM of their duties; disclosures necessary for the carrying out by Ministers, the OFT, the Competition Commission, the Consumer Panel or the Welsh Authority of duties

under this Act or other specified enactments; and disclosures made in connection with civil proceedings brought under this Act or other specified enactments.

856. In addition, *subsection (6)* provides that this section will not (i) limit information that may be published by OFCOM under sections 15 and 26 as results of research or as information or advice, in the Secretary of state's annual report under section 390 or in reports by OFCOM under any other provision of this Act or the Office of Communications Act 2002; (ii) prevent the disclosure of information for the purposes of a report of legal proceedings or (iii) apply to any information that has already been published or made public under (i) or (ii).

857. *Subsection (10)* makes it an offence for any person to disclose information in contravention of this section.

Section 394: Service of notifications and other documents

858. When any person is authorised or required to send a notification and/or document to another person under this Act, the Office of Communications Act 2002, the enactments relating to radio spectrum management not contained in this Act, Schedule 2 to the Telecommunications Act 1984 or the Broadcasting Acts 1990 and 1996, it may be delivered, left at the proper address or sent by post.

*The meaning of proper address is given in *subsection (7)* and *(8)*.

859. When the recipient is a company, a partnership or unincorporated association, the notification and/or document may be addressed to the person(s) specified, respectively, in *subsections (4), (5) and (6)*.

Section 395: Notifications and documents in electronic form

860. This section applies where a person is authorised under section 394 to give or send a notification or other document by delivering it to another person and does so either by transmitting it electronically by means of an electronic communications network or transmitting it by other means but in a form that means that other apparatus must be used to make it intelligible (e.g. sending a computer disk by post). If the intended recipient is not OFCOM, he must have agreed with the sender to that the notification and/or document may be delivered in that way and form (and not have withdrawn his agreement), and must have provided the sender with his address and other information needed to send them.

861. If the intended recipient is OFCOM, OFCOM must have indicated their agreement to receive the notification and/or document in the form in question and the thing transmitted and the means of transmission must comply with any conditions and procedures determined and published by OFCOM. When transmitting a notification and/or document, OFCOM may determine the means of transmission used and the form in which they may be transmitted (subject to *subsection (5)*).

862.   *Subsection (5)* provides that, if the intended recipient is not OFCOM, he must have agreed with the sender that the notification and/or document may be delivered in that way and in that form (and not have withdrawn his agreement), and must have provided the sender with his address and other information needed to send the notification or document.

Section 396: Timing and location of things done electronically

863.   The Secretary of State may by order make provision for determining the times and places at which things are done electronically under this Act, the Office of Communications Act 2002, the enactments relating to radio spectrum management not contained in this Act, Schedule 2 to the Telecommunications Act 1984 and the Broadcasting Acts 1990 and 1996.   The Secretary of State may also specify how anything carried out electronically for the purposes of those Acts, including any requirements relating to time and place, may be proved in legal proceedings.

Section 397: Purchase of Duchy of Lancaster land

864.   This section gives the Duchy of Lancaster a general power to sell land to persons who provide public electronic communications networks.

Section 398: Repeal of certain provisions of the Telecommunications Act 1984

865.   This section will repeal the spent provisions dealing with the privatisation of British Telecommunications set out in sections 60, 61(1) to (6), 62, 63(1) to (4), 64 to 67, 69 to 71, 72(2), (4) and (5) and 73 of the Telecommunications Act 1984. This section also amends section 68(2) of the 1984 Act to reflect the fact that the only outstanding liability of British Telecommunications plc for which the Secretary of State might be responsible is the payment of pensions, and repeals sections 93 and 97 of the Telecommunications Act 1984.

*Section 93 of the 1984 Act allows the Secretary of State (with the consent of the Treasury) to make grants towards fees or expenses incurred in the development or use of apparatus that is designed or adapted for disabled persons. Section 97 allows local authorities to contribute towards the cost of the provision by public telecommunications operators of telecommunications facilities that they consider to be of benefit to their area.

Section 399: Expenses

866.   Any expenditure by the Secretary of State in carrying out her functions under the Act, and any increase caused by this Act in sums payable under other Acts, shall be met from money provided by Parliament.

Section 400: Destination of licence fees and penalties

867.   Where OFCOM receive money in any of the circumstances listed in *subsection (1)*, they must pay it into the Consolidated Fund of the United Kingdom or Northern Ireland in accordance with *subsection (2)*. The circumstances in

subsection (1) include the imposition by OFCOM of a fine under Chapter 1 of Part 2, section 175 or Part 3 of this Act (including any imposed on the BBC), Part 1 or 3 of the 1990 Act or Part 1 or 2 of the 1996 Act and the receipt of fees for auctioned telephone numbers, of spectrum fees under the Wireless Telegraphy Act 1998 (c. 6) and of amounts paid to OFCOM under a Broadcasting Act licence by way of additional payments during the period for which the licence is in force and for subsequent years.

868.　OFCOM must prepare an annual account that shows the amounts received by them, the sums paid into the Consolidated Funds of the United Kingdom and Northern Ireland, the amount retained by them in accordance with any statement of principles they may make under section 401 and the cost to OFCOM of carrying out the functions to be covered by that retained amount. The report must be sent to the Comptroller and Auditor General, who must certify and report on the account. He must also lay a copy of OFCOM's annual account and his report before each House of Parliament.

Section 401: Power of OFCOM to retain costs of carrying out spectrum functions

869.　This section allows OFCOM, subject to the approval of the Treasury, to introduce a new system for meeting the cost carrying out their spectrum functions. Section 400(1)(c) provides for sums received by OFCOM under the Wireless Telegraphy Act 1998 to be paid to the Consolidated Fund. Under this section, OFCOM would be able to retain out of those sums sufficient amounts to cover the cost of carrying out most of their spectrum functions.

870.　*Subsections (1) and (2)* would enable OFCOM to make a statement of principles under which they could retain amounts received by them under the Wireless Telegraphy Act 1998. Under *subsections (3) and (4)*, the principles contained in any statement must secure, on the basis of such estimates of the likely costs as it is practicable to make, that on a year by year basis, the aggregate amount retained by OFCOM does not exceed the amount required to meet the annual cost to OFCOM of carrying out their functions in relation to the management of the radio spectrum. The amounts retained by OFCOM must be objectively justifiable and proportionate to the costs and the relationship between the costs and the amounts retained must be transparent. *Subsection (5)* excludes functions under sections 22(2), 28, 152(1), (2), (5) and (8), 155, 158, 168 and 175 to 177 of this Act and section 5 of the Wireless Telegraphy Act 1949 (since inclusion of those functions would be contrary to the EC Electronic Communications Authorisation Directive).

871.　As charges for licences covering several years are sometimes paid as a lump sum in one year, *subsection (6)* allows for amounts received in one year to be treated as referable to costs incurred in that year and in one or more subsequent years and to be brought into account in each of those years in accordance with an apportionment made in the statement of principles. *Subsection (7)* allows any deficit or surplus to be carried forward and taken into account in determining what is required by OFCOM in the following year to meet the costs of carrying out their spectrum functions.

872.   Where a statement of principles has effect for a limited period or is withdrawn, *subsection (8)* provides that it does not apply to any amounts paid to OFCOM after the end of the period or after the withdrawal takes effect. *Subsection (9)* enables OFCOM to revise a statement of principles. *Subsection (10)* requires the consent of HM Treasury to be given for the making, revision or withdrawal of any statement of principles. *Subsection (11)* requires publication of so much of a statement of principles as demonstrates compliance with the requirements of *subsection (3)*.

Section 402: Power of Secretary of State to make orders and regulations

873.   This section sets out how the Secretary of State is to exercise her powers to make orders or regulations under the Act (other than those conferred by Schedule 4), and makes additional provisions in respect of these powers.

Section 403: Regulations and orders made by OFCOM

874.   This section sets out how OFCOM are to exercise their powers to make orders or regulations under the provisions in the Act and provisions inserted in other Acts which apply this section, and makes additional provision in respect of these powers. The orders and regulations concerned must be made by statutory instrument; and where the provision in the Act and provisions inserted in other Acts under which the instrument is made provides for it to be laid before Parliament, OFCOM must send it to the Secretary of State for that to be done. *Subsections (4) to (6)* provide that OFCOM must give notice before making orders or regulations to which this section applies and must allow a period of at least one month for representations to be made on any proposal by them to make such orders or regulations. The procedural requirements in this section implement Articles 14(1) and 33 of the Universal Service Directive and Article 6 of the Framework Directive.

Section 404: Criminal liability of company directors etc.

875.   This section provides that, where an offence under this Act, the Wireless Telegraphy Act 1949, the Marine, &c., Broadcasting (Offences) Act 1967, or the Telecommunications Act 1984 is committed by a body corporate, then a director, manager, secretary or other officer of that body corporate (including a member of a body corporate which is managed by its members) will also be liable for prosecution if it is proved that he had given their consent to the offence or had connived in its commission or if the commission is attributable to neglect on the part of the person in question.

Section 405: General interpretation

876.   This section provides for interpretation of defined terms in the Act.

Section 406: Minor and consequential amendments, transitionals and repeals

877.   Schedule 17, which provides for minor and consequential amendments to

other legislation, and Schedule 18, which contains transitional provisions in connection with other legislation, have effect. Furthermore, the provisions set out in Schedule 19 are repealed or revoked as specified in that Schedule. These Schedules are described in more detail below. *Subsections (2), (3) and (5)* also give the Secretary of State a limited power and, in the case of some local legislation, a duty to make consequential amendments of other legislation by order. *Subsection (4)* confers a further power by order to make consequential modifications to enactments extending only to Scotland, enactments extending only to Northern Ireland, local enactments and subordinate legislation.

Section 407: Pre-consolidation amendments

878. The Secretary of State may by order modify enactments relating to the management of the radio spectrum (as defined in section 405), the enactments relating to broadcasting (the Broadcasting Acts 1990 and 1996, Part 3 of the Act and other provisions of the Act dealing with them) and other enactments referring to these enactments in order to facilitate consolidation. An order may not be made unless an Act for repealing and re-enacting the enactments has been presented to Parliament.

Section 408: Transitional provision for anticipatory carrying out of functions

879. This section applies where an order made under section 411 bringing into force any of the following provisions of the Act: (i) a provision of Part 2 of the Act, (ii) a provision of Chapter 1 of Part 5; or (iii) a provision of Part 1 or 6 relating to a provision of Part 2 or of Chapter 1 of Part 5 or any enactment relating to the management of the radio spectrum, states that such a provision is brought into force for the purposes of enabling specified networks and services functions, or specified spectrum functions, to be carried out during the transitional period by the Director General of Telecommunications or the Secretary of State.

880. Any provision brought into force during the transitional period has effect as if references in that provision to OFCOM and references to OFCOM inserted by that provision in any other enactment were references to either the Director General of Telecommunications or the Secretary of State, as the case may be.

> **Subsection (6)* defines *the transitional period. Subsections (7) and (8),* respectively, define *networks and services functions* and *spectrum functions.*

881. This section should be read with paragraph 2 of Schedule 18, which provides that steps taken by the Secretary of State or OFCOM before a power or duty is conferred or imposed on either of them or transferred to OFCOM are to be treated as satisfying any requirement for steps to be taken prior to the exercise of the power or duty. This provision also applies to steps taken by the Director General of Telecommunications or the Secretary of State when section 408 applies.

882. The provisions of the Act which implement the four EC Communications Directives will be brought into force very quickly between Royal Assent and the date

on which those Directives must be implemented: 25 July 2003. The necessary steps under the Act for OFCOM to be able to exercise its functions under these provisions have not yet been completed. As a result, these functions will initially be exercised by the Director General of Telecommunications and the Secretary of State under section 408; and they have taken preparatory steps in advance under paragraph 2 of Schedule 18.

Section 409: Modifications consequential on regulations implementing Directives

883.   This section permits the Secretary of State (by order, subject to approval of a draft by Parliament) to amend the Act if regulations have been made under the European Communities Act 1972 to implement the four Directives cited in subsection (4) prior to the passing of the Act. These Directives have to be implemented in the European Community on 25 July 2003. Subsection (2) permits the Secretary of State to repeal provisions of the Act which have become redundant, modify the Act as necessary in consequence of the regulations, revoke the regulations and make transitory or transitional provisions. In the event, regulations of the type described in subsection (1) were not made before the Act was passed, the condition in that subsection can never be satisfied and, accordingly, it is not intended that this section will be brought into force.

Section 410: Application of enactments to territorial sea and other waters

884.   This section permits Her Majesty by an Order in Council to apply the provisions of Part 2 of the Act, the enactments relating to the management of the radio spectrum not contained in Part 2 of the Act and any related provision in Chapter 1 of Part 5 of the Act to the territorial sea and other waters of the United Kingdom.

Section 411: Short title, commencement and extent

885.   This section gives the Secretary of State a power to bring the provisions of this Act into force by order on appointed days and different days may be appointed for different purposes. This section and sections 31(1) to (4) and (6) and 405 came into force upon Royal Assent. This section also provides that the Act extends to Northern Ireland and that it may, by Order in Council, be extended to the Channel Islands and the Isle of Man.

SCHEDULES

Schedule 1: Functions transferred to OFCOM

886.   This is described in the notes to section 2.

Schedule 2: Transfer schemes

887.   This is described in more detail in the notes to section 30. The property, rights and liabilities capable of being transferred under paragraph 1 of the Schedule is

intended to include the rights and liabilities of the ITC as the Principal Employer of
ITC Pension Plan.

Schedule 3: Amendments of Schedule 2 to the Telecommunications Act 1984

888.   This Schedule (together with sections 106 to 119) amends the
telecommunications code (set out in Schedule 2 to the Telecommunications Act 1984)
in order to translate it into a code applicable to apparatus used in electronic
communications networks and services. It will become known as the 'electronic
communications code'. The electronic communications code is designed to facilitate
the installation and maintenance of electronic communications networks. It confers
rights on operators to install and maintain apparatus in, over or under land and results
in considerably simplified planning procedures, similar to those given to other
utilities. The only substantive changes are to enable the application of the electronic
communications code to persons who provide systems of conduits that are to be used
for the provision of an electronic communications network, but who do not actually
provide an electronic communications network themselves; and to allow apparatus to
be shared without either of the sharers being in breach of their obligations under the
code because of what the other is allowed to do. The other change is the addition of
paragraph 29 to the code, which encourages the sharing of apparatus.

Schedule 4: Compulsory purchase and entry for exploratory purposes

889.   This is described in the notes to section 118.

Schedule 5: Procedure for grants of recognised spectrum access

890.   This is described in the notes to section 159.

Schedule 6: Fixed penalties for wireless telegraphy offences

891.   This is described in the notes to section 180.

Schedule 7: Seizure and forfeiture of apparatus

892.   This is described in the notes to section 182.

Schedule 8: Decisions not subject to appeal

893.   This Schedule lists the types of decision taken by OFCOM and the Secretary
of State that cannot be appealed under Chapter 3 of Part 2 of the Act (see also the
notes to section 192). These include certain decisions taken under the Act and also
decisions under the Wireless Telegraphy Acts of 1949 and 1998. They also include
decisions to institute, bring or carry on any criminal or civil proceedings, or to carry
out any preliminary steps towards this.

Schedule 9: Arrangements about carrying on of C4C's activities

894.   This is described in the notes on section 199.

Schedule 10: Licensing the public teletext service.

895.   This schedule is described in the notes on section 219.

Schedule 11: Approval, imposition and modification of networking arrangements

896.   This is described in the notes on section 294.

Schedule 12: Corresponding obligations of the BBC and Welsh Authority

897.   This Schedule sets out obligations that correspond to those in the regulatory regime for licensed providers and apply to the BBC and the Welsh Authority. Paragraph 2 provides that the BBC is under a duty to publicise OFCOM's functions under Part 5 of the 1996 Act (fairness and privacy) and any procedures established by OFCOM or the BBC for the handling and resolution of complaints about the observance by the BBC of standards set under section 319. The BBC is also under a duty to comply with the quota on independent productions detailed in paragraph 1 of Schedule 12, which mirrors the requirements applying to licensed providers. This quota applies across the whole of the television broadcasting services provided by the BBC, subject to sub-paragraphs (8) and (9), which allow the BBC Charter and Agreement to provide for the quota to apply to particular services or groups of services collectively.

898.   This Schedule also sets out a number of obligations of the Welsh Authority. Paragraph 3 sets out the duty of the Authority to secure that each of their public service remits for S4C, S4C Digital and other services authorised by the Secretary of State under section 205 is fulfilled. The public service remits of the Welsh Authority may be amended by order of the Secretary of State. However, before making any such amendment the Secretary of State must consult the Welsh Authority and, if the order relates to programmes that are not in Welsh, the Channel Four Television Corporation. Any order amending the public service remits of S4C or S4C Digital must be consistent with the requirement that those services should further the dissemination of information, education and entertainment and should include programmes a substantial proportion of which are in Welsh. Paragraph 4 requires the Authority to prepare an annual statement of programme policy, and to monitor their performance against the proposals contained therein. Such proposals must include the means by which the Authority intend to secure that the public service remits for their services are to be fulfilled. Each statement must also contain a report on the Authority's performance in carrying out the proposals they set themselves in the previous such statement. When preparing any statement the Authority must consider any guidance by OFCOM that is in force for the purposes of section 266 and any reports previously published by OFCOM under section 264 or 358.

899.   Paragraph 5 imposes must-offer obligations on the Welsh Authority in relation to their public digital services, requiring them to make such services available for broadcast or distribution by every appropriate network and for broadcast by means of every satellite service available for reception in Wales. The Authority must do their best to ensure that there are arrangements for the broadcast or distribution of their public digital services that result in their being available free of charge to as many of the intended audience for any given service as is practicable. "Appropriate network", "intended audience" and "satellite television service" are defined in sub-paragraph (8). Paragraph 6 places a duty on the Authority to join with the providers of other must-provide services to meet the requirements of section 274 to secure the reception of such services free of charge in areas where they would otherwise not be available.

900.   Paragraphs 7 and 8 detail the programming quotas for independent and for original productions that are to be secured by the Welsh Authority in relation to their designated public services (which, for these purposes, are to be taken together). The proportion of programming to be made up of original productions is to be agreed between OFCOM and the Welsh Authority, with a power of direction for OFCOM in the absence of an agreement.

901.   Paragraph 9 provides that the Welsh Authority are under a duty to ensure that their designated public services broadcast high quality news and current affairs programmes, at intervals throughout the period for which the service is provided and at times that include peak viewing times. Peak viewing times, for the purposes of paragraphs 8 and 9, will be determined by agreement between OFCOM and the Authority, with a power of direction for OFCOM in the absence of an agreement.

902.   Paragraph 10 requires the Welsh Authority to draw up, to revise from time to time and to comply with a code of practice setting out the principles they will apply when agreeing terms for the commissioning of independent productions. The code must be submitted to OFCOM for approval and will have effect only if approved by OFCOM.

903.   Paragraph 11 requires the Welsh Authority to grant to the public teletext provider, on payment of a reasonable charge, access to the facilities reasonably required for the provision of the public teletext service. In the event of a dispute about charges, the amount is to be determined by OFCOM.

904.   Paragraph 12 provides that the Welsh Authority are under a duty to ensure that S4C and S4C Digital observe the programme standards set under section 319. Paragraph 13 requires the Authority to comply with a direction by OFCOM with respect to the establishment of complaints procedures relating to programme standards under section 319.

905.   Paragraph 14 requires the Authority to comply with directions by OFCOM in relation to the exclusion of advertisements or types of sponsorship from their public television services. The Authority are also required, under paragraph 16, to comply with directions by OFCOM as to the amount of advertisements, the interval

between them and the frequency of advertising breaks.

906.   Paragraph 15 gives OFCOM the power to direct the Authority to broadcast a correction or statement of findings for a breach of programme or advertising standards. Paragraph 21 gives OFCOM the power, after consulting the Authority, to issue directions to the Authority to ensure compliance with all relevant international obligations. The Authority are required to comply with such directions.

907.   Paragraph 17 requires the Welsh Authority to secure the observance of the fairness code for the time being in force under section 107 of the Broadcasting Act 1996. Paragraph 18 requires the Welsh Authority to include party political broadcasts and referendum campaign broadcasts in their designated public services. They must also draft and publish a document setting out their policy with regard to such broadcasts and review and revise this policy periodically.

908.   Paragraph 19 sets out the duty of the Welsh Authority to publicise OFCOM's functions under Part 5 of the Broadcasting Act 1996 in relation to the Authority and any procedures established for the handling of complaints about the observance by the Authority of standards set under section 319. Paragraph 20 requires the Authority to retain recordings of programmes and, on request, to supply such recordings or scripts or transcripts to OFCOM.

909.   Finally, paragraphs 22 and 23 set out the duty of the Welsh Authority to observe the code under section 303 of the Act when providing services for the deaf and visually impaired, and to promote equality of opportunity.

Schedule 13: Financial penalties under the Broadcasting Acts

910.   Part 1 of this Schedule amends the provisions in the Broadcasting Act 1990 as regards financial penalties.

911.   Penalties may be imposed on the revocation of a Channel 3 or the Channel 5 licence, or a licence to provide the public teletext service. At the moment, under section 18 of the Broadcasting Act 1990, the maximum penalty which can be imposed on a Channel 3 licensee is 7 per cent of the qualifying revenue for the licensee's last complete accounting period falling within the licence period, or where the licence is revoked before the licensee has begun to provide the relevant service or before the end of the licensee's first complete accounting period falling within the licence period, 7 per cent of what the Independent Television Commission estimate would have been the qualifying revenue of the licensee for his first complete accounting period falling within the period for which the licence would have been in force. Paragraph 2 amends section 18 of the 1990 Act by keeping in place the arrangements for calculating penalties on the basis of qualifying revenue (by OFCOM) but providing that the maximum penalty will now be whichever is the greater of £500,000 or the amount calculated by reference to qualifying revenue.

912.   Under   section   41   of   the Broadcasting Act 1990, penalties may be

imposed on the holder of a Channel 3 licence or the Channel 4 or Channel 5 licences, if he fails to comply with licence conditions or the regulator's directions. Paragraph 3 amends section 41 so that the distinction between a first and a subsequent offence is removed and the maximum penalty is now fixed at 5 per cent of the licensee's qualifying revenue for his last complete accounting period falling within the licence period (instead of 3 per cent for a first offence and 5 per cent for any subsequent breaches). In cases where a penalty is imposed before the first such accounting period has ended, the penalty is to be 5 per cent of what OFCOM estimate would have been the licensee's qualifying revenue for that period.

913.   Paragraph 5 makes similar amendments to section 55 of the Broadcasting Act 1990, which deals with penalties which may be imposed on the holder of an additional services licence if he fails to comply with licence conditions or the regulator's directions.

914.   Under section 42B (for restricted services) of the Broadcasting Act 1990, penalties may be imposed on a restricted services licensee if he fails to comply with licence conditions or the regulator's directions. Paragraph 4 amends this section. The new penalties are whichever is the greater of £250,000 (instead of £50,000) or 5 per cent of the licensee's qualifying revenue for his last complete accounting period falling within the licence period or, where a penalty is imposed before the end of the first such accounting period, 5 per cent of what OFCOM estimate would have been the licensee's qualifying revenue for that period. Also, the distinction between a first and a subsequent offence is removed for both restricted and additional service.

915.   Under section 101 of the Broadcasting Act 1990, penalties may be imposed on the revocation of a national sound broadcasting licence. These provisions are amended by paragraph 6 to provide that the maximum penalty is whichever is the greater of £250,000 or 7 per cent of the qualifying revenue for the licensee's last complete accounting period falling within the licence period, or of what OFCOM estimate would have been the qualifying revenue of the licensee for his first complete accounting period falling within the period for which the licence would have been in force, where the penalty is imposed before the first such accounting period has ended. The basis for calculating qualifying revenue substantively duplicates the existing provision in section 101.

916.   Under section 110 of the Broadcasting Act 1990, penalties may be imposed on analogue sound broadcasting licensees, and under section 120, on additional service licensees, if they fail to comply with licence conditions or directions given under Part 3 of that Act. The existing provisions are amended, in the case of a national sound broadcasting licensee, to provide that the maximum penalty is whichever is the greater of £250,000 or 5 per cent of the qualifying revenue for the licensee's last complete accounting period falling within the licence period, or of what OFCOM estimates would have been the qualifying revenue of the licensee for his first complete accounting period falling within the period for which the licence would have been in force, where the penalty is imposed before the first such accounting period has ended. In other cases (e.g. local licences or radio licensable content service licences, by

virtue of section 250(3) of this Act) the maximum penalty is increased from £50,000 to £250,000. In the case of an additional services licensee, the maximum penalty is 5 per cent of qualifying revenue, calculated on the same basis as for a national sound broadcasting licensee. There is no distinction between a first and a subsequent offence for penalties under either section 110 or120.

917.   Part 2 of this Schedule amends the provisions of the Broadcasting Act 1996 as regards financial penalties.

918.   Under section 11 of the Broadcasting Act 1996, penalties may be imposed on the revocation of a television multiplex licence and, under section 53(5) penalties may be imposed on the revocation of a radio multiplex licence. In the case of a television multiplex licence, the existing provisions are amended to provide that, where the licence is revoked before the licensee has begun to provide the service or before the end of the first accounting period, the maximum penalty payable is whichever is the greater of £500,000 (instead of £50,000) and 7 per cent of what OFCOM estimates would have been the multiplex revenue of the licensee falling within his first accounting period for which the licence would have been in force. In any other case, the maximum penalty is £500,000 or 7 per cent of the multiplex revenue for his last complete accounting period falling within the licence period. For a radio multiplex licence, the maximum penalty is £250,000 in the case of a local multiplex licence (increased from £50,000); and in the case of a national multiplex licence it is whichever is the greater of £250,000 (also increased from £50,000) or a prescribed amount. The prescribed amount is 7 per cent of multiplex revenue, calculated on the same basis as for a television multiplex service (see section 53(6) of the 1996 Act).

919.   Penalties may be imposed under section 17, on a television multiplex licensee; under section 23, on a digital television programme licensee; under section 27, on a digital additional services licensee; under section 59, on a radio multiplex licensee; under section 62, on a digital sound programme licensee and, under section 66, on a digital additional sound services licensee, if he fails to comply with licence conditions or OFCOM's directions. In the case of sections 17, 23 and 27, the maximum penalties are raised to the greater of £250,000 (from £50,000) or 5 per cent of the licensee's multiplex revenue for his last complete accounting period falling within the licence period. In cases where a penalty is imposed before the end of the first such accounting period, the second figure is to be 5 per cent of what OFCOM estimate would have been the licensee's multiplex revenue for that period. For sections 59, 62 and 66, where the licensee holds a local licence the maximum penalty payable is £250,000. In the case of national licences the maximum penalty payable is whichever is the greater of £250,000 and 5 per cent of the licensee's multiplex revenue for his last complete accounting period falling within the licence period. In cases where a penalty is imposed on a national licensee before the end of the first such accounting period, the second figure is to be 5 per cent of what OFCOM estimate would have been the licensee's multiplex revenue for that period. Again, the distinction between a first offence (where a figure of 3 per cent of revenue had effect, instead of 5 per cent) and subsequent offences has been eliminated.

920.   Paragraph 9 gives the Secretary of State the power to amend, by order, the size of any of the penalties that may be imposed under the provisions of the Broadcasting Act 1990 that are set out in sub-paragraph (2). Paragraphs 16 and 22 amend existing powers to alter penalties in the 1996 Act. In particular, orders made under those powers will in future be subject to approval by resolution of each House of Parliament (as is the power in paragraph 9).

921.   These new provisions will only apply in relation to failures taking place after the commencement of this paragraph.

Schedule 14: Media ownership rules

922.   This Schedule establishes new rules on the ownership of television services and radio multiplex services, and outlines the scope for the Secretary of State to impose new rules by order on the ownership of analogue and digital radio services. These provisions are described in more detail in the notes to section 350.

Schedule 15: Amendments of Broadcasting Acts

923.   This Schedule amends the 1990 and 1996 Acts. Many of the amendments are simply to update those Acts in line with this Act, for example to change references to the Independent Television Commission and the Radio Authority into references to OFCOM or to add references to the Act where relevant to the application or interpretation of those Acts. Other amendments include–

(a)   additional powers for OFCOM to obtain information under sections 5(2) and 88(2) of the 1990 Act (see paragraphs 3 and 35) and sections 5(2) and 44(2) of the 1996 Act (see paragraphs 78 and 104) in connection with ownership restrictions in relation to television and radio broadcasting licences;

(b)   changes to make sections 15 to 17A of the 1990 Act (which concern the award of Channel 3 and Channel 5 licences) reflect, in particular, the self-regulation of the delivery of public service remits by those channels (see paragraphs 7 to 10);

(c)   amendments in section 89 (see paragraph 36), which disqualifies a person from holding certain radio licences if he or she has been convicted of certain broadcasting offences in the previous five years, and also provides that a licence holder must do all that he or she can to ensure that a person convicted of any such offence is not concerned in the operation of a wireless telegraphy station broadcasting the service. The list of offences is amended, and subsection (3) is amended to provide that a licence holder must also do all he or she can to ensure that a disqualified person is not concerned in the provision of the service or of programmes for inclusion in the service (and section 60 of the 1996 Act is amended to extend most of section 89 to digital sound programme licences – see paragraph 119). These amendments do not apply to offences committed before the amendments come in to effect;

(d)   to provide that no more than one member of the Welsh Authority may be a person who is a member or an employee of OFCOM (see paragraph 71);

(e)   amendments to provisions in the 1996 Act relating to "multiplex revenue" to take account of amendments elsewhere in this Act (see section 242 in particular) for the carriage of digital sound programme services on television multiplexes, and because broadcasting services (e.g. digital sound and digital television programme services) might in future be carried on general multiplex services (within the meaning given in section 362(1));

(f)   to bring the definition of "digital additional services" (section 24 of the 1996 Act) into line with concepts in this Act (e.g. "available for reception by members of the public") and to allow for such services to be carried on general multiplex services (see paragraph 93);

(g)   to bring Part 5 of the 1996 Act, which concerns the Broadcasting Standards Commission, into line with this Act (see paragraphs 132 to 137), in consequence of the repeal of provisions about standards complaints and the transfer of the Commission's functions as respects fairness and privacy to OFCOM (see also section 327).

Schedule 16: Further amendments in connection with media mergers

924.   This Schedule sets out further amendments in connection with media mergers.

Schedule 17: Minor and Consequential Amendments

925.   Schedule 17 sets out minor amendments to other legislation and amendments to other legislation that are consequential upon the Act. Paragraph 1 of the Schedule sets out the definitions that apply for the purposes of any Act or instrument amended by the Schedule.

926.   The majority of these amendments involve changes to terms contained in other legislation that is used in relation to the current telecommunications licensing regime and that is to be replaced by the Communications Act, to ensure, as far as possible, that the current term is replaced with an equivalent term for the purposes of the new regulatory regime. A number of these amendments are of a similar nature and include, for example, amendments to legislation such as the Opencast Coal Act 1958 and the Regional Development Agencies Act 1998 to replace references to the telecommunications code and telecommunications apparatus with references to the electronic communications code and electronic communications apparatus. The amendments also include amendments to disclosure of information provisions in various legislation (for example, the Greater London Authority Act 1999 and the Water Industry Act 1991), to provide an exemption from the general restriction on the disclosure of information in respect of OFCOM and the Communications Act.

927.   In addition, this Schedule sets out a number of minor and consequential amendments to the enactments relating to radio spectrum management. These include

the amendment of section 1D of the Wireless Telegraphy Act 1949 which is dealt with in more detail in the notes to section 169 and amendments requiring the Secretary of State's approval for orders and regulations made by OFCOM. For example, paragraphs 9(3) and 11(4) amend those sections of the Wireless Telegraphy Act 1949 which provide for regulations as to wireless telegraphy and regulations as to radiation of electro-magnetic energy, in order to require the Secretary of State's approval of any such regulations that are made by OFCOM. Similarly, paragraph 37(5) requires the approval of the Secretary of State for the making by OFCOM of any order under section 7 of the Wireless Telegraphy Act 1967, which places restrictions on dealing in, and custody of, certain apparatus. Paragraph 73 requires the approval of the Secretary of State for the making by OFCOM of any order under section 85 or 86 of the Telecommunications Act 1984 about information to be marked on or to accompany wireless telegraphy apparatus or to be given in advertisements for such apparatus.

928.   Schedule 17 also contains minor and consequential amendments with respect to broadcasting. These mainly reflect the changes to the regulatory structure so as to replace references to the existing regulators with references to OFCOM.

929.   The Welsh Development Agency Act 1975, section 19(1), which relates to the Agency and the media, is amended (by paragraph 50) so that references to "the appropriate authority" are replaced by a reference to OFCOM, and at subsection (11), the references to the Independent Television Commission and the Radio Authority are replaced by a reference to OFCOM. Similarly, references to the Independent Television Commission and the Radio Authority in section 92 and 93 of the Representation of the People Act 1983, which relate to broadcasting from outside the United Kingdom and broadcasting of local items during election periods are replaced by references to OFCOM (see paragraph 63).

930.   The Cinemas Act 1985 contains provisions, including a licensing regime, concerning premises which are used for "film exhibitions". The definition of "film exhibition" at section 21(1) is amended so that a film exhibition means any exhibition of moving pictures other than an exhibition of items included in a programme service within the meaning of Part 3 of the Communications Act that is being simultaneously received (or virtually so) by the exhibitor (see paragraph 76). The effect of the amendment is to ensure that cinemas which exhibit films transmitted to them via cable or satellite from a central source will not require licensing under the Communications Act; however films exhibited in such a way will continue to be covered by the licensing provisions of the 1985 Act.

931.   Various amendments have been made to the Copyright, Designs and Patents Act 1988 so as to bring these in line with the regulatory changes made under the Communications Act (see paragraph 91). In particular, these ensure that copyright is not infringed by the use by OFCOM in connection with the performance of their functions of material provided to them; or of any existing material which is transferred to them by a scheme made under section 30 of the Communications Act.

932. In section 33 of the Value Added Tax Act 1994, which relates to refunds of VAT in certain cases, the reference to the Channel 3 nominated news provider is replaced by a reference to the Channel 3 appointed news provider, to reflect changes made by the Act (see paragraph 129).

933. Schedule 9 to the Transport Act 2000, which contains disclosure of information provisions, has been amended so as to substitute OFCOM for the Independent Television Commission and so as to add the Broadcasting Act 1996 and the Communications Act to the list of specified enactments covered by those disclosure provisions (see paragraph 166).

934. The provisions relating to party political broadcasts and referendum campaign broadcasts contained in section 11 of and paragraph 4(6) of Schedule 12 to the Political Parties, Election and Referendums Act 2000 have been amended so as to remove the references in that section to Sianel Pedwar Cymru (paragraph 167). The effect is now that those provisions provide that the BBC shall have regard to the Electoral Commission's views when determining its policy with respect to party political broadcasts and referendum campaign broadcasts. The corresponding duty with respect to the Welsh Authority is now contained in Schedule 12 to the Communications Act.

935. The Schedule also includes minor amendments to the Office of Communications Act 2002 (paragraphs 171 and 172). Paragraph 8(1) of the Schedule to the OFCOM Act is amended to require OFCOM to conduct their affairs so as to secure that revenues from fees and charges which do not fall to be paid to the Consolidated Fund are at least sufficient to enable OFCOM to meet the cost of carrying out the functions to which they relate.

Schedule 18: Transitional Provisions

936. The principal paragraphs of this Schedule have been described in connection with the applicable sections.

937. Paragraphs 59 to 62 of this Schedule set out the transitional arrangements that will apply on commencement of the provisions of Chapter 2 of Part 5 of this Act.

938. Paragraph 59 provides that the new provisions introduced in this Chapter will not apply to any transfer of a newspaper or of newspaper assets that has already taken place as at the commencement date of these provisions. In addition, any transfer for which an application for consent has been made, but not determined, at the date of commencement will continue to be considered under the special newspaper merger provisions in the FTA 1973.

939. If, however, an application is made that falls within section 59(2) FTA 1973 because it is "expressed to depend" on the Secretary of State exercising a discretion in that Act not to refer the transaction to the Competition Commission, then the effect of paragraph 59(2) of this Schedule is that only   that   "expressed   to   depend"

application will fall within the transitional saving of the FTA 1973 provisions. If the Secretary of State's consent is not given without a reference, but the parties then decide to pursue the merger after the provisions of Chapter 2 of Part 5 of the Act take effect, it will then be treated as a merger under the EA 2002, as amended by these provisions.

940.   Paragraph 62 sets out provisions applying to conditional consents that have been given under the FTA 1973. On implementation of the provisions of Chapter 2 of Part 5 of this Act existing consents will be unaffected and will continue in effect as consents given under the FTA 1973. However, where these consents have conditions attached to them, such that the party concerned is subject to ongoing obligations, paragraph 62 provides that the Secretary of State may accept undertakings in lieu of the conditions on the consent. Acceptance of an undertaking will be at the Secretary of State's discretion but, if accepted, any such undertaking would then be treated as equivalent to an undertaking given to the Secretary of State in a public interest case under the EA 2002 (see paragraph 9 of Schedule 7 to the EA 2002). Such undertakings could relate to competition and/or to general public interest obligations and so in deciding whether to accept such undertakings the Secretary of State can, in particular, consult with the OFT and/or OFCOM.

Schedule 19: Repeals

941.   This Schedule sets out those provisions in other enactments that will be repealed as a consequence of the Act.

COMMENCEMENT

942.   The provisions of the Act will be brought into force on a day or days appointed by commencement order of the Secretary of State, save for sections 31(1) to (4) and (6), 405 and 411, which came into force upon Royal Assent.

DETAILS OF BILL'S PASSAGE THROUGH PARLIAMENT

Parliamentary Stage	Date	Hansard Reference
Introduction (Commons)	19th November 2002	**Hansard Reference**
Second Reading	3rd December 2002	Vol 394; Col 520
Committee	From 10th December 2002 – 6th February 2003 (26 Sittings)	Vol 395; Cols 782 – 865
Report	Day 1 - 25th February 2003 Day 2 - 4th March 2003	Hansard Standing Committee E; Cols 1-1072
Third Reading	4th March 2003	Vol 400; Cols 144 – 232 Vol 400; Cols 682 – 775
Introduction (Lords)	5th March 2003	Vol 400; Cols 775 - 787
Second Reading	25th March 2003	Vol 646; Col 873
Committee	Day 1 – 29th April 2003	Vol 647; Cols 655 – 790

	Day 2 – 6th May 2003	Vol 647; Cols 582 – 647 and 661 – 688
	Day 3 – 15th May 2003	Vol 647; Cols 972 – 1026 and 1042 – 1071
	Day 4 – 20th May 2003	Vol 648; Cols 317 – 361 and 382 – 436
	Day 5 – 22nd May 2003	Vol 648; Cols 703 – 768 and 784 – 820
	Day 6 – 3rd June 2003	Vol 648; Cols 940 – 1038
	Day 7 – 5th June 2003	Vol 648; Cols 1168 – 1233 and 1246 – 1312
Report	Day 1 – 23rd June 2003	Vol 648; Cols 1431 – 1480 and 1489 – 1563
	Day 2 – 26th June 2003	Vol 650; Cols 11 – 24 and 40 – 83 and 101 – 124
	Day 3 – 1st July 2003	Vol 650; Cols 383 – 426 and 454 – 511
	Day 4 – 2nd July 2003	Vol 650; Cols 737 – 803 and 819 – 870
Third Reading	8th July 2003	Vol 650; Cols 886 – 982
Commons Consideration of Lords Amendments	14th July 2003	Vol 651; Cols 138 – 209 and 220 – 261
Lords Consideration of Commons Amendments	16th July 2003	Vol 409; Cols 44 – 118

Royal Assent – 17th July 2003 - House of Lords Hansard Vol 651 Col 965
17th July 2003 - House of Commons Hansard Vol 409 Col 439

APPENDIX 1

The following is a list of expressions defined in the Act, and the sections and Schedules in which those definitions are to be found.

Defined Term:	Section/Schedule:	Applies to:
"the 1984 Act"	Paragraph 64, Schedule 18	Schedule 18
"the 1990 Act"	405(1)	the Act
"the 1996 Act"	405(1)	the Act
"the abolition of licensing"	Paragraph 64, Schedule 18	Schedule 18
"access"	405(1) & (4)	the Act
"access contract"	87(12)	Section 87
"the Access Directive"	151(1)	Part 2, Chapter 1
	Paragraph 9(16), Schedule 18	Paragraph 9, Schedule 18
"access radio licence"	359(5)	Section 359
"access-related condition"	151(1)	Part 2, Chapter 1
"accounting period"	177(11)	Section 177
"acquisition"	277(13)	Section 277
	Paragraph 1(14), Schedule 12	Paragraph 1, Schedule 12
	Paragraph 7(13), Schedule 12	Paragraph 7, Schedule 12
"additional radio service"	362(1)	Part 3
"additional television service"	362(1)	Part 3
"adoption"	151(1)	Part 2, Chapter 1
"the alleged offender"	Paragraph 7(1), Schedule 6	Paragraph 7, Schedule 6
"allocation"	151(1)	Part 2, Chapter 1
"alteration"	134(8)	Section 134
"analogue teletext service"	362(1)	Part 3
"ancillary service"	362(1)	Part 3
"apparatus"	405(1)	the Act
"apparatus market"	46(9)	Section 46
	151(1)	Part 2, Chapter 1
"apparatus for wireless telegraphy"	174(8)	Section 174
	Paragraph 8, Schedule 5	Schedule 5
"the application date"	227(8)	Section 227
"application programme interface"	74(3) & (4)	Section 74

Defined Term:	Section/Schedule:	Applies to:
"appropriate network"	271(7)	Section 271
	Paragraph 5(8), Schedule 12	Paragraph 5, Schedule 12
"the appropriate percentage"	217(7)	Section 217
	228(8)	Section 228
	253(13)	Section 253
	400(8)	Section 400
	Paragraph 7(7), Schedule 10	Paragraph 7, Schedule 10
"approval"	53(6)	Section 53
	54(8)	Section 54
"approve"	53(6)	Section 53
	54(8)	Section 54
"approved"	53(6)	Section 53
	54(8)	Section 54
"approved code"	120(15)	Section 120
"approved networking arrangements"	292(9)	Section 292
	293(8)	Section 293
"arrangements"	Paragraph 10, Schedule 9	Schedule 9
"arrangements proposed by OFCOM"	Paragraph 9(5), Schedule 11	Paragraph 9(5), Schedule 11
"assistance for disabled people"	362(1)	Part 3
"associated facility"	32(3)	the Act
	405(1)	the Act
"the Authorisation Directive"	Paragraph 13(8), Schedule 18	Paragraph 13(7), Schedule 18
"authorised person"	Paragraph 3(4), Schedule 6	Paragraph 3 of Schedule 6
"available for reception by members of the public"	361	the Act
	362(1)	Part 3
"the BBC"	405(1)	the Act
"the BBC Charter and Agreement"	362(1)	Part 3
"BBC company"	362(1)	Part 3
"the BBC's services"	198(9)	Section 198
"belief"	264(13)	Section 264
"body"	405(1)	the Act
"broadcast"	405(1)	the Act

Defined Term:	Section/Schedule:	Applies to:
"Broadcasting Act licence"	405(1)	the Act
"Broadcasting Act licence fee"	347(8)	Section 347
"Broadcasting Act powers"	317(1)	Section 317
"broadcasting provision"	318(5)	Section 318
"business"	405(1)	the Act
"business premises"	233(9)	Section 233
	248(9)	Section 249
"C4C"	405(1)	the Act
"C4 company"	362(1)	Part 3
"cable package"	330(6)	Section 330
	331(6)	Section 331
	332(10)	Section 332
"cash bid amount"	400(8)	Section 400
"Channel 3"	362(1)	Part 3
"a Channel 3 licence"	362(1)	Part 3
"Channel 3 programmes"	286(7)	Section 286
	351(10)	Section 351
"a Channel 3 service"	362(1)	Part 3
"Channel 4"	362(1)	Part 3
"Channel 4 licence"	297(3)	Section 297
"Channel 5"	362(1)	Part 3
"charging year"	38(12)	Sections 38 and 39
"citizens"	3(14)	Section 3
"code operator"	Paragraph 1, Schedule 4	Schedule 4
"code-related liabilities"	Paragraph 18(8), Schedule 18	Paragraph 18, Schedule 18
"the commencement day"	350(6)	Section 350
"Communications Directives"	409(4)	Section 409
"communications functions"	22(5)	Section 22
"communications matters"	3(14)	Section 3
	20 (7)	Section 20
	21(7)	Section 21
"communications provider"	405(1)	the Act
"communications service"	Paragraph 1(1), Schedule 17	Schedule 17
"competition test"	Paragraph 15, Schedule 11	Schedule 11
"conditional access system"	75(3)	Sections 75 and 76
"conduit"	106(7)	Section 106
"conduit system"	Paragraph 1(2), Schedule 17	Paragraph 1, Schedule 17
"connected person"	Paragraph 15(5), Schedule 10	Paragraph 15, Schedule 10
"connected services"	316(4)	Section 316

Defined Term:	Section/Schedule:		Applies to:	
"the Consumer Panel"	16(2)		the Act	
	405(1)		the Act	
"consumers"	405(1) & (5)		the Act	
"Content Board"	12(1)		the Act	
	405(1)		the Act	
"a content service"	32(7)		Section 32(2)	
"the continued provision"	Paragraph 9(3), Schedule 18		Paragraph 9, Schedule 18	
"the contracting party"	Paragraph 4(1), Schedule 18		Paragraph 4, Schedule 18	
"contravening provider"	102(6)		Section 102	
	142(6)		Section 142	
"the contravening provider"	42(1)		Section 42	
	98(1)		Section 98	
	100(1)		Section 100	
	124(1)		Section 124	
	124(2)		Section 124	
	140(1)		Section 140	
"contravening supplier"	102(6)		Section 101 and 102	
	142(6)		Section 141 and 142	
"the contravening supplier"	101(1)		Section 101	
"contravention"	405(1)		the Act	
"controlled"	362(6)		Section 362	
"the court"	Paragraph 13(12), Schedule 11		Paragraph 13, Schedule 11	
	Paragraph 3(8), Schedule 18		Paragraph 3, Schedule 18	
	Paragraph 4(8), Schedule 18		Paragraph 4, Schedule 18	
"customers"	405(1)		the Act	
"the decision-maker"	195(9)		Section 195	
"the defaulter"	Paragraph 13(1), Schedule 11		Paragraph 13, Schedule 11	
"defendant"	174(1)		Section 174	
"designated organisation"	333(6)		Section 333	
	Paragraph 18(7), Schedule 12		Paragraph 18, Schedule 12	
"designated universal service provider"	151(1)		Part 2, Chapter 1	
"digital additional sound service"	362(1)		Part 3	
"digital additional television service"	362(1)		Part 3	
"the digital public teletext service"	362(1)		Part 3	
"digital sound programme service"	362(1)		Part 3	

Defined Term:	Section/Schedule:	Applies to:
"digital television programme service"	362(1)	Part 3
"the Directives"	Paragraph 13(7), Schedule 18	Paragraph 13, Schedule 18
"the Director"	Paragraph 64, Schedule 18	Schedule 18
"director"	404(3)	Section 404
"disabled"	27(5)	Section 27
	337(9)	Section 337
	Paragraph 23(6), Schedule 12	Paragraph 23, Schedule 12
"disaster"	51(7)	Section 51
"dispute procedures"	54(8)	Section 54
"distribute"	405(1)	Section 405
"document"	394(9)	Section 394
"domestic and small business customer"	16(13)	Section 16
	52(6)	Section 52
	53(6)	Section 53
	54(8)	Section 54
"the dominant provider"	87(1)	Sections 87 and 88
	89(1)	Section 89
	90(1)	Section 90
	91(1)	Section 91
	92(1)	Section 92
"the dominant supplier"	93(1)	Section 93
"drama"	264(13)	Section 264
"EEA State"	362(1)	Part 3
"electro-magnetic interference"	51(6)	Section 51
"electronic communication"	56(10)	Section 56
	57(3)	Section 57
"electronic communications apparatus"	151(1)	Part 2, Chapter 1
	Paragraph 1(1), Schedule 17	Schedule 17
	Paragraph 9(16), Schedule 18	Paragraph 9, Schedule 18
"the electronic communications code"	106(1)	Part 2, Chapter 1

Defined Term:	Section/Schedule:	Applies to:
	151(1)	Part 2, Chapter 1
	Paragraph 17(7), Schedule 18	Paragraph 17, Schedule 18
	Paragraph 18(9), Schedule 18	Paragraph 18, Schedule 18
"electronic communications code"	Paragraph 1(1), Schedule 17	Schedule 17
	Paragraph 17(7), Schedule 18	Paragraph 17, Schedule 18
"electronic communications code network"	Paragraph 1(1), Schedule 17	Schedule 17
"electronic communications code operator"	Paragraph 1(1), Schedule 17	Schedule 17
"electronic communications network"	32(1)	the Act
	405(1)	the Act
	Paragraph 1(1), Schedule 17	Schedule 17
"electronic communications service"	32(2)	the Act
	405(1)	the Act
	Paragraph 1(1), Schedule 17	Schedule 17
"electronic programme guide"	16(13)	Section 16
	74(3)	Section 74
	232(6)	Section 232
	303(13)	Section 303
	310(8)	Section 310
	311(2)	Section 311
"eligible person"	220(4)	Section 220
"enactment"	405(1)	the Act
"the enactments relating to broadcasting"	23(5)	Section 23
	407(5)	Section 407
"enactments relating to the management of the radio spectrum"	405(1)	the Act
"end-to-end connectivity"	74(3)	Section 74
"end-user"	151(1)	Part 2, Chapter 1
	272(9)	Section 272
	Paragraph 5(10), Schedule 12	Paragraph 5(8), Schedule 12
"enforcement authority"	120 (15)	Section 120

Defined Term:	Section/Schedule:	Applies to:
"enforcement powers"	Paragraph 13(6), Schedule 18	Paragraph 13, Schedule 18
"European Court"	Paragraph 6(9), Schedule 11	Paragraph 6, Schedule 11
"existing licence"	215(1)	Section 215
"the existing licence"	225(8)	Section 225
	221(1)	Section 221
"the existing service"	221(11)	Section 221
"expenditure"	286(7)	Section 286
	288(5)	Section 288
	353(7)	Section 353
"fairness complaint"	Paragraph 49(3), Schedule 18	Paragraph 49, Schedule 18
"financial year"	347(8)	Section 347
	400 (8)	Section 400
"the first notional expiry date"	225(7)	Section 225
"the Framework Directive"	4(12)	Section 4
	151(1)	Part 2, Chapter 1
	197(3)	Section 197
	Paragraph 10(7), Schedule 18	Paragraph 10, Schedule 18
"former PTO"	Paragraph 1(1), Schedule 17	Schedule 17
"the former operator"	117(1)	Section 117
"formerly regulated radio service"	251(5)	Section 251
"formerly regulated television service"	240(5)	Section 240
"frequency"	405(1)	the Act
"general condition"	151(1)	Part 2, Chapter 1
"general duties"	3(14)	Section 3
"general multiplex service"	362(1)	Section 362
"gross revenue"	177(11)	Section 177
"guarantor"	Paragraph 18(2), Schedule 18	Paragraph 18, Schedule 18
"hardwired"	93(5)	Section 93
"holder"	405(1)	the Act
"information"	405(1)	the Act
"initial expiry date"	224	Section 224
"initial licensing period"	230(11)	Section 230
"installation"	410(7)	Section 410
"intelligible"	405(1)	the Act
"intended audience"	272(7)	Section 272
	273(7)	Section 273

Defined Term:	Section/Schedule:	Applies to:
	274(10)	Section 274
	310(7)	Section 310
	Paragraph 5(8), Schedule 12	Schedule 12
"interconnection"	151(1) and (2)	Part 2, Chapter 1
"interference"	155(2)	Section 155
	366(10)	Section 366
"intermediary service provider"	120 (15)	Section 120
"international meetings about communications"	22(5)	Section 22
"international obligation of the United Kingdom"	405(1)	the Act
"the ITC"	Paragraph 64, Schedule 18	Schedule 18
"land"	Paragraph 5(8), Schedule 4	Paragraph 5, Schedule 4
"lease"	134(8)	Section 134
"leased line"	92(4)	Section 92
"legal proceedings"	187(5)	Section 187
	393(12)	Section 393
"licence period"	228(8)	Section 228
	Paragraph 10, Schedule 9	Schedule 9
	Paragraph 14, Schedule 10	Schedule 10
"licensable service"	206(7)	Section 206
"licensed public service channel"	362(1)	Part 3
"licensed service"	316(4)	Section 316
	337(9)	Section 337
"licensed television service"	272(7)	Section 272
	273(7)	Section 273
	274(10)	Section 274
"licensing period"	228(8)	Section 228
	229(6)	Section 229
	230(11)	Section 230
"listed provision"	406(9)	Section 406
"LLU notification"	Paragraph 8(4), Schedule 18	Paragraph 8, Schedule 18
"local authority"	148(3)	Section 148
"local Channel 3 service"	287(8)	Section 287
"local digital sound programme licence"	362(1)	Part 3
"local digital sound programme service"	362(1)	Part 3
"local enactment"	406(8)	Section 406

Defined Term:	Section/Schedule:	Applies to:
"locally-made"	314(7)	Section 314
"local material"	314(7)	Section 314
"local programme"	287(8)	Section 287
"local radio multiplex licence"	362(1)	Part 3
"local radio multiplex service"	362(1)	Part 3
"local radio service"	320(7)	Section 320
"local sound broadcasting licence"	362(1)	Section 362
"local sound broadcasting service"	362(1)	Part 3
"the M25 area"	362(1)	Part 3
"the main service"	263(3)	Section 263
"market area"	83(6)	Section 83
"market power determination"	151(1)	Part 2, Chapter 1
"Minister of the Crown"	336(9)	Section 336
"misuse"	151(1)	Part 2, Chapter 1
"modification"	405(1)	the Act
"multiplex service"	175(6)	Section 175
	233(9)	Section 233
	248(9)	Section 248
	330(3)	Section 330
	331(6)	Section 331
	332(10)	Section 332
	360(9)	Section 360
"must-provide service"	274(10)	Section 274
"national Channel 3 service"	362(1)	Part 3
"national digital sound programme service"	362(1)	Part 3
"national radio multiplex licence"	362(1)	Section 362
"national radio multiplex service"	362(1)	Part 3
"national radio service"	320(7)	Section 320
	333(6)	Section 333
"national sound broadcasting licence"	253(13)	Section 253
"the National Telephone Numbering Plan"	56(1)	the Act
"network access"	4(12)	Section 4
	151(1) and (3)	Part 2, Chapter 1
	197(1)	Part 2, Chapter 3
"network access question"	105(6)	Section 105
"networking arrangements"	362(1)	Section 362
"networks and services functions"	408(7)	Section 408
"news"	318(8)	Section 318
"non-communications services"	77(9)	Section 77
"non-representational images"	362(7)	Section 362
"notification"	394(9)	Section 394
"the notified misuser"	129(1)	Section 129

Defined Term:	Section/Schedule:	Applies to:
	130(1)	Section 130
"the notified person"	139(1)	Section 139
"the notified charge payer"	41(1)	Section 41
"the notified provider"	36(1)	Section 36
	37(1)	Section 37
	95(1)	Section 95
	96(1)	Section 96
	111(1)	Section 111
	112(1)	Section 112
"number"	56(10)	Sections 56 and 63
"numbering conditions"	60(7)	Section 60
	61(9)	Section 61
"OFCOM"	1(1)	the Act
	405(1)	the Act
"OFCOM's standards code"	362(1)	Part 3
"operator"	Paragraph 1(1), Schedule 17	Schedule 17
"the operator"	114(1)	Section 114
	Paragraph 18(1), Schedule 18	Paragraph 18, Schedule 18
"the operator's network"	Paragraph 1, Schedule 4	Schedule 4
"the operator's system"	Paragraph 18(1), Schedule 18	Paragraph 18, Schedule 18
"original production"	351(10)	Section 351
	353(7)	Section 353
"other member State"	405(1)	the Act
"participant"	362(6)	Section 362(1)
"peak viewing time"	278(10)	Section 278
	279(5)	Section 279
	287(8)	Section 287
	351(10)	Section 351
	353(7)	Section 353
	Paragraph 8(11), Schedule 12	Paragraph 8, Schedule 12
	Paragraph 9(8), Schedule 12	Paragraph 9, Schedule 12
"the period under review"	22 7(8)	Section 227
"persistent" and "persistently"	151(1)	Part 2, Chapter 1
"pre-commencement licence"	Paragraph 8(5), Schedule 14	Paragraph 8(5), Schedule 14

Defined Term:	Section/Schedule:	Applies to:
"the person in contravention"	Paragraph 14(1), Schedule 14	Paragraph 14, Schedule 14
"pre-commencement regulator"	405(1)	the Act
"pre-transfer licence"	253(13)	Section 253
"pre-transfer local licence"	253(13)	Section 253
	Paragraph 44(4), Schedule 18	Paragraph 44, Schedule 18
"pre-transfer national licence"	253(13)	Section 253
	Paragraph 44(4), Schedule 18	Paragraph 44, Schedule 18
"premises"	233(9)	Section 233
	248(9)	Section 248
"premium rate service"	151(1)	Part 2, Chapter 1
"price control matter"	193(10)	Section 193
"primary functions"	Paragraph 10, Schedule 9	Schedule 9
"privileged supplier condition"	151(1)	Part 2, Chapter 1
"programme"	204(10)	Section 204
	277(13)	Section 277
	278(10)	Section 278
	286(7)	Section 286
	287(8)	Section 287
	288(5)	Section 288
	303(13)	Section 303
	309(6)	Section 309
	405(1)	the Act
	Paragraph 7(13), Schedule 12	Paragraph 7, Schedule 12
	Paragraph 8(11), Schedule 12	Paragraph 8, Schedule 12
"programme service"	321(8)	Section 321
	405(1)	the Act
"programming budget"	277(13)	Section 277
	Paragraph 1(14), Schedule 12	Paragraph 1, Schedule 12
	Paragraph 7(13), Schedule 12	Paragraph 7, Schedule 12
"promptness standards"	9(7)	Section 9
"protected programme service"	75(3)	Section 75
"provide"	405(1)	the Act
"provider"	151(1)	Part 2, Chapter 1

Defined Term:	Section/Schedule:	Applies to:
"provision"	362(1)	Part 3
"the provision of premium rate services"	Paragraph 9(16), Schedule 18	Paragraph 9, Schedule 18
"public communications provider"	151(1)	Part 2, Chapter 1
"public digital service"	Paragraph 5(8), Schedule 12	Paragraph 5, Schedule 12
"public electronic communications network"	151(1)	Part 2, Chapter 1
	397(2)	Section 397
	Paragraph 1(1), Schedule 17	Schedule 17
"public electronic communications service"	151(1)	Part 2, Chapter 1
	272(9)	Section 272
	Paragraph 5(10), Schedule 12	Paragraph 5, Schedule 12
	Paragraph 1(1), Schedule 17	Schedule 17
"public service broadcaster"	271(8)	Section 271
"public services"	207(9)	Section 207
"the public teletext provider"	362(1)	Part 3
"the public teletext service"	362(1)	Part 3
"purposes of public service television broadcasting in the United Kingdom"	405(1)	The Act
"qualified auditor"	67(9)	Section 67
	77(9)	Section 77
	91(8)	Section 91
"qualifying revenue"	215(12)	Section 215
	217(7)	Section 217
	221(12)	Section 21
"qualifying service"	362(1)	Part 3
"racial group"	27(5)	Section 27
	337(9)	Section 337
	Paragraph 23(6), Schedule 12	Paragraph 23, Schedule 12
"radio licensable content service"	362(1)	Part 3

Defined Term:	Section/Schedule:	Applies to:
"radio multiplex service"	362(1)	Part 3
"radio programme service"	362(1)	Part 3
"the radio transfer date"	405(1)	the Act
"the recipient"	395(1)	Section 395
"referendum campaign broadcast"	333(6)	Section 333
	Paragraph 18(7), Schedule 12	Paragraph 18, Schedule 12
"regional Channel 3 licence"	362(1)	Part 3
"regional Channel 3 providers"	292(9)	Section 292
"regional Channel 3 service"	362(1)	Part 3
"regional programme"	286(7)	Section 286
	287(8)	Section 287
	351(10)	Section 351
	Paragraph 7(5), Schedule 11	Paragraph 7, Schedule 11
"regional news programme"	287(7)	Section 287
"regulatory authorities"	151(1) and (5)	Part 2, Chapter 1
	197(1)	Part 2, Chapter 3
"regulatory international standards"	151(1)	Part 2, Chapter 1
"relevant amount of gross revenue"	177(1)	Section 177
"relevant ancillary service"	232(6)	Section 232
"relevant business"	97(5)	Section 97
"relevant change of control"	351(10)	Section 351
	353(7)	Section 353
"relevant connection facility"	90(6)	Section 90
"relevant date"	305	Section 305
"the relevant date"	356(6)	Section 356
"relevant electronic communications network"	134(8)	Section 134
"relevant existing licence"	240(5)	Section 240
	251(5)	Section 251
"the relevant facilities"	87(12)	Section 87
"relevant independent radio services"	312(5)	Section 312
"relevant international obligations"	Paragraph 21(4), Schedule 12	Paragraph 21, Schedule 12
"relevant international obligations of the United Kingdom"	335(2)	Section 335
"relevant licence"	229(6)	Section 229
	324(12)	Section 324

Defined Term:	Section/Schedule:	Applies to:
"relevant licence period"	Paragraph 10, Schedule 9	Schedule 9
"the relevant market"	91(1)	Section 91
"relevant markets"	3(14)	Section 3(15)
"the relevant multiplex"	Paragraph 12(4), Schedule 14	Paragraph 12, Schedule 14
"a relevant national newspaper proprietor"	Paragraph 13(2), Schedule 14	Paragraph 13, Schedule 14
"the relevant network"	87(12)	Section 87
"relevant offence"	Paragraph 1(2), Schedule 6	Schedule 6
"relevant officer"	Paragraph 13, Schedule 6	Schedule 6
"relevant period"	97(5)	Section 97
	237(3)	Section 237
"the relevant person"	50(8)	Section 50
"the relevant provider"	121(3)	Section 121
	122(5)	Section 122
	132(1)	Section 132
"relevant provision of this Act"	409(4)	Section 409
"relevant provisions"	60(7)	Section 60
"relevant public broadcasting service"	224(9)	Section 224
"relevant public service broadcaster"	243(7)	Section 243
"relevant regulatory authorities"	83(6)	Section 83
"relevant revenue"	400(8)	Section 400
"the relevant service"	120(9)	Part 2, Chapter 1
"the relevant six months"	Paragraph 3(6), Schedule 14	Sub-paragraphs (4) and (5), Paragraph 3, Schedule 14
"relevant sound service"	258(9)	Section 258(2)
"relevant television service"	241(9)	Section 241
"the relevant transfer date"	Paragraph 51(5), Schedule 18	Paragraph 51, Schedule 18
"the relevant year"	41(9)	Section 41
"renewal period"	217(7)	Section 217
	223(4)	Section 223
"request to be tried"	Paragraph 7(5), Schedule 6	Schedule 6
"repeated contravention"	173(1)	Section 173
"representation"	405(1)	the Act
"the representations period"	82(4)	Section 82
"restricted television service"	362(1)	Part 3
"S4C"	362(1)	Part 3

Defined Term:	Section/Schedule:	Applies to:
"S4C company"	362(1)	Part 3
"S4C Digital"	362(1)	Part 3
"satellite television service"	273(7)	Section 273
	Paragraph 5(8), Schedule 12	Schedule 12
"Schedule 2 public operator"	Paragraph 14(4), Schedule 18	Paragraph 14, Schedule 18
"schools programmes"	296(12)	Section 296
"the second notional expiry date"	225(7)	Section 225
"service interoperability"	4(12)	Section 4
	151(1)	Part 2, Chapter 1
"services market"	151(1)	Part 2, Chapter 1
"signal"	10(6)	Section 10
	32(10)	Section 32
"significant market power"	151(1)	Part 2, Chapter 1
"simulcast radio service"	362(1)	Part 3
"SMP apparatus condition"	Paragraph 9(16), Schedule 18	Paragraph 9 Schedule 18
"SMP condition"	151(1)	Part 2, Chapter 1
	Paragraph 9(16), Schedule 18	Paragraph 9, Schedule 18
"sound broadcasting service"	362(1)	Part 3
"sound service"	205(9)	Section 205
"special or exclusive rights"	77(9)	Section 77
"spectrum functions"	408(8)	Section 408
"standards objectives"	362(1)	Part 3
"stations for wireless telegraphy"	174(8)	Section 174
	Paragraph 8, Schedule 5	Schedule 5
"subordinate legislation"	405(1)	the Act
"subsequent notional expiry date"	225(7)	Section 225
"subtitling"	362(1)	Part 3
"tariff"	68(8)	Section 68
"the telecommunications code"	Paragraph 18(9), Schedule 18	Paragraph 18, Schedule 18
"telephone number"	151(1)	Part 2, Chapter 1
"telephone numbers"	1(8)	Section 1
"television and radio services"	405(1)	the Act
"television broadcasting service"	362(1)	Part 3
"television licensable content service"	232(1)	Part 3
	362(1)	Part 3

Defined Term:	Section/Schedule:	Applies to:
"television multiplex service"	362(1)	Part 3
"television or radio broadcasting"	22(7)	Section 22
"television programme"	405(1)	the Act
"television programme service"	362(1)	Part 3
"television receiver"	368(1)	Part 4
"the television transfer date"	405(1)	the Act
"the Television without Frontiers Directive"	362(1)	Part 3
"tender notice"	216(13)	Section 216
	222(13)	Section 222
	225(7)	Section 224
"the territorial sea"	410(7)	Section 410
"text service"	362(1)	Part 3
"the threshold number"	337(9)	Section 337
"the transfer date"	Paragraph 51(6), Schedule 18	Paragraph 51, Schedule 18
"the transitional period"	408(6)	Section 408
"transfer scheme"	Paragraph 6, Schedule 2	Schedule 2
"transparency objectives"	Paragraph 10, Schedule 9	Schedule 9
"the Tribunal"	197(1)	Part 2, Chapter 3
	Paragraph 15, Schedule 11	Schedule 11
"Tribunal rules"	197(1)	Part 2, Chapter 3
	Paragraph 15, Schedule 11	Schedule 11
"TV licence"	364(1)	Section 363
	405(1)	the Act
"the United Kingdom Plan for Frequency Authorisation"	153(1)	the Act
"universal service condition"	151(1)	Part 2, Chapter 1
"the Universal Service Directive"	151(1)	Part 2, Chapter 1
	Paragraph 9(16), Schedule 18	Paragraph 9, Schedule 18
"the universal service order"	65(1)	Sections 65 and 67
	151(1)	Part 2, Chapter 1
"vehicle"	233(9)	Section 233
	248(9)	Section 248

Defined Term:	Section/Schedule:	Applies to:
	366(10)	Section 366
"the Welsh Authority"	405(1)	the Act
"wireless telegraphy"	405(1)	the Act
"wireless telegraphy licence"	405(1)	the Act

APPENDIX 2

This table identifies which sections of the Communications Act implement which Articles of the four Directives set out below.

References in this table to:-

FD   = Framework Directive;

AuD = Authorisation Directive;

AcD = Access Directive; and

USD = Universal Service Directive.

Section	Article(s) implemented
Part 1 – Functions of OFCOM	
Section 4 – Duties for the purpose of fulfilling Community obligations	Article 7(1) and (2) of FD Article 8 of FD Articles 17(2) & 18 of FD Article 20(3) of FD Article 5(1) of AcD Article 7(3) of AuD
Section 16 – Consumer consultation	Article 33(1) of USD
Section 24 – Provision of information to the Secretary of State	Article 25 of FD Article 16 of AuD Articles 15(2) and 17 of AcD Article 36(3) of USD
Section 25 – Community requirement to provide information	Article 5(2) of FD Article 15 of AcD
Section 26 – Publication of information and advice for consumers etc.	Article 5(4) and (5) of FD Article 15(1) of AuD Articles 11(2) & 15(1) of AcD Article 21(2) of USD
Part 2 – Networks, Services and the Radio Spectrum	
Chapter 1 – Electronic communications networks and services	
Section 32 – Meaning of electronic communications networks and services	
ss.(1)	Article 2(a) of FD
ss.(2)	Article 2(c) of FD
ss.(3)	Article 2(e) of FD
ss.(4)(a)	Article 2(m) of FD
ss.(7)	Article 2(c) of FD
Section 33 – Advance notification to OFCOM	Articles 3(2) and (3) and 6(1) of AuD Condition 10 of Part A of Annex to AuD
Section 34 – Designations and requirements for the purposes of s.33	Article 6(1) of AuD

Section 35 – Notification of contraventions of s. 33	Article 10(2) of AuD
Section 36 – Enforcement notification for contravention of s. 33	Article 10(2) & (3) of AuD
Section 37 – Penalties for contravention of s. 33	Article 10(2) & (3) of AuD
Sections 38 & 39 – Fixing of charges	Articles 6(1), 12 and 13 of AuD Condition 2 of Part A of Annex to AuD
Section 40 – Notification of non-payment of charges	Article 10(2) of AuD
Section 41 – Penalties for non-payment of charges	Article 10(2) & (3) of AuD
Sections 42 & 43 – Suspending service provision for non-payment and enforcement of directions	Article 10(2) & (5) of AuD
Section 44 – Duty of OFCOM to keep publicly accessible register	Article 3(3) of AuD
Section 45 – Power of OFCOM to set conditions	
ss. (3)	Article 6(1) and Part A of the Annex to the AuD Article 4(1) and 4(3) of AcD
ss.(4)	Article 6(2) of AuD and Articles 3 to 7 and 9 to 11 of , and Part A of Annex I to, USD
ss.(5)	Article 6(2) of AuD and Articles 5(1) and (2) and 6 of AcD
ss.(6)	Article 13 of FD
ss. (7) and (8)	Article 6(2) of AuD and Articles 8 to 13 of AcD and Articles 17 to 19 of USD and Article 16(2) of FD
Section 46 – Persons to whom conditions may apply	
ss.(2)	Articles 2(a) and 6(1) of the AuD
ss.(3)	Article 6(2) of AuD Article 13 of FD
ss.(4)	Article 13 of FD

ss.(5)	Article 8 of USD and Article 6(2) of AuD
ss.(6)	Article 5(1)(a) of AcD and 6(2) of AuD
ss.(7)	Article 16(4) of FD, Article 8(2) of AcD, Article 6(2) of AuD and Articles 17 to 19 of USD
ss. (8)	Article 8(2) of AcD, Article 16(4) of FD and Articles 17 to 19 of USD
Section 47 – Test for setting or modifying conditions	Articles 6(1) and 14 (1) of AuD Articles 5(3) and 8(4) of AcD Articles 3(2), 9(5) and 17(2) of USD
Section 48 – Procedure for setting, modifying and revoking conditions	Article 6 of FD Article 14(1) of AuD, Article 33 of USD and Articles 5(3), (6) and 8(4) of AcD
ss. (1) & (6)	Article 15(1) AcD
ss.(3)	Article 6(3) of AcD
ss.(5)	Article 7(5) of FD
Section 49 – Directions and approvals for the purposes of a s.45 condition	Article 6 and 7 of FD
Section 50 – Delivery of copies of notifications etc. ss. (2) to (6)	Article 15(2) of AcD
ss.(2)	Articles 8(5) and 16(2) of AcD and 36(2) of USD
ss.(3)	Article 7(3) of FD
Section 51 – Matters to which general conditions may relate	Article 6(1) of, and Part A of the Annex to, AuD
ss. (1)(a)	Condition 8 of Part A of the Annex to the AuD and Articles 20-22, 25, 26 & 29 , Part B of Annex I, Annex II and Annex III of the USD
ss. (1)(b) and ss.(4)	Article 4(2) of, and conditions 3 and 14 of Part A of the Annex to, the AuD and Articles 4(1) and 4(3) of AcD
ss. (1)(c) and ss.(5)	Condition 15 of Part A of the Annex to the AuD and Article 23 of USD
ss. (1)(d)	Condition 1 of Part A of the Annex to the AuD and Article 13(4) of USD

ss. (1)(e)	Condition 12 of Part A of the Annex to the AuD and Article 23 of USD
ss. (1)(f)	Condition 13 of Part A of the Annex to the AuD
ss. (1)(g)	Condition 18 of Part A of the Annex to the AuD and Article 17(2) of FD
ss.(2)	Article 2 of USD – definition of "publicly available telephone service"
ss.(3)	Article 2(a) of AuD
Sections 52 to 55 – General conditions: customer interests	Article 34 of USD and Part A of Annex to AuD Article 6(1) of, and condition 8 of Part A of the Annex to, the AuD
Section 56 - The National Telephone Numbering Plan.	Article 10(3) of FD and Article 27 of USD
Section 57 – Conditions to secure access to telephone numbers	Article 6(1) of, and condition 4 of Part A of the Annex to, the AuD, Article 27 & 28 of USD and Article 10(1) of FD
Section 58 – Conditions about allocation and adoption of numbers	Article 10(1) of the FD, Articles 5(2) and 6(1) of the AuD
ss. (1) and (2)	Article 13 of and, conditions 1, 2, 3, 6, 7, 8 & 9 of Part C of the Annex to, the AuD and Article 30 of USD
ss. (1) and (3)	Condition 4 of Part C of the Annex to AuD
ss. (3)	Article 25(2) of USD
ss. (4)	Articles 5(3) and (4) of AuD
ss. (5) and (6)	Article 13 of AuD
Section 60 – Modification of documents referred to in numbering conditions	Article 14(1) of the AuD
Section 61(3) - Withdrawal of telephone number allocations	Article 10(2) and 10(5) of the AuD
Section 63 - General duty as to telephone numbering functions	Article 10(2) of FD and condition 2 of Part C of the Annex to the AuD
Section 64 – Must-carry obligations	Article 6(1) of, and condition 6 of Part A of the Annex to, the AuD and Article 31 of the USD
Section 65 – Obligations to be secured by universal service conditions	Articles 3 to 7 and 9 to 11 of and Part A of Annex I to USD, and Article 2(j) of FD

Section 66 – Designation of universal service providers	Article 8 of USD and Article 4(2) of AuD
ss. (8)	Article 36(1) of USD
Section 67 – Subject-matter of universal service conditions	Article 6(2) of AuD and Part A of Annex I to USD
ss. (1)	Articles 3 to 7 and 9 to 11 of USD
ss. (3) to (9)	Article 11 and Annex III of USD
Section 68 – Tariffs etc. for universal services	
ss. (1) and (2)	Article 9 of USD
ss. (3) and (4)	Article 10 of USD
Section 69 – Directories and directory enquiry facilities	Article 5(3) of USD
Section 70 – Review of compliance costs	Article 12 of USD and Annex IV of USD
Section 71 – Sharing of burden of universal service obligations	Article 13 of USD
Section 72 – Report on sharing mechanism	Article 14(2) of USD
Section 73 – Permitted subject-matter of access-related conditions	Article 6(2) of AuD
ss. (2)	Article 5(1) of and Part II of Annex I to AcD
ss. (3)	Article 12(2) of FD
ss. (4)	Article 5(2) of AcD
ss. (5)	Article 6 of and Part I of Annex I to AcD
Section 74 – Specific types of access-related conditions	
ss. (1)	Article 5(1)(a) of AcD
ss. (2)	Article 5(1)(b) of, and Part II of Annex I to, AcD and Article 18 of FD
ss. (3) and (4) -Definition of application programme interface	Article 2(p) of FD
Section 75 – Conditional access systems and access to digital services	
ss. (1)	Article 5(2) of AcD and Articles 17(2) of FD
ss. (2)	Article 6 of and Part 1 of Annex I to AcD

ss. (3) Definition of conditional access system	Article 2(f) of FD
Section 76 – Modification and revocation of conditions imposed under s.75	Article 6(3) of AcD
Section 77 – Imposition of privileged supplier conditions	Article 13 of FD
Section 78 – Circumstances required for the setting of SMP conditions	Article 14 of and Annex II to FD
Section 79 – Market power determinations	Articles 15 and 16 of FD
Section 80 – Proposals for identifying markets and for market power determinations	Articles 6, 7 and 16(1) of FD
Section 81 – Delivery of copies of notifications under ss.79 and 80 ss.(2) ss.(3)	 Article 16(2) of AcD and Article 36(2) of USD and Article 7(5) of FD Article 7(3) of FD
Section 82 – European Commission's powers in respect of proposals	Article 7(4) of FD
Section 83 – Special rules for transnational markets	Articles 2(b), 15(4) and 16(5) of FD
Section 84 – Review of services market identifications and determinations ss. (2) and (3)	 Article 16(1) of FD, 7(3) of AcD and 16(3) of USD
ss. (4)	Article 16(3) of FD and Article 18(2) of USD
Section 87 – Conditions about network access etc. ss.(1) and (2) ss (3) and (5) ss. (4) ss. (6)(a) ss.(6)(b) ss.(6)(c), (d) and (e) ss. (7) and (8) ss. (9), (10) and (11)	Article 16(4) of FD Article 6(2) of AuD Article 8 of AcD Article 12(1) of AcD Article 12(2) of AcD Article 10 of AcD Article 9(1) and 9(4) and Annex II of AcD Article 9(2) and 9(4) and Annex II of AcD Article 11 of AcD Article 13 of AcD
Section 88 – Conditions about network access pricing etc.	Articles 8 and 13 of AcD, Article 6(2) of AuD and Article 16(4) of FD

Section 89 – Conditions about network access in exceptional circumstances	Article 8 of AcD, Article 6(2) of AuD and Article 16(4) of FD
Section 90 – Conditions about carrier selection and pre-selection	Article 19 of USD, Article 6(2) of AuD and Article 16(4) of FD
Section 91 – Conditions about regulation of services etc. for end-users	Article 17 of USD, Article 6(2) of AuD and Article 16(4) of FD
Section 92 – Conditions about leased lines	Article 18 of and Annex VII to USD, Article 6(2) of AuD and Article 16(4) of FD
Section 94 – Notification of contravention of condition	Article 10(2) of AuD and Article 11(6) of USD
Section 95 – Enforcement notification for contravention of conditions	Article 10(3) of AuD and Article 11(6) of USD
Section 96 – Penalties for contravention of conditions	Article 10(3) of AuD and Article 11(6) of USD
Section 98– Power to deal with urgent cases	Article 10(6) of AuD and Article 11(6) of USD
Section 100 – Suspending service provision for contraventions of conditions	Article 10(5) of AuD and Article 11(6) of USD
Section 102 and 103 – Procedure and enforcement of Directions	Article 10(2) & (5) of AuD and Article 11(6) of USD
Section 105 – Consideration and determination of network access questions	Article 5(4) of AcD
Sections 106 to 109 and Schedule 3 – Electronic communications code	Articles 11 and 12(1) of FD and Articles 4(1) and 6(1) of, and condition 5 of Part A of the Annex to, the AuD
Sections 106, 107, 109 and 115 – Application, modification and revocation of electronic communications code	Article 6 of FD and Article 14(1) of AuD
Section 110 – Enforcement of restrictions and conditions	Article 10(2) of AuD
Section 111 – Enforcement notification for contravention of code restrictions	Article 10(2) & (3) of AuD
Section 112 – Penalties for contravention of code restrictions	Article 10(2) & (3) of AuD
Section 113 – Suspension of application of code	Articles 10(2), (5) and 14(2) of AuD
Section 114 – Procedure for directions under s.113	Article 10(2) of AuD
Sections 132 & 133 – Powers to deal with emergencies	These provisions are permitted by Article 3 AuD
Sections – 135 to 137 – Information provisions	Article 5 of FD, Articles 6(1), 10(1) and 11 of, and condition 10 of Part A of the Annex to, the AuD, Article 11(2) of AcD and Articles 11, 21 and 22 of (in so far as those articles necessitate the provision of information) USD

Section 138 – Notification of contravention of information requirements	Article 10(2) of AuD
Section 139 – Penalties for contravention of information requirements	Article 10(2), (3) and (4) of AuD
Section 140 – Suspending service provision for information contraventions	Article 10(2) & (5) of AuD
Sections 142 & 143 – Procedure for and enforcement of directions under ss.140 and 141	Article 10(2) & (5) of AuD
Section 144 – Offences in connection with information requirements	Article 10(2) & (3) of AuD
Section 146 – Provision of information by OFCOM	Article 9 of AuD
Section 151 – Interpretation of Chapter 1	
ss.(1)Def of public electronic communications network	Article 2(d) of FD
Defs of FD, AcD and USD	Article 2(l) of FD
Def of end-user	Article 2(n) of FD
ss.(2) - interconnection	Article 2(b) of AcD
ss.(3) & (4) – network access	Article 2(a) of AcD
ss.(5) – regulatory authorities	Article 2(g) of FD
Chapter 2 – Spectrum Use	
Section 153 - United Kingdom Plan for Frequency Authorisation	Article 5(3) of AuD
Section 154 – Duties of OFCOM when carrying out spectrum functions	Article 9(1) of FD
Section 158 – Special duty in relation to television multiplexes	Condition 1 of Part B of the Annex to the AuD
Section 164 - Limitations on authorised spectrum use	Article 7 of AuD
Section 165 - Terms etc. of wireless telegraphy licences (new subsection (2C) inserted into WTA 1949 s. 1 only)	Article 6(4) of AuD
Section 166 - Exemption from need for wireless telegraphy licence	Article 5(1) of AuD
Section 168 - Spectrum trading	Article 9(3) and (4) of FD and Condition 5 of Part B of the Annex to AuD
Section 169 - Variation and revocation of wireless telegraphy licences	Article 10(2), (5) and (6) and 14(1) of AuD
Section 171 - Information requirements in relation to wireless telegraphy licences	Article 11(1)(e) and (2) of the AuD

Section 172 - Contraventions of conditions for use of wireless telegraphy	Article 10(2) of AuD
Section 173 – Meaning of "repeated contravention" in s.172	Article 10(2) & (5) of AuD
Section 174 - Procedure for prosecutions of wireless telegraphy offences	Articles 10(2), (3) and (6) of AuD
Section 183 - Modification of definition of "undue interference"	Article 2(2)(b) of, and condition 3 of Part B of the Annex to the AuD
Chapter 3 – Disputes and Appeals	
Section 185 – Reference of disputes to OFCOM	Article 20(1) of FD
Section 186 – Action by OFCOM on dispute reference	Article 20(2) of FD
Section 187 – Legal proceedings . about referred disputes	Article 20(5) of FD
Section 188 – Procedure for resolving disputes	Article 20(1) and (4) of FD
Section 189 – Disputes involving other member States	Article 21 of FD
Section 191– OFCOM's power to require information in connection with dispute	Articles 5 & 20(1) of FD
Sections 192 to 196 and Schedule 8 - Appeals	Articles 4 and 11(3) of FD and 10(7) of AuD
Sections 310 & 311 – Regulation of electronic programme guides	Permitted by Article 6(4) of AcD
Section 393 – General restrictions on disclosure of information	Article 3(5) of FD
Section 403 – Regulations and orders made by OFCOM	Articles 14(1) and Article 33 of USD and Article 6 of FD
Schedule 17 - Minor and consequential amendments	
Paragraph 8(6)	Article 5(3) & 7(4) of AuD
Paragraph 8(10)	Article 6(1) of AuD
Schedule 18 – Transitional Provisions	
Paragraph 7	Article 8 of USD
Paragraphs 8 & 9	Article 27 of FD
Paragraph 9	Article 27 of FD, Article 7(1) of AcD and Article 16(1) of USD
Paragraph 10	Article 16(2) of FD, Article 7(3) of AcD and Article 16(3) of USD
Paragraph 13	Article 2(1) of FD

APPENDIX 3

The four transposition tables set out below identify how the requirements of each of the four Communications Directives have been dealt with in the Communications Act. **DIRECTIVE 2002/21/EC OF THE EUROPEAN PARLIAMENT AND OF THE COUNCIL ON A COMMON REGULATORY FRAMEWORK FOR ELECTRONIC COMMUNICATIONS NETWORKS AND SERVICES**

THE FRAMEWORK DIRECTIVE

Article Number	Section Number (s)
CHAPTER I	SCOPE, AIM AND DEFINITIONS
Article 1	Scope and aim
(1) to (3)	No implementation required. Identifies aim and scope of the Directive
(4)	Directive 1999/5/EC implemented separately by S.I. 2000/730.
Article 2	Definitions
(a)	s. 32(1)
(b)	s. 83
(c)	s. 32(2) & (7)
(d)	s. 151(1)
(e)	s. 32(3)
(f)	s. 75(3)
(g)	s. 151(1) & (5)
(h)	Not used in Act
(i)	This meaning not used in Act
(j)	s. 65
(k)	Not used in Act
(l)	s. 151(1) & paragraph 13(8) of Sch. 18
(m)	s. 32(4)(a)
(n)	s. 151(1)
(o)	**948. Not used in Act**
(p)	s. 74(3) & (4)
CHAPTER II	NATIONAL REGULATORY AUTHORITIES
Article 3	National regulatory authorities
(1)	OFCOM Act 2002
(2)	OFCOM Act 2002, section 1 and paragraphs 1 and 17 of the Schedule
(3)	As above
(4)	All task set out in various enactments, which are all published
(5)	s. 393 and Part 9 of the Enterprise Act 2002
(6)	To be done administratively

Article 4	Right of appeal
(1)	s. 192 to 196 and Schedule 8
(2)	Does not apply: appeal body in Act is judicial
Article 5	Provision of information
(1)	s. 135 to 137 & 191
(2)	s. 25
(3)	Nothing additional required, covered by common law breach of confidence
(4)	s. 26
(5)	s. 26(6)
Article 6	Consultation and transparency mechanism
	There are a number of provisions in the Act which require consultation including, sections 48 , 49, 80 , 106, 107, 109, 115 and 403
Article 7	Consolidating the internal market for electronic communications
(1)	s. 4
(2)	s. 4(4)
(3)	s. 50(3) & (4) and 81(3)
(4)	s. 82
(5)	s. 48(5), 49(9), 50(2), 50(6), 80(6) and 81(2)
(6)	Paragraph 9 of Schedule 18
CHAPTER III	TASKS OF NATIONAL REGULATORY AUTHORITIES
Article 8	Policy objectives and regulatory principles
(1)	s. 4 Technological neutrality – s. 4(6)
(2)	s. 4(3)
(3)	s. 4(4)
(4)	s. 4(5)
Article 9	Management of radio frequencies for electronic communications services
(1)	s. 154
(3)	s. 168
(4)	s. 168
Article 10	Numbering, naming and addressing
(1)	Will be implemented in the conditions set under s. 57 & 58
(2)	s. 63(2)
(3)	s. 56
Article 11	Rights of way
(1)	s. 106 to 109 and Schedule 3, plus Schedule 2 to TA 1984 (electronic communications code).

(2)	s. 106 (OFCOM apply code)
(3)	s. 192
Article 12	Co-location and facility sharing
(1)	s. 107(4)(c), 109(2)(d) & paragraph 29 of Sch. 2 to the TA 1984
(2)	s. 73(3)
Article 13	Accounting separation and financial reports
(1)	s. 45(6), 46(3) & (4) and 77
(2)	s. 77(3)(b) & (c)
CHAPTER IV	GENERAL PROVISIONS
Article 14	Undertakings with significant market power
	s. 78
Article 15	Market definition procedure
(1)	Action for European Commission
(2)	Action for European Commission
(3)	s. 79(2), (3) & (7)
(4)	s. 83
Article 16	Market analysis procedure
(1)	s. 79, 80 and 84(2) & (3), the Electronic Communications (Market Analysis) Regulations 2003 (S.I. 2003/330) and paragraph 10 of Schedule 18
(2)	s. 46(7) & (8), the Electronic Communications (Market Analysis) Regulations 2003 and paragraph 10 of Schedule 18
(3)	s. 84(4)
(4)	s. 46(7) & (8) and 87 to 92
(5)	s. 83
(6)	As above
Article 17	Standardisation
(1)	Action for European Commission
(2)	s. 4(9) & (10), 51(1)(g) and 75(1)
(3)	No immediate action for Member States
(4)	Action for European Commission
(5)	Action for European Commission
(6)	Action for European Commission
(7)	Directive 1999/5/EC implemented separately by S.I. 2000/730.
Article 18	Interoperability of digital interactive television services
	s. 4(7), (8), (9) & (10) & 74(2)

Article 19	Harmonisation procedures
	No immediate action for Member States. If action eventually required will be done by issuing of direction under s. 5
Article 20	Dispute resolution between undertakings
(1)	s. 185, 188 & 191
(2)	s. 186
(3)	s. 4
(4)	s. 188
(5)	s. 187
Article 21	Resolution of cross-border disputes
	s. 189
Article 22	Committee
	No requirement on Member States
Article 23	Exchange of information
	No requirement on Member States – action for Commission
Article 24	Publication of information
	This is to be dealt with administratively
Article 25	Review procedures
	s. 24
CHAPTER V	FINAL PROVISIONS
Article 26	Repeal
	No requirement on Member States
Article 27	Transitional measures
	Schedule 18 paragraph 8 & 9
Article 28	Transposition
Article 29	Entry into force
	No requirement on Member States
Article 30	Addressees
	No requirement on Member States
Annex I	No requirement on Member States
Annex II	s. 78(5)

DIRECTIVE 2002/20/EC OF THE EUROPEAN PARLIAMENT AND OF THE COUNCIL ON THE AUTHORISATION OF ELECTRONIC COMMUNICATIONS NETWORKS AND SERVICES

THE AUTHORISATION DIRECTIVE

Article Number	Section Number (s)
Article 1	Objective and scope
	No implementation required. Identifies aim of Directive
Article 2	Definitions
(2)(a)	s. 46(2) & 51(3)
(2)(b)	s. 183 & s. 19(5A) of the Wireless Telegraphy Act 1949
Article 3	General authorisation of electronic communications networks and services
(1)	Chapter 1 of Part 2 and s. 132 & 133
(2)	s. 33
(3)	s. 33(5), (6), (7) & (8) and s. 44
Article 4	Minimum list of rights derived from the general authorisation
(1)	s. 106 & 107
(2)	s. 51(1)(b), (4) & 66
Article 5	Rights of use for radio frequencies and numbers
(1)	s. 166 & section 1AA of the Wireless Telegraphy Act 1949
(2)	Will be implemented in the conditions set under section 58
(3)	s. 58(4), 153, Sch. 17 para. 8(6) and section 1D(4A) of the Wireless Telegraphy Act 1949
(4)	Ditto
Article 6	Conditions attached to the general authorisation and to the rights of use for radio frequencies and for numbers and specific obligations
(1)	s. 33 & 34 (notification) s. 38 & 39 (administrative charge) s. 45(3), 46(2), 47, 51, 52, 57, 58 & 64 (general conditions) s. 106 to 107 & 109 (Electronic communications code) s. 135 to 137 (Information provisions) Sch. 17 para 8(10) and section 1D(9) of the Wireless Telegraphy Act 1949 (spectrum)

(2)	s. 45(4), (5), (7) & (8). 46(3), (5), (6) & (7) and s. 67 (universal service conditions) s. 73 (access-related conditions) s. 87 to 92 (SMP services conditions)
(3)	See entry for Part A of Annex
(4)	s. 165 and section 1(2C) of the Wireless Telegraphy Act 1949
Article 7	Procedure for limiting the number of rights of use to be granted for radio frequencies
(1)	s. 164
(2)	s. 164
(3)	s. 4 & 164
(4)	Sch. 17 para 8(6) and section 1D(4B) of the Wireless Telegraphy Act 1949
Article 8	Harmonised assignment of radio frequencies
	Shall be secured if necessary by a direction given under s. 5
Article 9	Declarations to facilitate the exercise of rights to install facilities and rights of interconnection
	s. 146
Article 10	Compliance with the conditions of the general authorisation or of rights of use and with specific obligations
(1)	s. 135 to 137
(2)	s. 35 to 37 (enforcement of advance notification provisions) s. 40 to 43 (enforcement of administrative charge provisions) s. 61(3) (withdrawal of telephone number allocations) s. 94 to 100 & 102 to 103 (enforcement of conditions) s. 110 to 114 (enforcement of restrictions and conditions for which application of electronic communications code subject), s. 138 to 144 (enforcement of information provisions) s. 169 & section 1E of the Wireless Telegraphy Act 1949 and s. 172 to 174 (spectrum enforcement)
(3)	s. 36 & 37, 41, 95 & 96, 111 & 112, 139, 144 & 174
(4)	s. 139

(5)	s. 42 & 43 (administrative charge) s. 61(3) (withdrawal of telephone number allocations) s. 100, 102 & 103 (conditions of entitlement) s. 140, 142 & 143 (information provision) s. 113 (electronic communications code) s. 169 and section 1E of the Wireless Telegraphy Act 1949 and s. 173 (spectrum enforcement)
(6)	s. 98 s. 169 and section 1E of the Wireless Telegraphy Act 1949 and s. 174 (spectrum enforcement)
(7)	s. 192
Article 11	Information required under the general authorisation, for rights of use and for the specific obligations
(1)	s. 135 & s. 171 and section 13A of the Wireless Telegraphy Act 1949
(2)	s. 135(4) & 171 and section 13A of the Wireless Telegraphy Act 1949
Article 12	Administrative charges
(1)	s. 38 & 39
(2)	s. 38(9) & (10)
Article 13	Fees for rights of use and rights to install facilities
	s. 38(6)(g) s. 58(1)(b), (5) & (6)
Article 14	Amendment of rights and obligations
(1)	s. 47, 48 & 60 s. 106, 107, 109 & 115 s. 169 and section 1E of the Wireless Telegraphy Act 1949
(2)	s. 113
Article 15	Publication of information
	s. 26
Article 16	Review procedures
	s. 24
Article 17	Existing authorisations
	Abolishing current regulatory regime and replacing with a new regulatory regime. As such not necessary to bring old regime into line with Directives

Article 18	Transposition
Article 19	Entry into force
	No requirement on Member States
Article 20	Addressees
	No requirement on Member States
Annex	
Part A	Conditions which may be attached to a general authorisation
	s. 45(3), 51 & 52
(1)	s. 51(1)(d)
(2)	s. 38 & 39
(3)	s. 51(1)(b) & (4)
(4)	s. 57
(5)	s. 106 to 109, schedule 3 and Schedule 2 to the Telecommunications Act 1984
(6)	s. 64
(7)	This is currently addressed through the UK's implementation of the Telecommunications Data Protection Directive (Directive 97/66/EC) and from the 31 October 2003 will be dealt with by the UK's implementation of the Directive on Privacy and Electronic Communications (Directive 2002/58/EC).
(8)	s. 51(1)(a) & 52
(9)	Not taking up this option to set conditions for this purpose
(10)	s. 33(5) & 135 to 137
(11)	This is enabled through the Regulation of Investigatory Powers Act 2000, in accordance with Directive 97/66/EC and Directive 95/46/EC.
(12)	s. 51(1)(e) & (7)
(13)	s. 51(1)(f)
(14)	s. 51(1)(b) & (4)

(15)	s. 51(1)(c) & (5)
(16)	This is currently addressed through the UK's implementation of the Telecommunications Data Protection Directive (Directive 97/66/EC) and from the 31 October 2003 will be dealt with by the UK's implementation of the Directive on Privacy and Electronic Communications (Directive 2002/58/EC).
(17)	Exemption Regulations under proviso to section 1(1) of WTA 1949
(18)	s. 51(1)(g)
Part B	Conditions which may be attached to rights of use for radio frequencies
(1)	s. 158
(2)	Wireless Telegraphy Act 1949 section 1
(3)	s. 183 & section 19(5) & (5A) of the Wireless Telegraphy Act 1949
(4)	Wireless Telegraphy Act 1949 section 1
(5)	s. 168
(6)	Wireless Telegraphy Act 1998 sections 1 and 3
(7)	Wireless Telegraphy Act 1949 section 1
(8)	Wireless Telegraphy Act 1949 section 1
Part C	Conditions which may be attached to rights of use for numbers
(1)	s. 58(1) & (2)
(2)	s. 58(1) & (2) and 63(1)
(3)	s. 58(1) & (2)
(4)	s. 58(1)(d) & (3)
(5)	Option in Directive for maximum duration not taken up in Act
(6)	s. 58(1) & (2)
(7)	s. 58(1) & (2)
(8)	s. 58(1) & (2)
(9)	s. 58(1) & (2)

DIRECTIVE 2002/19/EC OF THE EUROPEAN PARLIAMENT AND OF THE COUNCIL ON ACCESS TO, AND INTERCONNECTION OF, ELECTRONIC COMMUNUCATIONS NETWORKS AND ASSOCIATED FACILITIES

THE ACCESS DIRECTIVE

Article Number	Section Number (s)
CHAPTER I	SCOPE, AIM AND DEFINITIONS
Article 1	Scope and aim
	No implementation required. Identifies aim of Directive
Article 2	Definitions
(a)	s. 151(3) & (4)
(b)	s. 151(2)
(d)	Regulation 3 of Advanced Television Services Regulations 2003 (S.I. 2003/1901)
(c) & (e)	Not used in Act
CHAPTER II	GENERAL PROVISIONS
Article 3	General framework for access and interconnection
	Nothing is required to ensure persons not restricted from negotiating access and interconnection
Article 4	Rights and obligations for undertakings
(1)	s. 45(3) & 51(1)(b) & (4)
(2)	Regulation 4 of Advanced Television Service Regulations 2003 (S.I. 2003/1901)
(3)	s. 45(3) & 51(1)(b) & (4)
Article 5	Powers and responsibilities of the national regulatory authorities with regard to access and interconnection
(1)	s. 4(7) & (8) s. 45(5) & 73(2)
(a)	s. 46(6)(a), 73(2) & 74(1)
(b)	s. 73(2) & 74(2)

(2)	s. 45(5), 73(4) & 75(1)
(3)	s. 47 to 50
(4)	s. 105
CHAPTER III	OBLIGATIONS ON OPERATORS AND MARKET REVIEW PROCEDURES
Article 6	Conditional access system and other facilities
(1)	s. 45(4), 73(5) & 75(2)
(2)	No action for Member States
(3)	s. 47 to 50 & 76
(4)	s. 310 to 311
Article 7	Review of former obligations for access and interconnection
(1)	Schedule 18, paragraph 9
(2)	No requirement for Member States - action for European Commission
(3)	s. 84(2) & (3) & paragraph 10 of Schedule 18 and the Electronic Communications (Market Analysis) Regulations 2003 (S.I. 2003/330)
Article 8	Imposition, amendment or withdrawal of obligations
(1)	s. 45(7) & (8), 87 to 89
(2)	s. 45(7) & (8), 46(7) & (8)(a) & 87(2)
(3)	s. 46(7) & (8)(b) & 89
(4)	s. 47 to 50
(5)	s. 50(2)
Article 9	Obligation of transparency
	s.45(7) & (8)
(1)	s. 87(6)(b)
(2)	s. 87(6)(c), (d) & (e)
(3)	As above
(4)	s. 87(6)(b), (c), (d) & (e)
(5)	Action for Communications Committee
Article 10	Obligation of non-discrimination
	s. 45(7) & (8)
(1)	s. 87(6)(a)
(2)	s. 87(6)(a)
Article 11	Obligation of accounting separation
	s. 45(7) & (8)

(1)	s. 87(7) & (8)
(2)	s. 26 & 135
Article 12	Obligations of access to, and use of, specific network facilities
	s. 45(7) & (8)
(1)	s. 87(3) & (5)
(2)	s. 87(4)
Article 13	Price control and cost accounting obligations
	s. 45(7) & (8)
(1)	87(9) & (10) & 88
(2)	s. 88(1)(b) & (4)(a)
(3)	s. 87(9)(d), (10) & 88(4)(b)
(4)	s. 87(11)
CHAPTER 4	PROCEDURAL PROVISIONS
Article 14	Committee
	No requirement on Member States
Article 15	Publication of, and access to, information
(1)	s. 24 to 26 & 48(1) & (6)
(2)	s. 24 to 26 & 50(2) to (6)
Article 16	Notification
(1)	This will be dealt with administratively
(2)	s. 50(2) & 81(2)
Article 17	Review procedures
	s. 24
Article 18	Transposition
Article 19	Entry into force
	No requirement on Member States
Article 20	Addressees
	No requirement on Member States
Annex I	
Part I	s. 73(5) & 75(2)

Part II	s. 73(2) & 74(2)
Annex II	s. 87(6)(b), (c), (d) & (e)

DIRECTIVE 2002/22/EC OF THE EUROPEAN PARLIAMENT AND OF THE COUNCIL ON UNIVERSAL SERVICE AND USERS' RIGHTS RELATING TO ELECTRONIC COMMUNICATIONS NETWORKS AND SERVICES

THE UNIVERSAL SERVICE DIRECTIVE

Article Number	Section Number (s)
CHAPTER I	SCOPE, AIMS AND DEFINITIONS
Article 1	Scope and aims
	No implementation required. Identifies aim of Directive
Article 2	Definitions
(c)	s. 51(2) The Act does not refer specifically to any of the other terms defined in this Article.
CHAPTER 2	UNIVERSAL SERVICE OBLIGATIONS INCLUDING SOCIAL OBLIGATIONS
Article 3	Availability of universal service
(1)	s. 45(4), 65 & 67
(2)	s. 47
Article 4	Provision of access at a fixed location
	s. 45(4), 65 & 67
Article 5	Directory enquiry services and directories
	s. 45(4), 65 & 67
(3)	s. 69
Article 6	Public pay telephones
	s. 45(4), 65 & 67
Article 7	Special measures for disabled users
	s. 45(4), 65 & 67
Article 8	Designation of undertakings
	s. 46(5), 66 and paragraph 7 of Schedule 18 and the Electronic Communications (Universal Service) Regulations 2003 (S.I. 2003/33)
Article 9	Affordability of tariffs
	s. 45(4), 65 & 67
(1)	s. 68(1)
(2)	s. 68(2)
(3)	s. 68(2)
(4)	s. 68(2)

(5)	s. 47
Article 10	Control of expenditure
	s. 45(4), 65 & 67
(1)	s. 68(3) & (4)
Article 11	Quality of service of designated undertakings
	s. 45(4), 65, 67 & 135 to 137
(1) – (3)	s. 67(3) to (6)
(4)	s. 48(2), 49(4), 67(7)
(6)	s. 67(8) & (9) & 94 to 100 & 102 and 103
Article 12	Costing of universal service obligations
(1)	s. 70
(2)	s. 70(4), (5), (6) & (7)
Article 13	Financing of universal service obligations
(1)	s. 71
(2)	s. 71(5)
(3)	s. 71(6)
(4)	s. 51(1)(d) & 71
Article 14	Transparency
(1)	s. 403
(2)	s. 72
Article 15	Review of the scope of universal service
	No requirement on Member States – action for European Commission
CHAPTER 3	REGULATORY CONTROLS ON UNDERTAKINGS WITH SIGNIFICANT MARKET POWER IN SPECIFIC MARKETS
Article 16	Review of obligations
(1)	Schedule 18 paragraph 9
(2)	No requirement on Member States – action for European Commission
(3)	s. 84(2) & (3) & paragraph 10 of Schedule 18 and the Electronic Communications (Market Analysis) Regulations 2003 (S.I. 2003/330)
Article 17	Regulatory controls on retail services
	s. 45(7) & (8) and 46(7) & (8)
(1)	s. 91
(2)	s. 47
(3)	s. 91(7)
(4)	s. 91(6)

(5)	s. 46(7) & (8)
Article 18	Regulatory controls on the minimum set of leased lines
	s. 45(7) & (8) and 46(7) & (8)
(1)	s. 92
(2)	s. 84(4)
(3)	s. 92(1)(b)
Article 19	Carrier selection and carrier pre-selection
	s. 45(7) & (8) and 46(7) & (8)
(1)	s. 90
(2)	s. 90
(3)	s. 90(4)
CHAPTER 4	END-USER INTERESTS AND RIGHTS
Article 20	Contracts
	s. 51(1)(a)
Article 21	Transparency and publication of information
(1)	s. 51(1)(a) and 135 to 137
(2)	s. 26
Article 22	Quality of service
	s. 51(1)(a) & 135 to 137
Article 23	Integrity of the network
	s. 51(1)(c), (e) & (5)
Article 24	Interoperability of consumer digital television equipment
	Regulations 5 to 8 of and the Schedule to the Advanced Television Services Regulations 2003 (S.I. 2003/1901)
Article 25	Operator assistance and directory enquiry services
	s. 51(1)(a) & 58(3)
Article 26	Single European emergency call number
(1)	s. 51(1)(a)
Article 27	European telephone access codes
(1)	s. 56
(2)	s. 57
Article 28	Non-geographic numbers
	s. 57
Article 29	Provision of additional facilities
	s. 51(1)(a) & (b)

Article 30	Number portability
	s. 58(1)(e) & 58(2)(f)
Article 31	"Must carry" obligations
	s. 64
CHAPTER 5	GENERAL AND FINAL PROVISIONS
Article 32	Additional mandatory services
	Option. No current plans to take.
Article 33	Consultation with interested parties
	s. 16, 48, 49 & 403
Article 34	Out-of –court dispute resolution
	s. 52 to 55
Article 35	Technical adjustment
	No requirement on Member States
Article 36	Notification, monitoring and review procedures
(1)	s. 66(8)
(2)	s. 50(2) & 81(2)
(3)	s. 24 & 25
Article 37	Committee
	No requirement on Member States
Article 38	Transposition
Article 39	Entry into force
	No requirement on Member States
Article 40	Addressees
	No requirement on Member States
Annex I	
Part A	s. 45(4), 65 & 67
Part B	s. 51(1)(a)
Annex II	s. 51(1)(a)
Annex III	s. 51(1)(a) & 67(3)(c)
Annex IV	s. 70

Annex V	No requirement on Member States
Annex VI	Regulations 5 to 8 of and the Schedule to the Advanced Television Services Regulations 2003 (S.I. 2003/1901)
Annex VII	s. 92

Printed in the UK by The Stationery Office Limited
under the authority and superintendence of Carol Tullo, Controller of
Her Majesty's Stationery Office and Queen's Printer of Acts of Parliament